ALAN SORRELL

THE MAN WHO CREATED ROMAN BRITAIN

Alan Sorrell: Self-portrait with daughter Julia (c. 1970). Oil on canvas, 66.55 × 38.3 cm
(COLLECTION OF JULIA SORRELL, © ESTATE OF ALAN SORRELL)

ALAN SORRELL

THE MAN WHO CREATED ROMAN BRITAIN

Julia Sorrell and Mark Sorrell

OXBOW | books
Oxford & Philadelphia

Published in the United Kingdom in 2018 by
OXBOW BOOKS
The Old Music Hall, 106-108 Cowley Road, Oxford, OX4 1JE

and in the United States by
OXBOW BOOKS
1950 Lawrence Road, Havertown, PA 19083

© The authors 2018

Paperback Edition: ISBN 978-1-78570-740-7
Digital Edition: ISBN 978-1-78570-741-4

A CIP record for this book is available from the British Library

Library of Congress Control Number: 2017963321

All rights reserved. No part of this book may be reproduced or transmitted in any form or by any means, electronic or mechanical including photocopying, recording or by any information storage and retrieval system, without permission from the publisher in writing.

Design and layout by Frabjous Books
Printed in the United Kingdom by Latimer Trend

For a complete list of Oxbow titles, please contact:

United Kingdom
Oxbow Books
Telephone (01865) 241249, Fax (01865) 794449
Email: oxbow@oxbowbooks.com
www.oxbowbooks.com

United States of America
Oxbow Books
Telephone (800) 791-9354, Fax (610) 853-9146
Email: queries@casemateacademic.com
www.casemateacademic.com/oxbow

Oxbow Books is part of the Casemate Group

Front cover: Alan Sorrell: *Hadrian's Wall, Walltown Crags* (1959) Watercolour, pen & ink, gouache & chalks, 42 × 59 cm (© Crown copyright. Historic England Archive)

Back cover: Left: *Roman Newgate* (1950). Watercolour, gouache, ink & pencil, 53 × 73 cm; right: *Drawing Water from a Well at Walbrook* (undated). Watercolour, gouache, ink & pencil, pastel 38 × 48 cm (both © Museum of London)

Contents

List of illustrations — vii
Acknowledgements — xiii

PART ONE. ALAN SORRELL: A BRIEF BIOGRAPHY
Julia Sorrell

1 Introduction — 2
2 Early life and education — 5
3 The British School at Rome 1928–1930 — 17
4 England 1930–1939 — 26
5 World War II — 37
6 The post-war years — 53

PART TWO. A LIFE DETERMINED
Mark Sorrell

7 Portrait of my father — 82
8 Beginnings and the National Museum of Wales — 111
9 Jarlshof, Shetland: a work in progress — 142
10 Years of achievement — 151

Appendix: finding list of reconstruction drawings by Alan Sorrell — 191
References — 199

List of illustrations

Fig. 1   *Caerleon Legionary Fortress* (1939)

Fig. 2   Edith, Ernest and Doris Sorrell (*c.* 1899)

Fig. 3   Alan Sorrell, aged about 2, with his father, mother, sister and aunt on a pleasure steamer off Southend

Fig. 4   Doris and Alan in a bath chair (*c.* 1909)

Fig. 5   Alan's earliest drawing (date unknown)

Fig. 6   Landscape by Ernest Sorrell (date unknown)

Fig. 7   Art competition drawing (date unknown)

Fig. 8   *A Land Fit for Heroes* (1936)

Fig. 9   Monomarks Designing Company working drawing plus notes (*c.* 1922)

Fig. 10   Detail of Caerwent working drawing, early Christian church (1938)

Fig. 11   RCA Life drawing (*c.* 1926)

Fig. 12   *The Outer Narthex of St Saviour in Chora, Istanbul during the Restoration of the Mosaics* (1954)

Fig. 13   Study for *People Seeking after Wisdom* (1928)

Fig. 14   Alan Sorrell, British School at Rome (Jan. 1930)

Fig. 15   Alan Sorrell's studio, British School at Rome (1930)

Fig. 16   Study for a copy of *The School of Athens* by Raphael in the Stanza della Segnatura, Vatican (autumn 1928)

Fig. 17   *Nestor's Palace, Pylos* (1954)

Fig. 18   Copy of *The Tower of Babel* by Benozzo Gozzoli in the Camposanto, Pisa (1929)

Fig. 19   *The Appian Way* (1932)

Fig. 20   Copy after *The Victory of Heraclius over Chosroes*, part of *The Legend of the True Cross* by Piero della Francesca in the Basilica of San Francesco, Arezzo (dated March 1929)

Fig. 21   *The Refitting of Admiral Blake's Fleet at Leigh, During the First Dutch War* (1933)

Fig. 22   a. Alan Sorrell with family (*c.* 1934); b. *Britannia Rules the Garden* (1936)

LIST OF ILLUSTRATIONS

Fig. 23   *South Icelandic Coast (Vik)* (1935)
Fig. 24   *Icelandic Farm* (1936)
Fig. 25   *The Roman Forum at Leicester* (1936)
Fig. 26   *Boats at Leigh-on-Sea* (1973)
Fig. 27   *The Falling Tower* (c. 1939)
Fig. 28   *Caerwent, Gwent. A Bird's Eye View of the Roman Town* (1937)
Fig. 29   *Marching through the Camp* (1942)
Fig. 30   a. *Recruits leaving the Camp at Bridgnorth* (Xmas 1941); b. Alan Sorrell leaving the RAF (May 1946)
Fig. 31   *RAF Hut* (1943)
Fig. 32   *A Cavern in the Clouds* (April 1944)
Fig. 33   *Southampton Dock* (1944)
Fig. 34   Elizabeth Tanner *c.* 1944
Fig. 35   Alan Sorrell 1944
Fig. 36   *RAF Aerodrome* (1945)
Fig. 37   Alan viewing the exterior and interior of the Daws Heath Chapel (1946)
Fig. 38   Marriage of Alan & Elizabeth Sorrell on 29 March 1947
Fig. 39   a. Elizabeth nursing Richard in the kitchen (1948); b. The Sorrell family in the studio at Thors Mead (c. 1963)
Fig. 40   *Working Boats from Around the British Isles* (1951)
Fig. 41   a. Knossos and b. Bronze Age Jericho, working drawings (1951)
Fig. 42   *Raising of the Sarsens, Stonehenge* (c. 1965). a. Finished drawing; b. with geometric structural lines added
Fig. 43   Mural over the north arch, St Peters Church, Bexhill-on-Sea (1951)
Fig. 44   *The Seasons* (1954)
Fig. 45   *Conversation Piece: The Senior Common Room at Magdalen College, Oxford. Winter, 1954*
Fig. 46   Hinkley Point interior (Sept. 1959 or June 1960)
Fig. 47   *Planting of the Trees* (1971)
Fig. 48   *The Stone Men* (1961)
Fig. 49   *The Spoilers* (detail) (1958)
Fig. 50   *The Assault* (1974)
Fig. 51   *Watch Office, RAF Station* (1944)
Fig. 52   a. Birthday Card for Elizabeth Sorrell (c. 1970); b. Doodle (late 1940s)
Fig. 53   *The Evening Meal in the Triclinium* (c. 1960)
Fig. 54   Alan holding an aerial view of Roman Colchester (1973)
Fig. 55   Sketchbook studies of Elizabeth (c. 1960)
Fig. 56   *Ferns in the Conservatory* by Elizabeth Tanner (1946)
Fig. 57   Alan, Elizabeth holding Strüdel, and Julia in the studio (c. 1970)

LIST OF ILLUSTRATIONS   ix

Fig. 58   a. Alan on horseback (third from right) wearing a Panama hat (1929); b. Alan wearing his bush hat purchased in Aswan (1962)

Fig. 59   Alan in his blue beret sketching at Stonehenge (1958)

Fig. 60   Hinkley Point: view of No 1 & No 2 Reactors from the Goliath Crane (Sept 1959)

Fig. 61   *Rock-Cut Tombs at Toshka, Nubia* (1962)

Fig. 62   *Walls of Theodosius, Istanbul* (1954)

Fig. 63   Alan Sorrell, by Elizabeth Sorrell (*c.* 1970)

Fig. 64   a. *Harlech Castle, Gwynedd, about the year 1290* (1957); b. *Conway Castle, Gwynedd* (1957)

Fig. 65   a. *Tintern Abbey, Gwent, as it might have appeared before its dissolution* (1959); b. *Jedburgh Abbey, Borders, late 14th century* (1957)

Fig. 66   Alan Sorrell drawing at Armenna, Nubia (1962)

Fig. 67   *Armenna, Nubia: excavation of a Coptic house, Pennsylvania-Yale expedition* (1962)

Fig. 68   a. Hirsute Mesolithic hunter wearing stag antler frontlet, from *Prehistoric Britain* (1968); b. *Abu Simbel: experimental drilling in the Great Temple* (1962)

Fig. 69   *Bishop's Palace, St David's, as it might have appeared* c. *1530* (1958)

Fig. 70   *Planting of the Trees*, British School at Rome drawing (*c.* 1930)

Fig. 71   a. *The Long Journey* (1936); b. *The Postman* (1931)

Fig. 72   *The Archaeologist in Nubia* (1965)

Fig. 73   *Artist in the Campagna* (*c.* 1931)

Fig. 74   *The Enormous Head* (1967)

Fig. 75   *Officers' Mess, RAF Station* (1943)

Fig. 76   Anglo-Saxon squatters occupying an abandoned Roman villa, from *Saxon England* (1964)

Fig. 77   *Caerlaverock Castle, Dumfries, its likely appearance in the 15th century* (1959)

Fig. 78   *Criccieth Castle, Gwynedd, late 13th century* (1961)

Fig. 79   *Machine Gun Range and Rifle Range, RAF Station* (1944)

Fig. 80   *Caerleon: Bird's Eye View of the Roman Legionary Fortress* (1939)

Fig. 81   Excavations beside the Jewry Wall, Leicester (1936).

Fig. 82   Roman assault on the eastern entrance of Maiden Castle, Dorset (1937)

Fig. 83   Watercolour drawing of Cyril Fox (1946)

Fig. 84a   *Caerwent, Gwent: a raid on the south-west corner of the Roman town*, preliminary drawing (1938); b. Final drawing (1938)

Fig. 85   *Llantwit Major Roman Villa, South Glamorgan* (1949)

Fig. 86   a. Caerwent, Gwent: preliminary drawing of Romano-Celtic temple complex (1955); b. *Caerwent: Romano-Celtic Temple Complex*, the final drawing (1955)

Fig. 87   *Roman London: The Cripplegate Fort* (1966)

x   LIST OF ILLUSTRATIONS

Fig. 88   a. Tinkinswood, South Glamorgan: interment ceremony, first sketch (1939); b. Outline drawing of a Neolithic bowl by Cyril Fox, from a letter (1940); c. *Tinkinswood, South Glamorgan: interment ceremony at the Neolithic chambered tomb.* The final drawing (1940)

Fig. 89   *Maen Madoc, Powys: Dervacus's Son Inspecting his Father's Monument* (1940)

Fig. 90   *Via Appia* (1970)

Fig. 91   Alan Sorrell sketching in Shetland (1949)

Fig. 92   *Jarlshof, Shetland: the Viking settlement, boats drawn up* (1949)

Fig. 93   Jarlshof: ground plan from official guide book (1953)

Fig. 94   Jarlshof: wheelhouse interiors (1951)

Fig. 95   Jarlshof: outline reconstruction sketch by John Hamilton (1951)

Fig. 96   a. Jarlshof: preliminary drawing of broch and wheelhouse settlement (1951); b. *Jarlshof Iron Age Settlement, as it might have appeared about AD 450* (1951)

Fig. 97   *Cheddar, Somerset: the Anglo-Saxon palace, period II, c. AD 930 to late 10th or early 11th century* (1963)

Fig. 98   a. *Framlingham Castle, Suffolk, the courtyard in the 13th century* (1960); b. *Castle Acre Priory, Norfolk, from the north-east, shortly before its suppression in 1537* (1958); c. *Lullingstone Roman villa, Kent, as it might have appeared c. AD 360* (1961)

Fig. 99   *Hadrian's Wall: Harrow's Scar milecastle and Willowford Bridge* (1956)

Fig. 100 a. Roman road making, page proof (*c.* 1948–9); b. Roman road making (1961)

Fig. 101 *Mawgan Porth, Cornwall: interior of long house, Dark Age settlement* (1955)

Fig. 102 a. Hadrian's Wall: Carrawburgh Mithraeum, working drawing (1951); b. *Hadrian's Wall: Carrawburgh Mithraeum Interior* (1951)

Fig. 103 a. Walbrook Mithraeum: study of apsidal end (1954); b. Walbrook Mithraeum: advertisement board (1954)

Fig. 104 a. *Walbrook Mithraeum, London: Exterior* (1957); b. *Interior* (1954); c. *Interior* revised version (*c.* 1971)

Fig. 105 Nestor's Palace, Pylos, working drawing (1954)

Fig. 106 *Roman London,* c. *AD 400: the snowbound city, with houses burned by raiders beyond the walls* (1956)

Fig. 107 Heathrow Temple, London, the Iron Age Settlement, preliminary tracing (1955)

Fig. 108 Heathrow Temple: sketch of portico with cows' skulls (1955)

Fig. 109 *Heathrow Temple*, the final drawing (1955)

Fig. 110 *Hadrian's Wall: Housesteads Roman Fort* (1956)

Fig. 111 a. *Stonehenge, Wiltshire: the completed circle as it might have appeared c. 1400 BC*; b. Exhibition of Ministry drawings at the Jewel Tower, Westminster (1957). Alan Sorrell (right) and Hugh Molson

Fig. 112 *Tilbury Fort, Essex, from the south-west, as it might have appeared about 1725* (1958)

LIST OF ILLUSTRATIONS   xi

Fig. 113   a. *Stonehenge: Lifting Gear in Position* (1958); b. Stonehenge: Alan Sorrell (left) and Professor Atkinson (1958)

Fig. 114   *Buhen, Nubia: Reconstruction of the Middle Kingdom Fortress* (1959)

Fig. 115   a. *Buhen, Nubia: the mud brick walls of the excavated fort* (1962); b. *New Kalabsha, Nubia: blocks from the deconstructed late Ptolemaic–Roman temple stored ready for re-erection* (1962)

Fig. 116   a. *Anglo-Saxon Cheddar, Period I, pre-c. AD 930* (1966); b. *Anglo-Saxon Cheddar, Period III, Late 10th to 11th Century* (1966)

Fig. 117   a. *Medieval Cheddar, Period IV, Later 11th Century to 12th Century* (1966); b. *Period V, Early 13th century* (1966)

Fig. 118   *Roman Wroxeter, the bath complex* (1972)

Fig. 119   a. Bath: panorama of the Roman city, working drawing (1972); b. the final drawing (1972)

Fig. 120   *Bramber Castle, Sussex, as it might have appeared in the early 12th century* (1973)

Fig. 121   *The Battle of Maldon* (1967)

Fig. 122   Pompeii, Changing Room in the Public Baths, working drawing (1973)

Fig. 123   *Bronze Age funerary rites on the banks of the Thames* (1974)

Fig. 124   *The Death of Hannibal* (1969)

Acknowledgements

The authors would like to express their gratitude to the following people and organisations for their help and cooperation in supplying images for this book: Grace Beaumont of the Arts Council Southbank Collection; Mike Evans, Javis Gurr and Charis Abrahams of Historic England; Simon Thurley, former Chief Executive of English Heritage; George Fox and Charles Scott-Fox; Melanie Gardner of Tullie House Museum and Art Gallery, Carlisle; Dr Andrew Gorsuch, St Peter's Church, Bexhill-on-Sea; Adrian Gibbs, The Bridgeman Art Gallery and Newcastle Library and Museums Service; Verity Hadfield of CADW; Clare Hunt, former director of Southend Museums Service (the Beecroft Art Gallery); Kay Kays and Dr Clare Smith of Amgueddfa Cymru – National Museum Wales; Paul Liss and Petra van der Wal of Liss Llewellyn Fine Art; Rachel Methar and Professor John Nightingale of Magdalen College, Oxford; Hugh Morrison and Michelle Anderson of Historic Environment Scotland; Andrew Parkin & the Society of Antiquaries of Newcastle; Neera Pattapital of the Imperial War Museums; Sam Richardson of The Potteries Museum & Art Gallery, Stoke-on-Trent; James Sainsbury of Adur and Worthing Councils; Phil Scoggins of the Shropshire Museums Service; Allison Sharpe and Andrew Cormack at the Royal Air Force Museum, Hendon; David Thompson of the Tate Gallery; Liz Waring of the Graves Art Gallery, Sheffield; Sean Waterman at the Museum of London. We would also like to thank Emeritus Professor Sir Barry Cunliffe, Hannah Ratford at the BBC Written Archives Centre, Clare Hunter at Liverpool Museums, Jeremy Johnson at the Guildhall Art Gallery and L. Taylor at London Metropolitan Archives for their help in trying to trace missing works by Alan Sorrell.

The authors would like to express their gratitude to the following people and organisations for their help and cooperation in supplying invaluable research material for this book: Dr Tim Copeland for writing regarding Alan Sorrell's influences on him; Carolyn Cheadle, Julie Taylor and Jody Deacon of Amgueddfa Cymru – National Museum Wales for locating correspondence between Alan Sorrell and Sir Cyril Fox, V. E. Nash-Williams and others; Dr Brian Foss and Dr Alistair Pearson for material regarding Alan Sorrell's wartime activities; Dr Pat Hardy and Kate Ormerod at the Museum of London for providing access to correspondence between Alan Sorrell and Professor W. F. Grimes, Ralph Merrifield and others; Dr Alan Powers for material regarding Alan Sorrell's mural paintings; Valerie Scott and Christopher Smith (former director) of the British School at Rome for providing access to Alan Sorrell's file at the BSR.

We should also like to thank Dr Ian Sanders for much of the background work on our behalf including photography of many images, and Henry Sanders for his Photoshop skills when needed. Gratitude is also due to Tish Kerkham, Richard Sorrell and Joan Oliver Smith for reading and commenting on various sections of the text.

A special thanks is due to not only the Trustees of the Marc Fitch Fund (and their administrator Christopher Catling) and Historic Environment Scotland for their generosity in providing a grant to help in the production of this book, but also to our editor, Dr Julie Gardiner for initiating the project, and for her infinite patience, guidance and enthusiasm in seeing it through to completion, as well as to all the staff at Oxbow Books; and to Val Lamb at Frabjous Books.

Oxbow Books is grateful to the Marc Fitch Fund and Historic Environment Scotland for financial assistance towards the publication of this book.

Part One

ALAN SORRELL: A BRIEF BIOGRAPHY

Julia Sorrell

To my husband, Dr Ian Sanders, thanking you for all your tireless help and support to both Mark and myself to make this book possible. With love, Julia

Chapter 1

Introduction

BEFORE BEGINNING, it is necessary for me to make it clear to the reader that I am not an archaeologist, I am not an academic, I am not a writer, but I am an artist, and I am Alan Sorrell's daughter. As a little girl, on one of our many trips to Roman sites up and down the country, I remember asking my father: "Why do they have all your pictures at these places?" Mischievously, he replied: "You must remember I created Roman Britain." And, of course, I believed him.

The archaeological world realised their good fortune:

> "in being able to attract the services of a man like Alan Sorrell though service is perhaps too stark a word for the loving care which he lavished on each and every one of his brilliant reconstructions. To those of us whose interests were kindled and nurtured by the remarkable wave of popular archaeology in the 1950s the name of Alan Sorrell was as well known as those of Glyn Daniel and Sir Mortimer Wheeler."

So wrote Professor Barry Cunliffe in his foreword to *Reconstructing the Past*. He concluded:

> "Alan Sorrell's drawings have been an inspiration to amateur enthusiasts and professional archaeologists alike. Their accuracy, their timeless quality and the fact that they are works of art in their own right will ensure that they continue to inspire for generations to come." (in Sorrell 1981, 8)

Whether they be museum directors, archaeologists, teachers, or mere enthusiasts they all affectionately reminisce: "Of course I remember Sorrell's work." My father was scrupulous about replying to every young enthusiast who wrote to him, and would have been particularly moved by the archaeologist Tim Copeland who recently wrote:

> "Alan Sorrell's work has been crucial to my career as an archaeologist … I must have been about eight years old when I walked on my own the six miles to Caerleon one summer's day to see the remains. I never made it as I was picked up by the police as a 'missing child'… At sometime around ten years old I entered a drawing competition in my local children's library

INTRODUCTION 3

FIG. 1. *Caerleon Legionary Fortress* (1939). Gouache, pen & ink, chalks & watercolour, 43 × 55.5 cm
(COLLECTION OF AMGUEDDFA CYMRU – NATIONAL MUSEUM WALES)

and copied the barracks reconstruction. I won and my prize was to be taken to the Roman town of Caerwent which I had chosen because I had a guide book with three of Alan's reconstructions: the town, the forum and temple, and shop. I eventually got my father to take me to Caerleon on the bus. I think he was a bit embarrassed about his son wanting to be an archaeologist when we lived in the tough area of Newport Docks" (Copeland, pers. comm. 2014)

"Anyway," he continues "apparently when we got to the amphitheatre I was hugely upset that it was not like Alan's famous reconstruction, but a ruin."

Alan Sorrell's work inspired many people and yet few know about him as an artist and even fewer about his life. So I want to take the reader on a journey through this extraordinary man's life. Those who know Alan Sorrell's archaeological reconstruction drawings from visiting sites, television, museums or books will be surprised that this was only part of his artistic career. He painted murals; he travelled – recording pending changes; he painted imaginative, romantic pictures; he painted portraits, and so on. His output was prodigious. As for his personality, let us read what my mother wrote in 1945:

"When I remember that you told me how you had been on the verge of suicide once – it seems quite incredible – and quite unlike you – because you are so alive – your work, your letters, the way you walk and talk, your expressions, the way you love me – everything about you vibrates with life – so that the thought of you of all people thinking about death seems fantastic. I have never met anyone quite so brimming over with life." (Sorrell & Tanner 1944–7, undated, ?Sunday 1945)

However, when I was only 19, my father unexpectedly died, and we became rudderless without this stable anchor. I had just returned home from College for the 1974 Christmas holidays, and one morning my parents went shopping. They were involved in a car accident, both being injured. After a few days we collected my mother from hospital, but my father had to have his right arm, his writing arm, pinned. Mr Frank Todman, a patron, amateur artist, local solicitor and friend visited my father in hospital and told the surgeon to make a good job of the mend "as Alan Sorrell's contribution to art is enormous". On 21 December Alan rang my mother, Elizabeth, who due to her internal injuries including broken ribs, had to ask my father to stop "cracking so many jokes". My father's last words, unwittingly, were "take good care of Strüdel" (our dog). I mention this as Alan had always jokingly considered what his last words would be – having seen so many death-bed scenes in westerns! As we were due to collect Alan that afternoon, we all sat down for a celebratory lunch with my aunt and uncle. The phone went again: "I think you had better come to the hospital." My uncle drove us down – no-one spoke. When we got there we were told that Alan had had a massive heart attack on getting out of bed and had died. I remember the doctor turning to me and saying: "he was no spring chicken". Not having heard the phrase before, I was angry that my father was being compared to a chicken. My mother decided to see Alan for the last time; I did not – I regret this now, but I was young. She said "I have never seen him look so calm." My mother was to live another 17 years, but never recovered from this loss.

In trying to convey an impression of Alan Sorrell, I shall let him speak as often as I can as he left many unpublished manuscripts, enhanced by my mother's anecdotes she told whilst we sewed together on many a long evening. Maybe, like my mother, it may meander in its telling, as I link all the threads together, showing how circumstances influenced his direction to being an artist and his involvement with archaeology, as well as answering frequently asked questions such as: "Why DID he paint so many stormy skies?" At times, the text could be interpreted as self-indulgent. From my experience, most artists are shy, and working in isolation can lead to periods of self-doubt, neurosis and anxiety. My father, unlike many artists, had the honesty to express these sentiments as well as concerns about being ignored or considered out of fashion. Alan wanted to be valued as an artist, but at times felt threatened, as in the case of photography, whereby the general public may question whether there is still a need for an artist to visually record a scene. I elaborate on all of this in the chapters that follow and hope it will be entertaining – a "good read" and not too biased!

Chapter 2

Early life and education

ALAN ERNEST SORRELL was born 11 February 1904 in Tooting, London to Edith and Ernest. Even from the moment of conception, Alan's life was traumatic, he always believing this accounted for his nervous disposition. His parents had been told not to have any more children after the birth of Doris, 7 years Alan's senior. With that birth, Ernest had had to choose between his wife and child – the presumed priority then being the potential heir. Ernest chose Edith, who may have had pre-eclampsia with her pregnancies. Fortunately both mother and daughter survived. Not surprisingly, Edith was very stressed throughout her second pregnancy. Alan was born with a supposed weak heart and was a "difficult feeder". He would often say "Oh Cow & Gate, you know I was their first baby – my life was saved by them," adding: "Oh let's have Cow & Gate and help promote them." Such would be his parting words to my mother leaving for Hadleigh, Essex, to get free backing boards from Mr Buttery, the chemist, for Alan's completed reconstruction drawings. Mr and Mrs Buttery kept all the cardboard adverts for my mother after they had finished displaying them in their window. Once home, my father would look at them and laugh

Left: FIG. 2. Edith, Ernest and Doris Sorrell (*c.* 1899) (SORRELL FAMILY COLLECTION)

Right: FIG. 3. Alan Sorrell, aged about 2, with his father, mother, sister and aunt on a pleasure steamer off Southend (SORRELL FAMILY COLLECTION)

considering which would entertain the archaeologists more, the smiling baby or maybe the lovely ladies' legs – ah yes the one showing the recovery from varicose veins using this amazing new cream. You can imagine, then, my amusement on seeing a group of academics at the Society of Antiquaries examining the reverse of one of my father's drawings and pondering the significance of the Cow & Gate baby or the lovely legs! Interestingly, in 1904 Dr Killick, medical officer of health for Leicester, had asked the West Surrey Central Dairy Company Limited to supply powdered milk to help feed children of poor families. In 1908, the resultant high-protein *Cow & Gate Pure English Dried Milk* was first marketed on a large scale.

Ernest, himself a frustrated amateur artist, had been obliged to enter the family jewellery business. The Sorrells, of Huguenot descent, had lived and worked for generations as craftsmen in and around Pennington Street, London, after fleeing France and supposedly entering Britain in a basket of apples! As my brother Richard asked: "Which variety?" Without knowing this family history, Alan found that a Richard and Elizabeth Sorrell had owned Hyde Hall, near Great Waltham, Essex, in the 17th century. Alan romanticised that they were his ancestors: "I feel I belong to that part of England, as indeed I do because my people have lived thereabouts since 13 hundred and something which is a long time" (Sorrell & Tanner 1944–7, postmarked 19 June 1945). We went and just sat in the car looking at it and Alan even dreamed of living there.

Less salubriously our immediate Sorrell branch came from Bow, then moving to Tooting. On Alan's maternal side, Edith's family were Irish, her maiden name being Doody, and had moved from Galway, southern Ireland to Shifnal in Shropshire for work. Her father was a civil engineer, working in the mines, and produced a well drawn chart of the rock strata for the mine.

Edith and Ernest decided to relocate his business and young family to near Southend in Essex. They were a comfortable, lower middle-class family who appreciated the opportunity to leave London.

Alan was a timid and, supposedly, delicate child. Years later, in August 1940 at *Sunnyside*, Shifnal, Alan wrote a short story *The Shadow* (also referred to as *The Gun*) – obviously auto-biographical:

> "After that night he would have his bedroom door open, and as he came to know fear better and screamed so pitifully at its (*the gun*) onset, he was given a night light. His mother didn't call him a naughty boy now but she would come and stroke his hot forehead until at last he fell asleep. After a time a doctor came and they played with

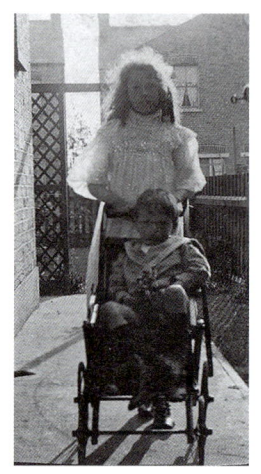

FIG. 4. Doris and Alan in a bath chair (*c.* 1909) (SORRELL FAMILY COLLECTION)

FIG. 5. Alan's earliest drawing (date unknown) (SORRELL FAMILY COLLECTION)

a funny thing called a stethoscope and (*he*) heard him say 'heart' to his father. After that he had to stay in bed for weeks and weeks although he felt quite well."

And:

"thinking that *(he)* was interested in guns rather than frightened of them his father gave him a box of toy-soldiers. [We still have a box of toy lead soldiers which Alan, as a child, painted and then re-enacted battle scenes.] He was also given 'a *GUN*. How fearfully he handled it, and what odd excuses he invented for not firing it!' … His fear caused all his relatives to speak of him as 'the artist.' It seemed to be a rather good occupation for so frightened and delicate a person – he would evidently be of no use in the family warehousing and removal business." (Sorrell 1940a, 5–6)

Alan spent a lot of his childhood in a bath chair but would later admit that against his friends he was "the healthiest looking with ruddy cheeks". Perhaps his mother, father and sister were over-protective. After all, when staying in the 1940s with his mother, she then being in her 80s, Alan wrote: "Yesterday I was out all day and did quite a nice sketch … mother came and brought some lunch". And, on hearing Alan had shingles, Elizabeth wrote: "Has your mother seen your room? I should think she would be worried if she knew that your landlady doesn't cook for you – are you feeling fit now?" (Sorrell & Tanner 1944–7, postmarked 14 Oct. 1945; undated ?Sept. 1946).

Ernest would keenly go painting at weekends taking his young son with him, and one can imagine them walking over the hills with their painting equipment, selecting such subject matters as Hadleigh Castle, which had

FIG. 6. Landscape by Ernest Sorrell (date unknown). Oil, 30 × 21 cm
(COLLECTION OF JULIA SORRELL)

been epitomised by John Constable. On these outings, Alan not only painted, but also would collect a piece of stone, which was carefully wrapped in cotton wool and added to his museum collection. A lasting impression was made on Alan and in 1946 he wrote to *The Times* about Hadleigh Castle where he pointed out that it was in danger of "losing its likeness to the picture because the North Tower was crumbling" (ASA). In 1910, however, these painting excursions were to end abruptly for 6-year-old Alan, with the sudden death of Ernest from pneumonia at only 49. "A drop of brandy could have saved him", the doctor told Edith, who had become a strict teetotaller following her father "dying of the bottle".

Edith and Ernest were strict Congregationalists although their wedding certificate showed them marrying in a Wesleyan Methodist Chapel. Years later, when referring to his feeling of exhaustion in Greece, Alan would write:

> "This was an excellent opportunity for meditation and, even, for soliloquy, but whatever tendencies I ever had to these habits, were driven out of me when I was a child; 'meditation' was called 'wool gathering', and soliloquy considered to be a sign of weakening sanity ... The idea of real tea, greatly attracted me, but my artistic conscience, bolstered up as always, by a Nonconformist upbringing, urged me to make another drawing before succumbing to such a voluptuous temptation." (Sorrell *c.* 1962, 24, 28)

Alan retained a strong protestant work ethic, being always haunted by guilt. By the time I knew him, a sense of abstemiousness had largely disappeared. This had begun in Rome where "he manfully drank a bottle of beer". (Sorrell *c.* 1938, 222: *Barbarians in Rome* is autobiographical, but written in the third person).

I was recently asked at an exhibition of Alan's work: "Well, what sort of artist was your father? Was he forever propping up the bar?" I laughingly replied – "that was NOT my father".

With the death of Ernest it was not just the painting excursions but life generally that was to radically change, from seeming comfort and ease to financially and emotionally painful episodes. Alan did not talk much about his childhood and early life, but we are able to form an insight from his writings and paintings. Alan developed an intolerable stammer which was to considerably affect him throughout his life. In Rome (1928–1930) he recalled that as he "could not talk very well ... he would retire from these discussions and soothe his jealous feelings by playing the Kreutzer Sonata on the common room gramophone." And "being very lonely ... he would go for long solitary walks, always at a tremendous pace." Feeling unconfident he "made many mistakes and the worst was his stony refusal to interest himself in the [Italian] language". He:

"reasoned that as he would never be able to say the words or the sentences there could be no point in his suffering agonising half hours with Marchi – and spending such a lot of money ... That tiresome stammer was both the expression and the cause of most of the trouble and all the actions led to it for sometimes he would, with ridiculous boldness, try to say things that he knew would be particularly difficult for him to test himself and then at other times he would run away from his difficulties, and suffer agonies of humiliation as the result. He couldn't under these circumstances behave like a rational being." (Sorrell *c.* 1938, 247)

Alan was never able to do public speaking or even confidently ask for his bus fare. I remember many incidents where the word simply did not materialise. Fortunately Elizabeth was supportive and on reading *Barbarians in Rome* (Sorrell *c.* 1938) she wrote:

"I can't think why you make yourself appear so timid though – or why you should be so self-conscious about the stammer – are you really self-conscious about it? If it does worry you, we'll cure it, but personally I think it's attractive ...". (Sorrell & Tanner 1944–7, undated, ?Sunday, 1945)

When, as a baby, my brother Richard was ill, my mother and father had been asked to open a local exhibition. Out of courtesy my mother was invited to speak first, followed by my father. Worrying about Richard compounded the situation, and all he could stutter was: "Now you can see why I paint." Generally people were patient, but sometimes, as at a Royal Watercolour Society meeting where Alan was struggling to express a point of view, he was shouted at by another artist "hurry up and get on with it". So much for artistic sensitivity! My mother was furious, my father humiliated.

As a little boy Alan was forced to write with his right hand, his left hand being tied behind his back. Although he did write with his right hand, he always set the table for a left-handed person, and in the car accident, he instinctively protected his dominant arm, hence his right arm was damaged. However, one advantage was that Alan would give equal importance to both the bottom right and left-hand corners of his paintings (usually a right handed artist will neglect the right hand corner and vice versa).

Alan was clumsy. In Rome he remembered how "he had never played ping-pong before and was very clumsy; he found calling the points spoilt the game because some of the numbers made him stammer" (Sorrell *c.* 1962, 39). He actually was to become quite good at ping-pong (table tennis) and every Christmas we all played and invariably Alan won! A school-friend commented on how Alan missed a lot of his schooling due to ill health. It could have been due to his health or "task avoidance" due to many things including his stammer and clumsiness, but he did tell a journalist that he started school at 10 years old (Mories 1939, 85). He once told me that he was unable to read till he was 10 – maybe he wanted to console me as I, too, was a late reader. He added that once he could read, he read Walter Scott's Waverley Novels! However he was not considered "grammar school material" and, due to lack of finances, private schools were completely out of the question. The only option was to finish his schooling at Chalkwell Hall School – then a "board school" – with pupils leaving at 14. His *Who's Who* entry in 1951 read "privately educated"; it should have been self-educated! Pre-1950s a large proportion of artists and archaeologists including John Piper, Lucian Freud, Graham Sutherland and Aileen Fox were private or public-school educated, whilst grammar schools offered an education to able students from poorer backgrounds, like Henry Moore and Sir Mortimer Wheeler. One archaeologist who did come from similar beginnings as Alan was Cyril Fox but he, like Alan, was unusual. Therefore, it is obvious how an intelligent and sensitive ex-board school pupil must have felt working

FIG. 7. Art competition drawing (date unknown). A statue on a plinth was to become a recurring compositional theme, see Figs 8 & 27. Gouache, watercolour & pen & ink, 37 × 36 cm
(COLLECTION OF JULIA SORRELL © ESTATE OF ALAN SORRELL)

and mixing in such a stratified society. Again I refer to *Barbarians in Rome* (Sorrell *c.* 1938) where a wealthy student arrived and it transpired that his preparatory school was near to where Alan "had spent his childhood, and he was fearful lest" this student "should enquire what his school had been and then he would have had to say" that his "was a board-school." Then "on meeting an educated German who spoke such good English," Alan "felt as never before, the inadequacy of his board school education." (Sorrell *c.* 1938, 168)

When Alan was 14, his sister Doris died of TB, aged 20. Edith had tried all the then recommended and supposed cures including sanatoriums around the country. Doris had been working as a secretary in London before she became ill and Alan believed her TB had been triggered by commuting daily by train, so when I went to college in London he was adamant I lived up there! Edith owned a few properties in Bow which she gradually sold to pay for Doris's treatment, the result being that there was little money left after Doris died. How did all this affect Alan? Could his low attendance at school have also been due to Doris being ill? For Alan coping with all this emotional stress may have been another reason for staying at home. Perhaps he also craved attention. Had he not been that delicate child Doris had pushed around in a bath chair? We can just conjecture, but we do know how neurotic he became. In Rome he wrote how "forgetting for once his old maidish fear of typhoid (or what the disease is that comes from eating not very pure ice cream) he bought one, and survived" (Sorrell *c.* 1938, 222). When Elizabeth was ill, Alan wrote: "Anything connected with

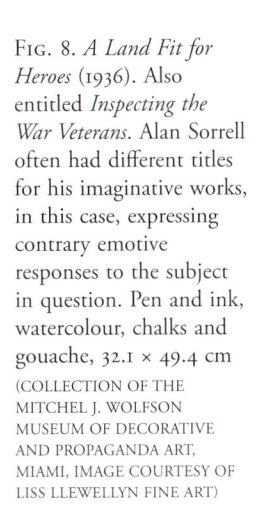

Fig. 8. *A Land Fit for Heroes* (1936). Also entitled *Inspecting the War Veterans*. Alan Sorrell often had different titles for his imaginative works, in this case, expressing contrary emotive responses to the subject in question. Pen and ink, watercolour, chalks and gouache, 32.1 × 49.4 cm
(COLLECTION OF THE MITCHEL J. WOLFSON MUSEUM OF DECORATIVE AND PROPAGANDA ART, MIAMI, IMAGE COURTESY OF LISS LLEWELLYN FINE ART)

the lungs makes me nervous" (Sorrell & Tanner 1944–7, ?Feb. 1945). If I ever coughed, Alan became frantic. I did not know why until my mother explained how Alan remembered, as a boy, hearing "Doris coughing up blood in her bedroom every night"; for how many years we do not know but probably much of his childhood. What was Alan doing when at home? Was he drawing? It would not be surprising considering the maturity of the perspective and composition of a painting he produced at this time which won a children's competition. Interestingly he included a figure on a plinth which he repeated in later works such as *Inspecting the War Veterans* (1936).

Money, or rather the lack of it, troubled Alan: "You must SAVE money, not spend it" (Sorrell *c.* 1938, ASA). At times he became resentful: "First-class, red plush, third class austere boards, so third class" for Alan "for the fantasy of the virtue of discomfort died hard" (Sorrell *c.* 1938, ASA). Twenty-five years later, in 1954, he expressed the same sentiments when travelling to Greece and Istanbul: " … but if one has only the third part of a mere cabin, with fans buzzing like angry hornets, and pipes hissing like a nest of vipers, throbbing engines and snoring humans, then perhaps a feeling of depression may be permitted" (Sorrell *c.* 1962, 8).

When Alan left school at 14 what was he to do? First of all he went to Clark's College for a secretarial training, but that seemed to be short-lived, which is not surprising. I remember him typing up *Last Boat to Nubia* (Sorrell *c.* 1974) with just one finger! Certainly not the expected 60 words a minute. He would sit in the studio/sitting room with a rhythmic tap-tap of the loud key on the old Olivetti type-writer with the bell ringing at the end of each line. My mother and I were watching a television programme with this tap-tap going on behind us. So Alan transferred to the kitchen where a fainter tap-tap continued. This was repeated every evening for months and the work was completed shortly before his death. Determined yes, but not secretarial material!

Alan had always wanted to be an artist, but was under family pressure to support his mother. Edith, however, encouraged Alan in his wish – after all had not Ernest wanted to paint and been deterred by his family? Alan attended the Junior Art Department of the Southend Municipal College to be trained as a

FIG. 9. Monomarks Designing Company working drawing plus notes (*c.* 1922)
(COLLECTION OF JULIA SORRELL, © ESTATE OF ALAN SORRELL)

commercial artist. He later wrote:

> "– I don't know – I spent 4 years in a J.A.D., and came out of it terribly untrained, but that was because of bad teaching, and teaching is the whole crux of the matter. Really and truly I am deeply pessimistic about all movements which set out to encourage the arts in any way – but that's neither here nor there". (Sorrell & Tanner 1944–7, postmarked 23 June 1945)

In 1923 he found himself Assistant Designer for *Monomarks Designing Company*, Kensal Rise in London. He later remarked:

> "... when I was employed as a designer of labels for dairymen, I had sent forth into the world scores of them decorated with magnificent cows whose noble lineaments derived also from Royal Academical genius. In all seriousness, the picking of other artist's brains is in no sense unworthy, so long as the thought is reborn in the process". (Sorrell 1939d: 102)

Often Alan would look at a cream pot and say to us children "I wonder if those are my designs." One benefit that did materialise from his employment was working to strict deadlines as well as not being proud. In other words: "the customer is always right". Hence his commercial designs are full of notes and amendments. The same process would be repeated years later between Alan and archaeologists such as Sir Cyril Fox and V. E. Nash-Williams regarding the Caerwent dig. Correspondence was written around the cartoon until the information was accurate. I recall lengthy discussions between Alan and the archaeologists regarding the flag of St Mawes Castle.

FIG. 10. Detail of Caerwent working drawing, early Christian church (1938). Pencil, pen & ink, crayon & gouache on tracing paper, 61.5 × 48 cm
(SORRELL FAMILY COLLECTION)

Was this finger-nail sized flag a Union or Pre-Union flag? His commercial art training gave him the humility and mentality necessary to undertake such commissions.

Although Alan's ambition was to be a "Fine Artist", he was delighted to be offered a place at the Royal College of Art by the Principal Sir William Rothenstein, even if it was as an illustrator. When interviewed by Percy Horton in 1955, Alan acknowledged that "the qualities of his work together with the independence and integrity of his character and outlook had attracted the attention of Sir William Rothenstein" (Horton 1955, 18). Alan felt, however, a lasting sense of inadequacy when described as "illustrative"; hence even as late as 1972 he would be writing:

> "'Illustration' is today often used as a term of denigration, though when one realises that nine-tenths of European drawing and painting is illustration, sometimes on a huge scale, as in the splendid rhetoric of Rubens' pictures of scriptural and classical subject matter, and coming right down to 'book-size' with Rembrandt's drawings and etchings, and then to the minute with Calvert's *Chamber Idyll*." (Sorrell 1972b: 25).

Earlier in the 1940s he again felt it necessary to justify

> "the reason I don't experiment is that I consider myself to be merely an illustrator (Giotto also was an illustrator!) I mean it doesn't seem to matter what the tone of my voice is (to alter the metaphor) so long as I can be understood. Of course, its easy to pick holes in such a theory and prove it to be a fallible one but I mean I am not likely to spend years experimenting with, say impressionistic colour (so called) or in anatomical dissection or with 'abstract form.' You will be pleased to hear I have sold my 'thatching' drawing for 20 guineas". (Sorrell & Tanner 1944–7, postmarked 22 Apr. 1945)

In due course Alan was able to transfer to the decorative mural department. He had to finance his time at the RCA by doing commercial art at night (Mories 1939, 85), hence missing out on a relaxed student's life. He would later tell Elizabeth not to hide away, adding: "I used to be very ill adjusted to life and its cost me a good many wasted years and a great deal of unhappiness – getting adjusted" (Sorrell & Tanner 1944–7, postmarked 17 Aug. 1944).

In 1954, when visiting the Church of the Holy Saviour in Chora, Istanbul, Alan met Ernest Hawkins, a Byzantinist and a mosaic conservator:

> "When I disclosed my identity, we discovered that, as students, we had both sat at the feet of the same reverend professor at South Kensington. We talked for some time about Professor Tristram [a medievalist art historian and Professor of Design at the Royal College of Art] of his extraordinary remoteness from contemporary trends in art and design,

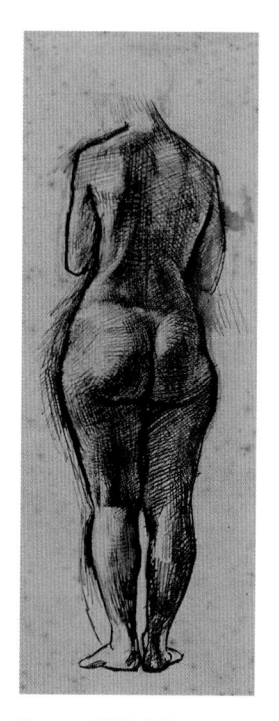

Fig. 11. RCA Life drawing (*c.* 1926). Chalks & pencil, 40 × 20 cm (COLLECTION OF JULIA SORRELL, © ESTATE OF ALAN SORRELL)

and how valuable that remoteness had been to his students. They could always rely on his criticisms being utterly unbiased by the fashion of the day, entirely objective, and without fussy complications related to technical methods and machinery. The Professor had always been very kind to me, he approved my doing commercial drawings out of College hours and said it 'kept my feet upon the ground'. In his remoteness he did not realise, perhaps, that if one keeps ones feet upon the ground they are likely to become muddied, and mud sometimes takes a long time to clean off. Commercial art, so called, is, of course, an inferior kind of art, in that the artist is required to twist his personal views so as to please the customer: therefore it is inevitably insincere and second-rate. This desire to please is the mud which I later found so difficult to remove. I fear the Professor did not like my work very much: he invariably used two expressions when looking at it – 'very able' and 'I should do a series of these'. I quickly realised they both signified disapproval, but that increased my respect for his judgement". (Sorrell *c.* 1962, 182)

Ernest Hawkins, who had been instrumental in Alan being able to draw at S. Saviour, invited him to his flat:

"The dinner that Mrs Hawkins had cooked was delicious, but my enjoyment of it was tempered by anxiety as to what my host would say about the drawings which he had asked me to show him. He had used the word 'slick' in commendation of my drawing of St Saviour, and this had sunk deep into my soul, a veritable dagger thrust into the vitals of my self-respect … Slick has an even more serious derogatory connotation than Professor Tristram's 'able' for whilst 'able' suggests only a dreary level of accomplishment with a basis of unimaginative honesty, 'slickness'

FIG. 12. *The Outer Narthex of St Saviour in Chora, Istanbul during the Restoration of the Mosaics* (1954).
(WHEREABOUTS & SIZE OF ORIGINAL UNKNOWN; ASA COPY)

implies superficiality of the more dashing sort with a fundamental basis of dishonesty, a rapid skating over the ice, the breaking of which would land the artist in difficulties beyond his power of solving. So the shock of having this fashionable quality of 'slickness' applied to my work had displeased me greatly, but, fortified, or perhaps mollified by the effects of the excellent dinner which Mrs. Hawkins had cooked for us, my censor now revised his verdict, though in a slightly oblique way, by saying that the large amount of work I had done indicated 'great ability'. In this phrase I seemed to hear a far off whisper of Tristram, but with this I had to be satisfied, and if I fell silent and glum, it was because I was trying to deduce what Hawkins really did think of the work. He was the first artistically literate person to see these drawings, and although I (with the armour-plated vanity which is part of the essential make-up of the artist) thought it was good, doubts now began to seep in. Suppose it was poor, even just average, commonplace, thin – all these mean sounding adjectives sprang up before me like miserable little yellow faced midgets; some of them collapsed immediately, but a few survived, grinning horribly".

Later on Alan writes: "It was a long time before I slept, which shows that a single word, spoken in no way unkindly, can keep one writhing unhappily for more hours than a physically hurtful blow" (Sorrell *c.* 1962, 192–3). These are long passages but, after reading them, one has a keen insight into Alan's lack of self-esteem.

Chapter 3

The British School at Rome 1928–1930

RECOGNISING ALAN'S assiduous and rapid development at the Royal College, Sir William Rothenstein suggested he should consider entering for the *Prix de Rome,* a long-established French scholarship for young artists which was then a highly celebrated accolade. The British version of the *Prix de Rome* had first been awarded in 1881 as part of the recognition of mural painting as a distinctive art form. "By 1911 The British School at Rome was established with special emphasis on decorative painting and the study of Renaissance murals in Italy" (Willsdon 2000, 15). Alan, along with three others, presented their work to a panel of judges including Augustus John. Alan won the scholarship in 1928 as a Decorative Muralist with a composition entitled *People Seeking after Wisdom.* When interviewed by the Evening Standard, Alan said "after being in Rome for two years I intend on going in for decorative painting as a career" (*Evening Standard*, ASA archive cutting undated, late April 1928).

On leaving England Alan was delighted as "had he not been one of that hurrying crowd only a few weeks ago". Remembering the rigidity of commercial art he observed that "boredom and greyness breed adventurers and from the office stools and the monotonous rumble come 'the true romantics'… He was wondering whether he was a 'true romantic' not *quite* the type maybe" (Sorrell *c.* 1938, 1, 241). Of course he was!

Alan arrived in Rome on 29 September 1928. The students were given a studio with a balcony bedroom, there was a communal dining room. The building is imperious with a Classical feel up a flight of steps which were accessed via Villa Borghese Gardens about 1½ miles (2.4 km) from Central Rome. In the British School at Rome there was a tennis court, probably to maintain the British feel and a charming enclosed garden.

Its architect had been Sir Edwin Lutyens. What a cultural shock for Alan, whose travelling had been limited to London and Essex apart from trips to

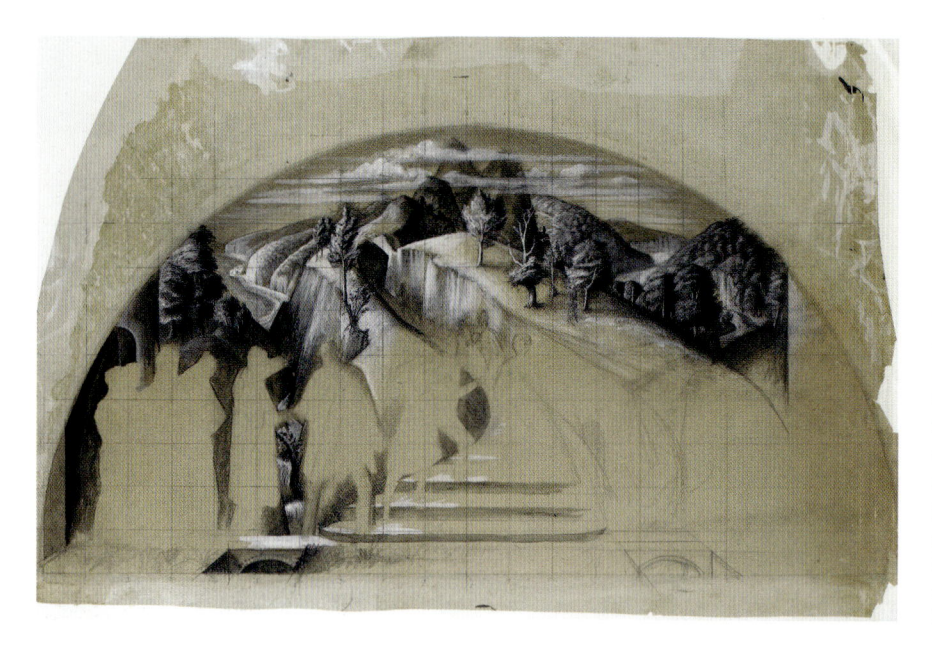

FIG. 13. Study for *People Seeking after Wisdom* (1928). Preliminary study for his submission piece for the British School at Rome scholarship in decorative mural painting. Pencil, ink and gouache on paper, 49.5 × 79 cm
(IMAGE COURTESY OF LISS LLEWELLYN FINE ART)

his maternal family in Shropshire. Socially, he would meet a diverse group of people from artists to archaeologists, historians, classicists and architects, some of whom would become lifelong friends and work colleagues. They included Colin Hardie (classicist), Reginald Brill (artist) and Ian Richmond (archaeologist). On visiting the School, Aileen Henderson (later Lady Fox) noticed Alan: "a dark, thin young man with a stammer, diffident yet determined" (Dykes 1980, 5).

In *Barbarians in Rome*, an autobiographical novel Alan completed in the 1930s, he gives us a real insight into this young man's intellectual and social inadequacies: "a gawky young man and his extreme nervousness rather spoils his dramatic pause …". Alan continues that this being the first time he had had two years to entirely devote himself to his artistic development, he "found it daunting and did not know where to begin". It was imperative, though, to educate himself, establish a concrete direction, be receptive and question many contrary opinions.

> "Yes he would COPY a fresco, a picture which would TEACH him something, – Raphael's *School of Athens* at the Vatican. Every young artist must perforce begin as a primitive, and this one was far too immature to really love this ripest fruit of the Renaissance any more than he could appreciate Baroque architecture, but he knew it was acknowledged a supreme work, and in his rather oppressively honest enquiring way he wanted to discover for himself the secrets of its presumed great merit. Perhaps copying would explain them to him … He argued that it was extraordinary that students should avoid copying good pictures because

THE BRITISH SCHOOL AT ROME   19

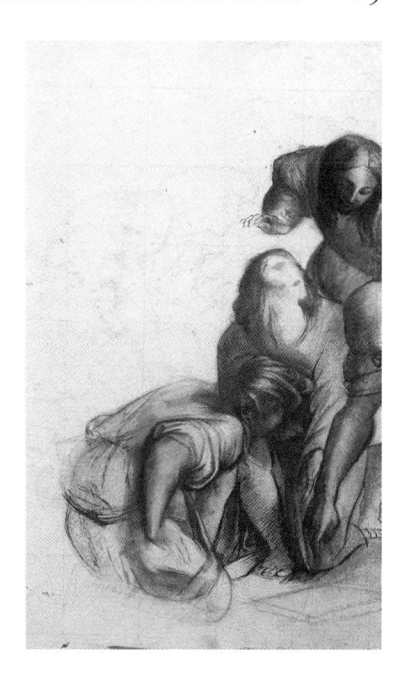

Left to right:

FIG. 14. Alan Sorrell, British School at Rome (Jan. 1930). Taken in the corridor with the studios along the right
(SORRELL FAMILY COLLECTION)

FIG. 15. Alan Sorrell's studio, British School at Rome (1930). The sleeping area was above
(SORRELL FAMILY COLLECTION)

FIG. 16. Study for a copy of *The School of Athens* by Raphael in the Stanza della Segnatura, Vatican (autumn 1928)
(IMAGE COURTESY OF LISS LLEWELLYN FINE ART)

it seems such a logical way of accustoming themselves to good form. You can't begin to properly express your own ideas until you have the experience of the possibilities and limitations of your particular medium. Find out WHY the masters did things in their own special way, how they grouped their figures, for instance, and then do likewise – well – not exactly that perhaps, but your enquiries will make you sound yourself, make you THINK and find out some of the fundamentals of picture making – save you years of blind ineffectual slogging." (Sorrell *c.* 1938, 32)

He continued that considering himself an original person he would not

"be likely to become a mere echo of the man you study; actually and paradoxically, nothing stimulates originality more than a dive into other people's minds … Yes, artists are funny fellows, he mused, they draw from the figure, and study anatomy and perspective, but refuses to study actual works of art". *ibid.*)

Obviously this was an intelligent man "hungry" for education.

Alan wondered if "an *intelligent* Fine Artist" could be a romanticist or had to be purely academic and analytical? Following a tour of Tuscany, he was directed to the School's library and in particular a book entitled *Art* by Clive Bell (1914). He "swallowed with avidity his [Mr Bell's] astonishing pronouncements on the good and bad in art. They completed the stirring up process which the five weeks tour had started." Alan "found himself to be in a queer state of glorying in his rich memories of Tuscan renaissance art, and at the same time clinging with almost religious fervour to a conviction

[Mr Bell's] that between the Byzantines and Mr Paul Cezanne European art had been in a state of almost obscene decay." Alan

> "reviewed the large drawing of the hills and trees, and quickly decided that he must deprive the world of the not-yet-started-painting since it seemed to be noticeably deficient in 'Pure Form.' That was the phrase, 'Pure Form.' Away with this golden calf of representational; the cylinder and the cube are the new tablets of the law, straight from Bloomsbury. Then to complicate matters still further he read another book, which in a series of elaborate charts and many pages of pseudo-scientific explanation, settled for once and for all the difficulties of colour, and, working on the lines indicated, he produced a mauve and pale green picture."

Alan considered that the drawback to this theory,

> "was that every colour seemed to become in the end either mauve or pale green. But for the moment he believed he had found the solutions for all his technical worries, and with the Tuscans, growing less vivid in his memory, he became quite satisfied that Cézanne was the only artist worthy of emulation and he viewed his own earlier work with a kindly but condescending pity." (Sorrell *c.* 1938, 203)

By 'Pure Form' Clive Bell (1914) means the analytical reduction of the subject matter to basic fundamental geometric shapes of circle, square, rectangle, etc, devoid of any emotion. Oddly enough Alan's

> "devotion to 'Pure Form' did not prevent his doing a little painting of *The Prodigal Son*; oddly, certainly, since his idol, Mr Cézanne, had spent his life in the contemplation of apples on plates. However, one must make allowance for national foibles, and what an apple on a plate is to a Frenchman, a Prodigal Son is to an Englishman, one must suppose. But in spite of all this confusion of thought and purpose and this dogmatism of immaturity …"

Alan was beginning "to grow up as an artist".

In reference to colour, an artist has a limited palette that concentrates on the harmony and balance of the complementary warm and cool hues. In his continual search for truth and honesty, Alan found it was his

> "weak colour sense that made painting so difficult, but instead of admitting the weakness and realising that the best and obvious course would be to use colour merely to decorate and not to express forms, he must needs try to increase his sensitiveness by mere headwork – theorising in the pseudo-scientific method of the Impressionist doctrinaires, those intrepid fellows who, not content to use Nature as an inspiration, called in the chemists to analyse her colour so that they might imitate it more exactly."

He consistently referred to Bell who surely as a Cambridge intellectual should know! After all had not

> "Mr Clive Bell commanded him to look at things 'objectively' and now he would have considered a piece of the True Cross as either a significant or an insignificant piece of form. And so he even examined the pathetic casts of engulfed Pompeiians in this unsentimental and so inevitably unimaginative way too. It was all a question of form, Pure Form. *But he did conscientiously wander up and down the Pompeiian streets, and their chariot ruts for a moment startled him out of his chilly objectivity.*" (Sorrell *c.* 1938, 245)

Earlier he had visited the Colosseum which

> "he was initially disappointed by but "when you leave the place you begin to *rebuild* it in all its former splendour, and as the years go by the sunlight will become more vivid, the shadows more richly violet and the sky tropically blue." (*Ibid.*, 26)

It is obvious that Alan had something different to offer than just "Pure Form." He had an innate, romantic ability to visualise and re-create a former civilization from what were often patchy ground plans, as described in his 1954 trip to Greece. Professor Carl Blegen, an American archaeologist, showed Alan the plans of his excavation of the Palace of King Nestor at Pylos. Blegen "then became even graver in manner, and said he thought there were very, very, serious difficulties in the way of reconstruction drawing of the site". As described in greater detail in Chapter 10, Alan there and then reconstructed the palace in a drawing showing how it could work as a three-dimensional structure, leaving the skeptical Blegen not only convinced that it was possible, "but desirable, a splendid idea" (Sorrell *c.* 1962, 53). So these innate seeds set tentatively in Rome would later bear fruit!

FIG. 17. *Nestor's Palace. Pylos* (1954). Produced for Professor Carl Blegen for an *Illustrated London News* article

(SIZE, MEDIUM & LOCATION OF ORIGINAL UNKNOWN, ASA COPY)

Alan was always a very driven and competitive man. In his second year he felt he had a strategy to achieve this goal. Alan's

> "outlook was certainly not sentimental, and was becoming increasingly strained and grim. He had a natural delight in small forms, the embroidering of a theme with a hundred relevant but tiny facts, which gave the quality of jewellery to his best work; that was his instinct, but now he would have none of these 'unessentials,' his forms must be large and powerful and passionate, he would be a 'great' painter or nothing. He was chock full of theories of art based on the pictures he had seen and the books he had read recently." (Sorrell *c.* 1938, 268)

He decided

> "he would adhere rigidly to those two precious sketches he had made in England, and he'd develop as large paintings, one after the other. He'd begin first the smaller painting of the Annunciation; the angular woman seated beneath a tree and a kneeling winged masculine angel embracing her ear. These figures would occupy nine-tenths of the canvas, but there would be room for a *livid* sky with a small tree flattened against the light. The second and larger design of the cripple girl being raised by the travelling preacher would be the *greater* work."

There

> "was to be a background of yellow stormy sky here too, with wind tossed trees as a 'secondary rhythm.' He would, he vowed approach these very literary subjects in the severely objective manner of Cézanne. He wanted in fact the best of both worlds … the trees were to be trees *yet* not trees – just shapes, the figures to be figures, yet *not* figures. They were to be passionately romantic, and yet coldly intellectual arrangements of abstract forms. And the colour was to be the pseudo-scientific prismatic scheme as propounded in that little book he had read last session." (*Ibid.*, 255)

Why was Alan prepared to paint so disparate from his natural instincts? The reason being he wanted to "strike a new note" which

> "would place him in such a favoured position that on his return to England patronage, commissions, and teaching appointments of the most lucrative and informal kind, would pour down upon him; the future would be a triumphant progress, and he visualised himself as being in a few years time as a person most attentively listened to, sought after, wined and dined, and immensely popular. His *manner* he decided would be slightly aloof and enigmatic, with a 'certain dignity' and he would wear the most beautiful clothes in a properly careless manner. No wonder he chose romantic subjects for the engines which were to be the prime cause of this marvellous metamorphosis. Meanwhile he hesitated to put his pencil to paper. Was that, you wonder because he was afraid by so doing he would destroy his dream of mastery and success?" (*Ibid.*, 255)

He dreamed of "phone calls in the dead of night from illustrious enthusiasts – the Chantrey Bequest – commissions – friendships with great and famous men, (on grounds of absolute equality, of course) – a romantic marriage with a Baroness, an Austrian Baroness for preference …" (*ibid.*, 282). This desire for success could have been influenced by his friendship with the successful sculptor Francis William Sargant, who lived and worked near San Minato in Florence. However, at the end of year exhibition, he felt inadequate in comparison with his peers. Alan

> "was full of envy, and in a sudden panic he ran to look at his own work the sight of which convinced him so strongly of his total incapacity and the hopelessness of keeping on trying to be an artist that only a desperately long walk could assuage the silly misery." (Sorrell *c.* 1938, 205)

In fact Alan was the only student to sell that year! It was his copy of Benozzo Gozzoli from the Campo Santo bought by Captain Scott-Moncrieff, the translator of Proust.

Towards the end of his *Prix de Rome* Alan "was still obsessed by the strangling quietude of Piero and his architectonic structure and his disdain of human playfulness and small things." Alan

> "viewed it critically and far from striving to preserve its instantaneous passion, he deliberately substituted for it a cold 'intellectual' arrangement of *shapes*, whose interest for him was no longer human but formal and abstract. In short instead of being natural he became affected." (*Ibid.*, 274)

Fig. 18. Copy of *The Tower of Babel* by Benozzo Gozzoli in the Camposanto, Pisa (1929). Pencil
(WHEREABOUTS OF ORIGINAL UNKNOWN, ASA COPY)

Initially Alan felt hugely inadequate. Was it because of "that confounded stammer coming upon him, not insidiously, but chokingly, and the less he said, or tried to say the better". Or was his Nonconformist background causing him to be frightened of raucousness and disapproving of drunkenness which he had never seen before. He "feared horseplay, and the necessity for taking part in it". He self-consciously thought or knew that his fellow students "were giggling and smirking at him". Alan was grateful when a fellow student organised and lead an outing and by sticking "to him like a shadow, was glad to conceal his inefficiency in these matters from the fair maidens".

Imagine the students' surprise then with Alan's gradual "emergence as an actor instead of a mere onlooker which had previously been his role". For example when Christmas arrived Alan had made for the play "ingenious wire and head pieces for the actors". And he made an enormous contraption for another student "to wear on his head at dinner". Then there was the Via Appia walk which was a very special occasion even though Alan

> "wasn't responsible for originating the idea of a moonlight tramp from San Paolo along the Old Via Appia returning with daylight to San Sebastiano, but he certainly did take it to himself as though it were his own, and even obstinately persist in spite of the fact of the Director letting it be known that he disapproved all such projects as being 'irregular.'" (Sorrell *c.* 1938, 290)

For the first time Alan had become a ringleader: "he tried to believe that this emergence was due to his 'undoubted strength of character,' but perhaps more truly he was able to seize this opportunity," as one of his friends was visiting Florence and he conjectured that "there are disadvantages in having dominating friends". Throughout the Via Appia walk they

> "talked all the time about nothing in particular, just to themselves remembering that they were trespassing on an ancient haunted grave-yard. The moon began to decline at about two o'clock and it sank at last into the pale mist that came creeping gently round the ruins, making them huge and sinister and leaving the tops of the stone pines hanging like great bats flying on their secret nocturnal journeys." (Sorrell *c.* 1938, 291)

Although nearly 30 years later my father had learnt to compensate and disguise many uncertainties in his personality, his spirit remained intact as expressed in October 1972 when describing a recent drawing of Via Appia involving

FIG. 19. *The Appian Way* (1932). Pencil, ink and gouache on paper, 51.5 × 65.5 cm
(PRIVATE COLLECTION, IMAGE COURTESY OF LISS LLEWELLYN FINE ART)

FIG. 20. Copy after *The Victory of Heraclius over Chosroes*, part of *The Legend of the True Cross* by Piero della Francesca in the Basilica of San Francesco, Arezzo (dated March 1929). Oil on panel, 49.5 × 33.8 cm
(PRIVATE COLLECTION, IMAGE COURTESY OF LISS LLEWELLYN FINE ART).

"a recollection of an experience many years ago. Moonlight has always fascinated me, and here it defines the eccentric mutilated shapes of monuments and statues and helps to establish a sympathetic relationship between them and the people walking into the picture." (Sorrell 1972c, 47)

Alan left Rome having travelled extensively around Italy as well as visiting countries en route back and forth to England. The whole experience had proved invaluable and enlightening both intellectually and emotionally. In the future he would not forget the influence upon him. In 1939 Alan reflected on his younger self when discussing his painting *The Miracle*:

"The first and large version was a student work and was painted in Rome. It was going to be a 'great' work, but, alas! It became a mere dull pedestrian exercise, partly because of the painter's inexperience, and partly because of the Influence; the capital letter is well deserved because it refers to no less a personage than Piero della Francesca. I had copied his work in the church at Arezzo and had come completely under the charm of his marvellous quietude and dignity; *here* then was the man to model myself on, and only in retrospect does this naively vainglorious attempt seem fantastically ridiculous … The influence did at any rate teach the student that every shape in the jig-saw pattern of the picture should be a *good* shape." (Sorrell 1939c, 68)

Chapter 4

England 1930–1939

ON ALAN'S RETURN to England in 1930 he had the recurring worry of money. This continuously haunted him whether it be in Rome where having "bought the flask his small tradesman's desire to get his money's worth would force him to drink to the dregs" (Sorrell *c.* 1938, 222); or years later when writing to my mother "No I don't want to teach, but I must earn some money to live" (Sorrell & Tanner 1944–7, postmarked 11 Aug. 1944). I too remember him with the milk bottle patiently standing there draining the last drip of milk into the milk jug. On reading his diaries there is a continual reference to money. I have chosen my date of arrival as an example. It reads: *went to see Betty & in the evening drew £10.00 – Balance £31.15 shillings, Julia born 11.50 pm* (ASA Business Diaries 1955–74, 4 Aug. 1955).

I have digressed.

Alan was offered part-time teaching at the Royal College of Art by Sir William Rothenstein, but, above all, he wanted to practise as a muralist. He felt that unless he "soon procured a 'job,' a picture to paint, the very desire to work would entirely disappear, swallowed up by that feeling of uselessness which is one of the fundamental troubles of the artist of today". Perchance, he "recalled the reading room of the public library at Southend" and he imagined "What could be more truly picturesque than its pier thrusting out into the grey estuary with that astonishing four-storied structure called the Pier Head, and the promenade, thronged with people, and the myriad small craft offshore? Pictures of such scenes would be genuine historical painting of the only history we can know – that of our own time." He approached the Chairman of the Committee who "listened sympathetically; and then had his say: We would have decorations, assuredly, and the subjects would be historical; not contemporary history though; but medieval, Cromwellian, and Regency," adding not the reading room, "but those four upright recesses flanked by pilasters in the vaulted gallery upstairs." Alan then enquired "The subjects?" "Oh yes: The Re-fitting of Admiral Blake's fleet at Leigh; The Building of

Prittlewell Church Tower; and we must include Southend somehow or other. Yes, of course, The Arrival of the Mail Coach at Southend in 1806."

"Naturally" Alan remarked "I was delighted and grateful, in spite of my disappointment at being set history book themes" adding: "perhaps only an artist can understand that the painter of today desires more than anything else the opportunity to serve the community of which he is a member" (Sorrell 1942, 86, 88). Alan believed that the artist "is never really happy until he knows (or thinks he knows) he is not only wanted, but needed, and that he is welcomed by his fellows as a useful and valuable workman … and since it expresses my attitude it will in a measure explain my feeling of exhilaration when I was told to go ahead with the sketches for the library decorations" (Sorrell 1943a, 104). Years later he would write to Elizabeth: "Your attitude to exhibitions and earning money is all wrong you know, my dearest darling. What's the use of work that's never seen" (Sorrell & Tanner 1944–7, postmarked 28 Oct. 1944).

These murals are particularly relevant to Alan's development and would train him how to approach his future archaeological work and I shall concentrate on the first one, *The Re-fitting of Admiral Blake's Fleet at Leigh*. Alan wrote that if the artist does not know his subject he "must *learn* it before he can properly paint it, and this learning the subject was to be my great problem with these four large paintings … I would soak myself in the theme in a *literary sense* before advancing a pictorial conception of it." He continues: "When an artist is confronted with such a problem, where the antiquarian element plays so important a part, he must not let the mere temporary external forms hide the external qualities which they partly obscure" (Sorrell 1943a, 104).

Alan began by borrowing a local history book from the Chairman of the Committee – a "keen historical scholar and an archaeologist of note". Alan thought it "a good idea to submit a questionnaire of nine questions:

> "Here it is: Year, 1652. 1. Commonwealth Navy frequently anchored off Leigh Road, so one may assume the existence of store houses etc.? 2. Where or what was Leigh Road? Blake was re-fitting for two months – sixty men o' war – Penn, Lawson, Dean, reinforced by 1200 soldiers."

and so on (Sorrell 1942, 88).

Having sent them off Alan "spied out the land and made studies". He went to the Victoria & Albert Museum in London for information on ships, rigging etc. A box of Dutch engravings dated 1671 were found.

> "They dealt with dockyard scenes and ships and (whisper it very softly) I made tracings of as many of them as I could, contravening, no doubt, all print room regulations and art morality … One particularly useful

FIG. 21. *The Refitting of Admiral Blake's Fleet at Leigh, During the First Dutch War* (1933). Oil on board, 280 × 137 cm (SOUTHEND MUSEUMS SERVICE)

engraving showed a ship heeled over (like the 'Royal George' of Cowper's poem) and held in position with two lighters with tall masts whose blocks and tackle could evidently regulate the ship's tilt. Some men were working with the capstan which controls the ropes." (Sorrell 1943b, 136)

He even persuaded a local fisherman to take him out in his boat to study the waves and to view the coast-line from the sea:

"The old salt would certainly take me out in the '*Saucy Anne*' and out we went, and then I discovered that the sea was quite choppy … Applying paint to palette was difficult but transferring that paint to canvas was not only difficult but comically like a one sided game of darts; I had to pounce rather than paint, and my aim was not always that accurate." (Sorrell 1943a, 104–5)

Alan found a studio to work in Leigh where he proceeded to finalise the composition before transferring it to the final canvas: "The Dutch tracings fitted in beautifully, even the little incident of the two men bending down and lifting up the box found its place" (Sorrell 1943b, 137). Prior to the Admiral Blake painting Alan had had always a worry of plagiarism: "my work must before all things be 'original'. If, in the past, he had found any resemblance to another painting "my own design was altered to make it different" (Sorrell 1943e, 64). In Rome, however, Alan had "acquired information for paintings from different sources of life and the antique". After all "What do the sources of information matter if you can transmute the facts into your own personal idiom? All original thought is really based on the conscious or unconscious absorption of either other people's ideas, or actuality, or both" (Sorrell *c.* 1938, 80). Decades later when I had worried that I might have cheated at school, my father had quietly said "so like me".

Alan believed that "one gets ideas from *seeing*; they rarely emerge from what is called 'the inner consciousness'" (Sorrell 1943a, 104) For example he "made the barrels of clay, and over them spread a wet piece of linen starched so that it set in the desired folds" or he hired models and "went to Nathan's, the theatrical costumiers, for the cloaks, and hats and breeches" (Sorrell 1943c, 9). "The design was [then] traced through on to a sheet of brown paper and worked out in body-colour, some pastel and Indian ink." This and the other three preliminary drawings were "highly approved of" (Sorrell 1943b, 137). Alan "transferred to the RCA for working on the final painting". He put 13 colours on his palette: "flake white, cadmium, yellow ochre, burnt sienna, burnt umber, Venetian red, crimson, alizarin, vermillion, viridian, Prussian blue, ultramarine, lamp black … I worked resolutely over the whole canvas, from top to bottom – resolutely though not confidently." As a result he was easily influenced by Cezanne who "had not glazed or scumbled, so they must be bad methods" (Sorrell 1943d, 47), or Constable who suggested the use of "shadows flying across the sea and concealing the too great complexity of sail and rigging; shadows describing the shapes of objects". In another incident he removed some of the figures from the group on the quay after a visitor had said "You've got to find your way through that group you know." Eventually he relaxed and realised that

> "you could do anything with a scumble, obliterate entirely, veil and lighten the underlying colour or deepen it to a prodigious extent ... All the stupid inhibitions regarding glazing and scumbling had now gone by the board." (Sorrell 1943e, 64)

And his Romantic spirit triumphed over theory with:

> "the great drama of wind and sea, the wind whipping the sea into foam and fluttering the pennons, bellying out the sails of the vessels and bending the trees on the hills, must take precedence over that interest which is concerned only with uniforms and historical accuracy. What I have tried to express is something of the activity and alertness which I mentioned earlier in this essay – the activity of preparation for war and the alertness which goes with it." (Sorrell 1934)

The painting was well received at the Royal Academy (RA) Summer Exhibition, had good reviews with the result that he had positive funding for the three other panels. Alan remarked that he hoped it would encourage the "fostering a healthy pride in the history of a place" (Sorrell 1943e, 65). Alan now saw a reason and had the motivation for depicting historical subjects, as well as enjoying the necessary research. In fact he had created a template for his subsequent archaeological reconstruction drawings, which he would adhere to and refine further with future experience.

FIG. 22.
Left: a. Alan Sorrell with family (*c.* 1934). Photograph from about the time of Alan's marriage to Mary Sorrell. Alan is standing back middle, Mary may be the woman in front of him; Edith Sorrell (Alan's mother) is on her right
(SORRELL FAMILY COLLECTION)

Right: b. *Britannia Rules the Garden* (1936). The only known drawing which includes both Alan and Mary Sorrell. The Britannia theme links to *A Land Fit for Heroes* (see Fig. 8). Ink and gouache on paper, 37.2 × 45.1 cm
(ARTS COUNCIL COLLECTION, SOUTHBANK CENTRE, LONDON. © ESTATE OF ALAN SORRELL)

Alan's future seemed promising but he was to make an unfortunate mistake. This was the meeting at a social function in 1933, and the subsequent marrying, of Irene Agnes Mary Oldershaw. On their marriage certificate her profession was "professional singer" – it could account for his dislike of opera! Quite quickly he realised his error, to which his mother was in agreement, and subsequently it was a subject not to be mentioned. So you can imagine my surprise on arriving home from school at the age of 15 to see a sudden influx of furniture. On questioning their source, it was briefly mentioned that his first wife had just died. This marriage had lasted 13 years. Why so long? Firstly: thinking it *must be love* – after all Irene was sympathetic and patient with his shyness, and stammer: "That tiresome stammer was both the expression and the cause of most of the trouble," and he tried "to say things that he knew would be particularly difficult for him to test himself and then at other times he would run away from his difficulties, and suffer agonies of humiliation as the result" (Sorrell *c.* 1938, 247). Secondly, he came from a strict Congregational background, which was commented on in Rome by a visiting eminent artist on seeing Alan's "pale/serious face said: 'We don't want any little missionaries or Jesus Christs here'" (*ibid.*, 66). Later on he wrote: "My feelings about religion are difficult to explain: all I know is, that if they are attacked or ridiculed I react in a violent way" (Sorrell & Tanner 1944–7, postmark 23 Mar. 1947).

Alan describes, in another autobiographical short story *The Shadow* or *The Gun*, how he:

> "went to stay with [her] people at Shuttleford. He had quite decided to marry [her]. What more could a man want – intelligence, kindliness, good looks and an income of her own. Unfortunately, the visit, instead of being the beginning of a new and happier chapter, provided the incident which finally quenched [his] happiness and set him on the path – to fame perhaps – and certainly misery too." (Sorrell *c.* 1940b, 19)

In *The Retired Life of Henry Myers*, another short story written around this time about a newly retired school-master married to a controlling headmistress, Alan wrote: "His eight days alone at Chalwell had given him a chance to realise his own tepid way of life, to recall his lost youth and wasted opportunities, his mistakes, his slavery, yes, that's what it came to, his slavery" (Sorrell *c.* 1940c, 11). In yet another short story *Nothing Changes Except in Name*, about an outsider who commits suicide, Alan wrote:

> "If a man considers himself to have been so badly treated by life that existence has become unendurable, then suicide is justifiable, and by taking such direct action he is revenging himself for all the insults and sorrows that have been inflicted upon him; why should he not destroy that cruel devil, life?"

FIG. 23. *South Icelandic Coast (Vik)* (1935). Gouache and pen and ink on paper, 34 × 50 cm
(GRAVES ART GALLERY, SHEFFIELD © ESTATE OF ALAN SORRELL)

adding, on a suicide note: "What I've never known: A woman's love, a child to call me 'father', a home and friends" (*ibid.*, 13). To Elizabeth he wrote: "… am torn to shreds, what is right to do, how selfish should one be, is one selfish to think of ones own happiness and work and so on" (Sorrell & Tanner 1944–7, postmark 2 Mar. 1945). From these quotes one can deduce an unhappy yet guilty man.

However, Irene and Alan did travel together to places like Italy and Iceland. "The paintings of Iceland" wrote Alan "were done after a summer holiday in that strange and inaptly named country" (Sorrell 1939d, 101). Percy Horton (1955, 18) wrote: "Sorrell visited Iceland, the stark character of which made a special appeal to him and inspired some thirty watercolours, which were shown at the Walker Gallery in Bond Street." Here Alan's stormy skies, which were to become his signature for much of his later work, appeared for the first time, and I conjecture a link between the storm and a break of light in the distance with his emotionally traumatic life – the stress and depression with a sense of hope. He had "endeavoured to express a landscape mood." Iceland was important in his artistic development, as seen in *South Icelandic Coast* where he was relying on his memory, due to the appalling weather conditions.

> "Since there must be an interval between the visual impression and the registering of it on paper, all drawings might be properly called 'memory' drawings, but this South Icelandic Coast deserves the title more than most because two years elapsed before I actually made the picture. The first

attempt was a monochrome, but my memory of that morning's colour seemed to grow so fresh and strong when the facts were once on paper, that I threw aside this preliminary drawing and sketched a second one for colour, on white paper. The actual form of the cliffs and boat I copied from a few lines in my sketch-book. I employed body-colour from the beginning, applying it in thin liquid washes. The sea was finally coloured with pastel rubbed with the finger and then fixed, and black conté crayon was used with some delicacy on the cliffs and on rock forms in the glacial valley. Finally the boat was completed with a black pen-line. I stole the sea-gull from a reproduction of an old Royal Academy picture, thus putting into practice the advice of the late Professor Lethaby, who once said: 'Steal as much as you can, and make it your own.' This is called 'putting old wine into new bottles'." (Sorrell 1939d, 102)

Of another Icelandic painting *Travelling in Iceland* Alan says:

"The only preliminary work for this picture was a little pencil scribble, and the design was drawn quite freely on white Whatman paper ..." (*ibid.*, 102)

"Since true imagination springs from a hypersensitive appreciation of fact, it becomes evident that, without a deep study of fact, the artist will find himself empty of inspiration, and then it is that he turns to fantasy; since he is too indolent to study the strangeness of actuality, he will invent peculiar forms and impossible situations. Naturally they will not carry conviction; the feeling of absolute reality that earns conviction is the implicit quality of an imaginative painting." (Sorrell 1940e, 131)

FIG. 24. *Icelandic Farm* (1936). Alan's signature stormy skies first appear here. Watercolour, pen & ink, gouache 35.4 × 58.5 cm
(COLLECTION OF AMGUEDDFA CYMRU – NATIONAL MUSEUM WALES, © ESTATE OF ALAN SORRELL)

The trip to Iceland also taught him that there was a role as an artist akin to a visual journalist. This would be particularly apparent with his later trips to Greece, Istanbul and Nubia, as well as archaeological sites. A good example is his diary entries where he was making sketches and notes for Hadrian's Wall: 24 May 1956 "went to Corbridge", 25 May "went to Housesteads & Birdoswald". Of course the final drawing took much longer! (ASA, Business Diaries 1955–74, 24 & 25 May 1956).

Fig. 25. *The Roman Forum at Leicester* (1936). Alan's first reconstruction drawing produced for publication in the *Illustrated London News* (DESTROYED IN WW2, ASA COPY)

In 1936 Alan and Irene were visiting her parents in Leicester and, being bored, he happened to notice an archaeological excavation going on in the city centre and did some sketching (see Chapter 8 and Fig. 81). The archaeologist in charge, Dr Kathleen Kenyon, approached him and asked if he would like to do a drawing to accompany an article she had been asked to write for the *Illustrated London News*. Alan agreed and the finished drawing was submitted to the *ILN*'s director Sir Bruce Ingram. He replied "Couldn't you also do a re-construction drawing of it?" My father agreed to this, and liaising with Dr Kenyon, a finished drawing was produced. Unwittingly a long relationship with the *Illustrated London News* had begun (see Part II), although he never was to have a good relationship with Leicester! Not only did his in-laws live there, his sister Doris had gone to a sanatorium there. Years later Alan was unhappy when my brother Mark applied to Leicester University.

Following the publication of the Leicester drawings, Alan was contacted by Sir Mortimer Wheeler and invited to visit his excavation at Maiden Castle in Dorset, where evidence for a Roman assault of the Iron Age hillfort had been discovered. Alan visited and, duly, a reconstruction drawing appeared in a future *ILN* issue. This was followed by an approach from Sir Cyril Fox and V. E. Nash-Williams of the National Museum of Wales, who were responsible for an excavation at Caerwent. They again were writing a feature in the *ILN* and needed reconstruction drawings. So began the work that Alan is predominantly remembered for today, and his association with the leading archaeologists of the day, although he was not alone. During the late 1930s, following the rediscovery of the artist Thomas Guest (1754–1818) (today remembered as the 'recorder' of Beakers found in

Fig. 26. *Boats at Leigh-on-Sea* (1973). Watercolour, pen & ink, 24 × 38 cm
(SOUTHEND MUSEUMS SERVICE)

excavations of barrows at Winterslow, Wiltshire whilst working alongside Rev. A. B. Hutchins), there was a wave of other living artists inspired by the growing enthusiasm for archaeology. These included Paul Nash, John Piper, Graham Sutherland, Henry Moore and Eric Ravilious, many of whom were my father's friends. To varying degrees they represented part of a modern British movement which often steered towards abstraction, surrealism and romanticism whilst visualising our heritage and landscape (Hauser 2007, 22; Piggott 1978, 48; Smiles 2005, 11).

In 1937, Alan was elected a member of the Royal Watercolour Society about which he had mixed feelings. In 1944 he wrote "I'm not on very good terms with the RWS precisely because of the fact that I'm always – or nearly always – well noticed in their exhibitions" (Sorrell & Tanner 1944–7 illegible postmark, ?May 1946). Later on:

> "You will be surprised to hear I have finished the war drawing and it really looks very well and extremely powerful. I am sorry to send it to the RWS but am wondering if they have power to not hang a member's work. I'm not sure. But this one will make R. Flint really peeved if he sees it. You've no idea how wedded these people are to the pure traditional type of watercolour." (Sorrell & Tanner 1944–7, postmarked 3 Mar. 1946)

When Elizabeth's sister Audrey remarked that "she doesn't seem to think much of the RWS", Alan added: "I can't say I blame her." However it was a venue for Alan to exhibit and he encouraged Elizabeth by writing "Have you written to the RWS? Why not? You're not old, but you must have lost a year or two somewhere – or maybe I am forgetting my own barren years." (Sorrell & Tanner 1944–7, postmarked 28 Oct. 1944) In due course Elizabeth became a member too and, as a child, I remember many trips and a big feast once a year at the old gallery in Conduit Street, when all members took food with them. It all seemed very friendly and one year I was toasted by Vincent Lines as the "little Renoir". Alan was not always diplomatic. My mother told me many stories whilst we sewed together late into the evenings. One of them was how Alan was asked to show people around a RWS show, and on arrival at the paintings of the then President Sir William Russell Flint, Alan said: "now let me show you some pornography" and turning around he saw the President! However Alan and Elizabeth remained members and I remember him saying: "Betty, how are the finances?" "Not good," she replied. "Oh well, I had better go and paint some boats at Leigh, they always sell at the RWS." It was to remain a vital continuous link with the art world however critical he may have felt at times.

Chapter 5

World War II

THROUGHOUT WORLD WAR II, Alan would develop both emotionally and artistically. He was on the verge of breaking out of his chrysalis. One can see this butterfly emerging through correspondence written to various people including the archaeologist Sir Cyril Fox and my mother, Elizabeth Tanner. Alan's intrepid determination and keenness is obvious, and him being needed and appreciated were crucial. Whether it be trying to arrange a visit to Sir Cyril Fox at the Museum in 1937:

> "On Monday, Tuesday, Thursday and Friday I teach at South Kensington in the evening. However I have Wednesdays quite free. There is a train leaving Paddington at 8.55am arriving at Cardiff at 11.43." (NMW 1937–60, museum stamped 22 April 1937)

Or September 1938 relating with excitement and enthusiasm how he was:

> "becoming increasingly interested in Roman history and have even taken to reading Tacitus, and see now where R. Graves got all his tit-bits from." (*Ibid.*, museum stamped 2 September 1938)

The shift, decay, and fragility of civilisation became central to many artists and writers in the inter-war period, especially as the impending war approached. Yeats, in his poem *The Second Coming* (1919, first published in the *Dial* 1920) wrote:

> "Things fall apart; the centre cannot hold;
> Mere anarchy is loosed upon the world."

Alan would express it visually in paintings such as *The Falling Tower* reminiscent of both Trafalgar Square in London and Piazza del Popolo in Rome. These feelings, perhaps initiated by his growing interest in the ruins of a past civilisation, would become a central theme in much of his consecutive imaginative work for the rest of his life. Alan also saw the similarities militarily, as shown when he wrote to Sir Bruce Ingram at the *ILN*:

FIG. 27. *The Falling Tower* (c. 1939). Perhaps Alan's first painting depicting the destruction of heritage. Notice the figure on a column used to create a leaning upright within a tilted oval formed by the church and shadow. Gouache, ink, watercolour and pastel on paper, 48.5 × 61 cm
(COLLECTION OF JULIA SORRELL © ESTATE OF ALAN SORRELL)

> "the curiously topical nature of these reconstructions – an even cursory examination will show that the Roman Legionary fortress and the present day militia camp are practically identical in layout, detail, and appearance." (NMW 1938–60, 28 December 1940)

Before the war commenced, Alan was already thinking of what his role might be. This is evident by him keeping a copy of a *Picture Post* article printed April 1939 on camouflage (*Picture Post* 1939). In September 1939 Alan:

> "was still waiting for a war job. Apparently it is to be in camouflage work for which they are building up an organisation at the College. It's all very official – but appallingly slow." (NMW 1938–60, museum stamped 18 September 1939)

The Ministry of Labour had received over 2000 applications for camouflage war work by the beginning of September, and only a fraction were to be employed or put onto the waiting list (Foss 2007, 16).

Running parallel to this was the creation of the War Artists' Advisory Committee (WAAC), which was to first meet on 23 November 1939 at the National Gallery. It consisted of Kenneth Clark (the gallery's director), artists Muirhead Bone, Percy Jowett, Walter Russell and E. M. O'R. Dickey and one representative from each of the armed forces. Names were put forward by members of the committee, and on 15 December a radio broadcast was

FIG. 28. *Caerwent, Gwent. A Bird's Eye View of the Roman Town* (1937). Gouache, chalks, pen & ink & watercolour, 70 × 93.5 cm
(COLLECTION OF AMGUEDDFA CYMRU – NATIONAL MUSEUM WALES)

put out inviting applications, so that by the end of February, 755 names had been considered, 247 were given employment, and 141 were put onto the reserve list (Foss 2007, 21–3) Alan had applied, like his friends John and Paul Nash, Vivian Pitchforth, Edward Bawden and Eric Ravilious. Alan, along with other friends including Robert Austin, Gilbert and Stanley Spencer, Henry Moore, Percy Horton and Alan Gwynne-Jones (Alan's RCA tutor) were put on the reserve list, although in the case of Alan, he seems not to have been told this, and assumed that he had been rejected.

Alan restlessly remarked, on 17 November, that "apart from having a balloon blown onto the house and nearly catching fire things are quiet here" (NMW 1937–60, AS to Cyril Fox, 17 November 1939). He was still on the teaching staff at the Royal College and although it initially closed in 1939, it re-opened in January 1940, only to suffer bomb damage and to be closed again in September 1940. The RCA was relocated to Ambleside taking with it staff unfit for service in the war (Cunliffe-Charlesworth 1991, 211; Frayling 1987, 119–21). As for Alan, he enlisted in the RAF on 18 December 1940. Due to his age this was not compulsory and, jokingly, he later told Elizabeth: "most men joined up to fight for their country. As for me I joined up to escape my wife". In fact he was very patriotic and, wanting to contribute, he suggested that having produced aerial views for the archaeologists, he could produce aerial views for use on bombing missions. However, he initially underwent military training and, writing from RAF Bridgnorth Disciplinary Training Camp on 31 December as 1273153 A/C Sorrell, he felt sure that he had:

> "done the right thing in volunteering for the R.A.F. and as a matter of fact I find the new experiences rather stimulating. It's rather fun – excepting getting up at 6.15 a.m. – and parading at 8.15! I may be here 4–5 weeks but it may be only 3." (NMW 1937–60, AS to Cyril Fox 31 December 1940)

When possible, Alan was producing drawings even though he:

> "had rotten bad luck at the Tate after all. I heard from J.R. [John Rothenstein] and he said the Trustees decided not to purchase 'after

prolonged discussion' but they want to see more work later on. I was awfully disappointed because this particular gouache drawing is really good, and J.R. was keen. I'd like to know (what) happened." (*Ibid,*, AS to Cyril Fox, museum stamped 31 Dec. 1940)

However, by the end of the war, 26 of Alan's drawings and paintings were in fact bought for the nation by the WAAC, being later passed on to museums including the Imperial War Museum and the Tate.

Alan was soon transferred to Farnborough where there was a "specialist unit" developing terrain model-making techniques to aid pilots on difficult bombing missions. His security vetting was equivalent to that of the staff at Bletchley Park and, having signed the *Official Secrets Act*, he was to maintain this secrecy for the rest of his life (A. W. Pearson, pers. comm. 2011):

"In about a fortnight I move onto permanent quarters near Reading. I believe I wrote to you from Bridgnorth and gave you some idea of the life. Really you know, I've never been so uncomfortable physically, but that was more than compensated by the fact that I saw some things that simply asked to be painted and I hope to get down to them before long. They were chiefly early morning scenes, all rather grim, but to me at any rate extremely moving and dramatic. Of course, the whole Bridgnorth episode was comic when looked at in a reasonable way, and I would not have missed it for worlds. Here at Farnboro' conditions are easier and naturally the work is more interesting but the camp is good and I am carefully memorising various objects which I hope to organise into a picture." (NMW 1937–60, AS to Cyril Fox undated, ?Jan. or later 1941)

Alan again contacted John Rothenstein, who in turn, wrote to the WAAC secretary E. M. O'R. Dickey on 6 May 1941 saying that Alan was:

"a most competent artist, who, though he is not wanting in imagination, has during past years devoted his efforts largely to making somewhat poetic records of a variety of places, such as Iceland. He has also been employed by the National Museum of Wales to make pictorial reconstructions of ancient civilizations, and has carried out an important decoration for Southend Public Library.

At the present moment he is serving with the R.A.F. When he wrote to me I promised that I would recommend him

FIG. 29. *Marching Through the Camp* (1942). Part of Alan's first series RAF camp life drawings based on his month spent at RAF Bridgnorth Disciplinary Training Camp Dec. 1940–Jan. 1941. Chalk, ink & wash on paper, 27 × 35 cm
(COURTESY OF ROYAL AIR FORCE MUSEUM, HENDON)

to you, and suggested he should send you some examples of his work or photographs." (IMW 1941–6, 6 May 1941)

On 19 May Alan followed this with a friendly letter to E. M. O'R. Dickey, whom he knew through the RCA:

"You will probably be surprised to hear from me on such oddly headed notepaper and from such an address. The fact is I volunteered for the R.A.F. in December for special duties and I have been here since January. But first of all I was at a 'disciplinary training camp', at Bridgnorth where it was a bit too cold but otherwise rather amusing. Well I've seen and am seeing some jolly good things to make pictures of, I am memorising a good deal and getting it on paper in quite a precise way. But some sketching facilities would be very useful and Dr. Rothenstein has advised me to write to you to enquire of the likelihood of this being granted. I should be so grateful if you could do something. I hope, by the way, you do remember me, it's rather a long time since we met. I hope Mrs. Dickey is well and, also your son. I wonder whether you're still at Richmond. I liked Henry Moore's drawings at the National Gallery show, especially, and a lot of the work is good isn't it?" (*Ibid.*, 19 May 1941)

On 23 May Dickey replied:

"The Artists' Advisory Committee at their meeting on Wednesday recommended that you should be given such facilities for sketching as may be compatible with your duties and I expect the Air Ministry representative on the Committee will shortly communicate with your Commanding Officer. We very much hope that you will be able to tackle some of the interesting subjects you have found and look forward with interest to seeing your work." (*Ibid.,* 23 May 1941)

On 31 July, Dickey again wrote to Alan:

"I am asked to thank you on behalf of the Artists' Advisory Committee for having been good enough to let them see your three drawings of incidents at a Royal Air Force hutment camp in winter. The Committee have recommended that they be purchased at 15 guineas for the three." (*Ibid.*, 31 July 1941)

Alan replied on 22 September:

"Many thanks for your letter which has been forwarded to me. I think they certainly should be called 'drawings' and in 'chalk, pen and wash' if you think that alright?" (*Ibid.*, 22 September 1941)

Of course drawing materials were difficult to obtain, hence Alan's request, and perhaps the monochrome nature his and other contemporaries' work at this time.

The above letters give an excellent insight into a determined man refusing to be ignored by anyone, whatever their official status may be. He realised

FIG. 30.

Left: a. *Recruits Leaving the Camp at Bridgnorth* (dated on the back Xmas 1941). Chalk, ink and wash on paper, 38 × 41 cm
(SORRELL FAMILY COLLECTION)

Right: b: Alan Sorrell, kitbag on shoulder, leaving the RAF. Sketch from a letter, May 1946. Pencil
(© IMPERIAL WAR MUSEUMS)

there were opportunities for him as an artist, and the above letters encapsulate his approach and stamina not only in the War, which he would maintain throughout his working life. He was determined to "live by his art".

Alan was not just an artist in the war, but was an airman living and working alongside the other service men without any special privileges. On 23 May 1941 he wrote to Cyril Fox:

> "As you see we are still in Farnboro' but expect to move to permanent quarters next week (This move has been going on for at least 4 months!). We alternate between periods of intense activity, and times of no-work-at-all. A curious thing has happened, the Air Ministry has fished me out of a list for a civilian camouflage post and they're trying to get my discharge from the R.A.F. As it would mean more activity (with a lot of flying) I should like the change. It's rather funny after volunteering. I've had several week-ends away and have just returned from London where as you can imagine the Jerries have made a sad mess. On Sunday morning there was a smoke pall over the south part of the city from some wretched fire and thousand of pieces of blackened paper were falling down most of the day. But of course London goes on magnificently just the same and will continue to do so."

He adds:

> "It is surprising in a way that I have next to no news, but without being monotonous, the days are certainly much like each other. Anyway I shall always be grateful to the RAF for giving me a new angle on things, just when I badly needed it. You'll see I am now Leading Aircraftman! But not Sergeant yet!" (NMW 1937–60, 23 May 1941)

From July 1941 Alan was assiduously employed in the V-section of the Central Interpretation Unit (CIU), RAF Medmenham at Danesfield House in Buckinghamshire. Alongside other artists, in a cramped vaulted basement room they interpreted aerial reconnaissance photographs and maps, turning them into terrain models, using cardboard, egg cartons and presumably any other suitable materials to hand (Pearson 2002, 231–7). However, he never interpreted them as aerial views, since these were unsuitable for pilots who might approach a target from more than one direction (A. W. Pearson, pers. comm. 2011).

On 8 September 1941 Alan left the RAF and was transferred to the Air Ministry at Adastral House, London as a camouflage officer, with probably higher status and better pay. On 1 December a letter from Sir Cyril Fox had reached Alan at the Air Ministry via Farnborough and Medmenham, and Alan replied:

> "It appears I may be kept at Air Ministry Headquarters – with frequent excursions to inspect aerodromes in various parts of the country. I have just returned from Leicestershire and a week or two ago I went round Gloucestershire by plane, train and car. Very interesting. I passed through Bristol and wished I could have come across to Cardiff somehow or other. I am still managing to do some drawing, and Rothenstein likes my RAF pictures and wants one for Carlisle – he buys for the gallery there, and as I have just done one of a hut interior I hope he will like that." (NMW 1937–60, 8 Sept 1941)

Fig. 31. *RAF Hut* (1943). Part of Alan's second series of RAF camp life scenes. Watercolour, gouache, ink & pastel on paper, 26 × 35 cm
(COLLECTION OF MARK SORRELL, © ESTATE OF ALAN SORRELL)

This may refer to the one RAF drawing still remaining in our family collection.

When writing to Dickey on 21 September Alan added:

> "You will see I am no longer in the RAF. I am at the A.M. for a few weeks and shall then be sent away to supervise camouflage on aerodromes. It should prove interesting." (IMW 1941–6, 21 September 1941)

The work included not only disguising buildings with paint and netting, but as the war progressed, the grass runways were being replaced by concrete. These had to be toned down and painted over to simulate hedgerows and trees in an attempt to merge them with the surrounding fields (Air Ministry 1956, 234–55; Goodden 2007, 78–88). Alan spent long periods in the air studying the landscape and this later would enable him to visualize his aerial views with greater acuity.

In May 1944 at RAF Squire's Gate, Alan wrote:

> "My wife has called to see you, I believe, with a drawing showing an R.A.F aerodrome through the clouds: I do hope your Committee will like it. The incident was one I experienced whilst flying to Ireland last year." (IMW 1941–6, AS to Mr Gregory, WAAC, undated)

This was *Cavern in the Clouds* – a beautifully romantic, pen and ink drawing. His experiences had certainly given Alan a new perspective to his work.

As at RAF Medmenham, Alan's war work was secret, and we have only a

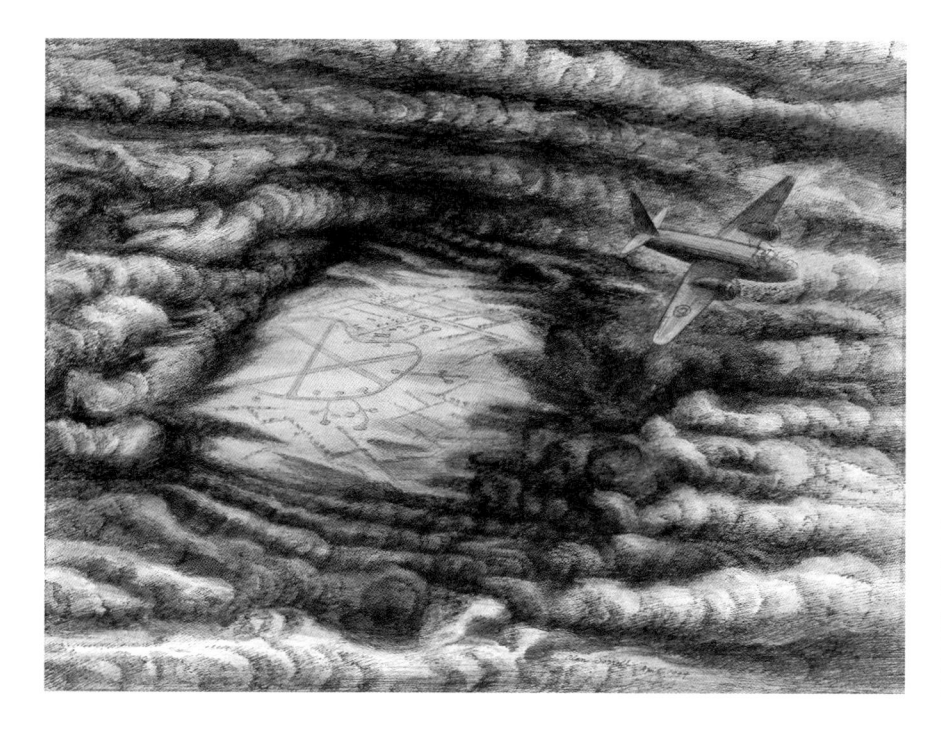

Fig. 32. *A Cavern in the Clouds* (April 1944). Gouache and ink on paper, 29.4 × 39.8 cm (PRIVATE COLLECTION, IMAGE COURTESY OF LISS LLEWELLYN FINE ART)

few glimpses about what he did from some of the remaining correspondence. From a letter to the WAAC, 4 February 1943, we know the Air Ministry had posted him to Framlingham, in Suffolk, where a new airfield was being constructed for the US air force:

> "I have had a large and, in some respects, unique position of these hutted camps in that I have lived in them as an airman (for 9 months), visited them and flown over them as an Air Ministry Officer and finally (or more properly, firstly) assisted in the sighting and planning of them. I feel rather keenly that this camp life lived by so vast a proportion of airmen in this country has been somewhat over-looked by War Artists, and I am wondering whether there is any likelihood of your Committee making it possible for me to produce a series of paintings and drawings from this abundant subject matter – which interests me extremely." (IWM 1941–6, 4 Feb 1943)

On 9 March 1943 he continued:

> "There is in fact, (an) enormous mass of unheroic but exciting stuff in and around these camps, and I don't think it has yet been touched. So I shall look forward to hearing from you favourably regarding this delay. May I remind (you) of the matter later on?" (*Ibid.*, 9 March 1943)

By 13 March, Alan received an official letter:

> "I write to confirm that you are asked to undertake for the Ministry of Information drawings of RAF Hutted Camps. For this work I am authorised to offer you a fee of 25 gns. It is agreed that, in consideration of the above fee, the property in the original drawings and all rights of reproduction in any form shall be vested solely in the Crown. I am authorised to offer you third class travelling expenses, and should you have to work away from here, maintenance allowance of a flat rate of £1 per day of each absence of 24 hours, and a day allowance of 6/8 for an absence from home for more than 10 hours. I am enclosing a form on which your claim for travelling and maintenance expenses should be made." (*Ibid.*, 13 March 1943)

Alan was keen to get the work even though he was paid less than many other war artists. (Foss 2007, 159) On 3 May he wrote:

> "The head of my A.M. department tells me he has no objection to my being absent for a month from June 1st so if you could approach the Director General of Works again I think we could count on my being given leave." (*Ibid.*, 3 May 1943)

By this stage of the war, aerodrome camouflage was cut back due to the expense and it being largely unnecessary (Air Ministry 1956, 235; Goodden 2007, 91). This may explain why he was given leave to work as a war artist. By 1944 "Censorship rules further limited the types of subjects that could be sketched, painted or exhibited. These led to exhibition and reproduction prohibition being placed" (Foss 2007, 129). This corroborates one of my mother's stories: every day Alan went past a place on the way to his digs and he would peer over or through a chink in the fence; he would memorise what he saw and once home jot it down in his sketch-book. He repeated this many times until he had enough information and made a drawing of it in pen, watercolour and gouache. At this point Elizabeth would smile, remembering how Alan had sold it to the WAAC who could not exhibit it because of censorship, and it was later acquired by the Tate. The drawing in question is probably *Southampton Dock*, his only non-RAF painting, which shows the construction of a Mulberry artificial harbour in preparation for D-Day. It is highly detailed, with comprehensive sketches, making this story credible. As an Air Ministry camouflage officer, was Alan involved in the disguising of secret D-Day preparations?

Years later, in his account of his trip to Nubia, Alan would write briefly why he left the Air Ministry and returned to the RAF on 1 May 1944 – an event which would prove to be a pivotal moment in his life. The RAF may have wanted him back as a model maker for the Central Intelligence Unit who, at that time, were expanding and sending model makers to North Africa for missions against Italy (Pearson 2002, 229–31).

Fig. 33. *Southampton Dock* (1944). A drawing of the building of the Mulberry Harbour in the No. 7 King George V Graving Dock. This was Alan's only non-RAF themed painting purchased by the War Artists Advisory Committee and presented to the Tate Gallery in 1946. Watercolour, pen, ink & crayon on paper, 51.1 × 62.5 cm

(© TATE, LONDON 2017)

> "I did serve in the R.A.F., something which I thought fit to gloss over, though Andorf [a German Alan had met] might have been pleased had I told him that I staged a successful one-man mutiny whilst in uniform when I refused to become involved in making recognition models for bombing places which I considered to be of irreplaceable artistic importance. My punishment was not to be shot at dawn, but to be sent to Blackpool, there to make models of ships suitable for destruction." (Sorrell *c.* 1974, 169)

Having been very much involved in the construction and camouflage of the bomber airfields in eastern England, he must have been all too aware of the destructive power now being unleashed on not only Germany but also France and Italy. For example, the historic city of Lubeck had been destroyed, parts of Rome, the monastery of Monte Cassino and even the refectory containing Leonardo's *Last Supper* in Milan (HM Stationery Office 1945, 30–1; 1946a, 30–4; 1946b, 44). Disquiet was felt by some at the Air Ministry (Hastings 1979, 201–10), and a few lone voices in the public at large, such as Vera Brittain (1944) and the Rev. George Bell, the Bishop of Chichester, who wrote about his condemnation of the Allied practice of area bombing to *The Times* in 1941. Later, on 9 February 1944, he said in the House of Lords: "How can the War Cabinet fail to see that this progressive devastation of cities is threatening the roots of civilization." (Hastings 1979, 209; Lambourne 2001, 8).

In *Barbarians in Rome* (Sorrell *c.* 1938, 145, 150) Alan had expressed his feeling for Italian heritage:

> "they turn to the outer wall which is a tapestry of pale colour contrived by cunning fellows Benozzo Gozzoli, Orcagna, Simone Martini and others unknown [*bombed, 1944*]. Here for the first time [he] savoured the ineffable sweetness of Italy of Fra Angelica and St. Francis. Every quarter of an hour the Cathedral bell chimed and that was the only outside sound that penetrated into this separate world … After much hesitation [Alan] decided to make a drawing of Gozzoli's fresco of the Tower of Babel [*recently restored*]. All [Alan's] Pisa wanderings seemed to lead him to the Piazza del Duomo, and the night before he left for Lucca he came upon it by moonlight, and that memory remained with him always."

Remembering his visit to Arezzo and seeing Piero della Francesca's frescoes he wrote:

> "Piero's work has a peculiar quality of precise dreaminess. The happy accident, beloved of the romantics, is entirely ruled out, and every line and every tint appear to be the result of cool thought and reconsideration." (*Ibid.*, 192)

Wasn't this the true Alan rather than the man pondering over "Pure Form" in a pseudo- intellectual yet cold manner? How could he be in any way involved in what he would have considered such senseless destruction?

His punishment for refusing to obey orders was to be reinstated as Leading Aircraftman in the RAF, and assigned to a ship reconnaissance training squadron at RAF Squire's Gate, Blackpool. He wrote to Mr Gregory (WAAC secretary from 1942):

> "I seemed to have fallen on a rather good place, (apart from the distance from London) and I only hope I stay here whilst I am in the RAF. I am living quite comfortably in an hotel and if things continue so I shall have good opportunities for work." (IWM 1941–6, undated, ?1944)

In a later letter he comments that "Blackpool is disgustingly prosperous with a perpetual summer holiday quality about it" (*ibid.*). A chance meeting on 30 June 1944 would change Alan's life for ever. On visiting Blackpool Art School to obtain drawing materials, he asked to see the Principal Mr Hayes who was out. "Perhaps I can help you, Mr. Sorrell" volunteered a young woman who was Head of the Junior Art Department. Turning to face her and immediately struck by her beauty, he asked: "How do you know my name?" "Because you taught me at the Royal College." Alan always contended "it was love at first sight".

He was as persistent with this young lady, Elizabeth Tanner, as with his work. He immediately asked her out for tea and then suggested a ride on the Big Dipper, which was totally out of character – he hated heights! He then proceeded to bombard her with letters once or twice a day and failing that, telegrams. Fortunately love was mutual. Being socially unconfident, the sheer joy of meeting an intelligent, like-minded woman was obvious:

> "I have been reading and re-reading Tennyson's 'Morte d'Arthur' do you know it, it is superb – all about 'clashing harness' and 'juts of pointed rock.' I could go on meandering like this for hours – and I may say you're the only person I can do this to – but I mustn't try your patience. I'm awfully glad my dear to learn that you are working away at your painting. You haven't read Mrs. Gaskells 'Charlotte Bronte'? It's a classic in its own right." (Sorrell & Tanner 1944–7, postmarked 28 Oct. 1944)

Elizabeth expressed her admiration and belief in him and he replied:

> "You touch me very much by your references to my work and give me faith in myself. Before the war I had all but lost that and what you say does cheer me. I wish I could be the great man you would like me to be! But I seem to need boosting all the time. These war subjects are a kind of boosting; but the phase will end soon enough. I love to hear from you, I feel you love me for myself which is true isn't it?" (*Ibid.*, postmarked 4 Aug. 1944)

Alan admired Elizabeth:

> "I should certainly be very disappointed if you did not completely express yourself as an artist" (*ibid.*, undated ?1946)

Left: Fig. 34.
Elizabeth Tanner
c. 1944
(SORRELL FAMILY COLLECTION)

Right: Fig. 35.
Alan Sorrell 1944.
Photograph taken just after he was made a corporal in August that year
(SORRELL FAMILY COLLECTION)

and encouraged her:

> "You know that painting of yours of the field of flowers, well, do you know, I believe the Medici Society would very likely buy it for reproduction. Why not spend a few days in London in the summer and take it to them." (*Ibid.*, undated ?1945)

For all his supposed confidence, a lack of self-esteem is only too apparent:

> "You are a kind of sheet-anchor to me you know, without you I should have no direction. I wonder whether you realise that our relative positions have changed, haven't they? I'm glad for you to say 'Do this' or 'Do that' because I trust you utterly, and believe in your goodness." (*Ibid.*, postmarked 3 June 1945)

Later:

> "I'm a bit like an old man to-day as I have just been to St. George's Hospital to have my leg injected. It must have been a strong injection because it affected me in various ways – eyes head and so on. I've got to go back several more times but it will be worth it and I'm sure you'll love me more when I haven't an obvious flaw, won't you, my pet." (*Ibid.*, undated ?June 1946)

These are just a few extracts from three volumes of love letters written from 1944–1947. Yes, both Elizabeth and Alan were happily in love.

However, Alan was married, albeit unhappily. He wrote to Elizabeth in 1945:

> "You know I live miserably, and make my wife unhappy, but you can't understand how difficult it is to inflict the final and sharp injury by saying 'I am going to leave you'. There is no bond between my wife and myself. We torture each other and I am in the process of being ruined. And yet my wife tells me she is sad because the 'person she loves best is no longer hers'. You may imagine how that makes me feel, how I try to be less unkind, and so on, all the while knowing it's no use, and that I am only riveting the chains which will one day strangle me." (*Ibid.*, postmarked 2 May 1945)

Unsurprisingly, Alan felt awkward, as expressed in July 1945, when

> "today I hear from my wife and it rather embarrasses me; she has been to the Leicester Galleries about some journalism she is doing, and got talking and the upshot was that she got them to ask for my drawing of the wood for a forthcoming exhibition." (*Ibid.*, postmark date dated Sunday, 1945?)

Coincidentally Elizabeth noted that:

> "A friend of mine wrote the other day, that she went into the Leicester Galleries to the Artists of Fame and Promise exhibition and she came across a very nice drawing of a wood and thought 'Betty would like this' – and then she looked to see the name of the artist and saw it was by Alan Sorrell!!" (*Ibid.*, postmark dated Sunday, 1945?)

The drawing sold in July 1945.

We know very little about Irene (often known as Mary) but, in 1965, she wrote a book *Out of Silence* discussing her recovery from a stroke, and, for us, a little insight is given into her personality.

> "My aunt, with whom I lived for many years, was a maiden lady. She was devout and had a great influence on me. Every week I went to see my parents and my brother – especially my mother – and even when my aunt was extremely strict I was happier with her, although she did not always understand me, for I was a rebellious girl as well as being withdrawn." (Mary Sorrell 1969, 14)

She was a student in London and when staying with her aunt in Leicester she would write or paint.

> "I loved and revered words, and next to words I loved art." (*Ibid.*, 17)

There is one reference to her marriage to Alan:

> "But I am not concentrating on earlier years that were both exhilarating and sad; nor on a marriage that was filled with nostalgic happiness and sorrows. My life began again as a journalist, but alas, without God. He would have helped me in those days as He does now." (*Ibid.*, 16)

She was seemingly sensitive:

> "The morning dew on that sparkling cobweb made me swallow my tears. It was so perfect and so precious." (*Ibid.*, 17)

WORLD WAR II 51

Little wonder Alan developed shingles "due to worry and nervous strain" and guilt. To Elizabeth he wrote "Love me and believe in me, and maybe a happy path will be found for everybody" (Sorrell & Tanner 1944–7, postmarked 1 Feb. 1945).

The war ended 1945. For Alan, his last day of service was 14 May 1946 with his release leave on 10 July 1946. In his release book there is a statement of aptitudes:

> "This airman has been employed in making a pictorial research for historical record purposes of runway and aerodrome construction and the lay-out of RAF stations. He has a natural artistic ability and is strongly recommended for employment as an artist or art teacher."

Early in 1944, Alan had proposed the idea of a series of aerodrome pictures as a necessary historical record (IWM 1941–6, undated, ?1944), and it took many months before a decision was finalised. During the final months of the war, Alan travelled as a commissioned war artist around different aerodromes such as RAF Marham, Norfolk, and RAF Tuddenham, Suffolk, gathering information. Amongst other works, Alan produced two large aerodrome oil paintings – the second *Construction of a Runway at an Aerodrome* finished 1946.

With the first one, an aerial view of a RAF Hendon in London, Alan describes in detail its execution, which took many months and was completed in the autumn of 1945. This was typical of Alan and oil paint, and so unlike his confident use of drawing media. Obviously there is a common prejudice of oil painting being the "real art" as opposed to linear drawing. In this painting, Alan was very influenced by opinions

FIG. 36. *RAF Aerodrome* (1945). In this large-scale work, Alan has put many of the typical features of aerodromes including both spectacle and frying pan dispersal areas to the left of the aerodrome ring-road. Notice his rain clouds and cast shadows forming a compositional oval. His experiences in the RAF enabled greater confidence in his aerial views. Oil on canvas, 86.4 × 188 cm
(COURTESY OF ROYAL AIR FORCE MUSEUM, HENDON)

"I had one or two people to see it and they weren't really enthusiastic. I felt it was somehow a bit dull and lacking in vitality. Anyway on Monday I was very fed up and in a bad temper with the world generally, and suddenly decided I would lash out at the picture and either ruin it completely or make something of it. So I went for it in a 'hit and miss' way and hacked it about with the utmost abandon working very quickly and the effect was excellent as it began to come to life. Well I only did about two hours work then, but next day I slashed at the precious sky and re-painted it entirely [in] 1 & 1/2 hours! Well today I finished it – about 7 hours work! It is now a different picture entirely and has a lot of movement and life: I think (even) you may (perhaps) like it, darling I've got an official coming to see it to-morrow." (Sorrell & Tanner 1944–7, postmarked 2 Nov. 1945)

Fortunately not only Gilbert Spencer came and admired, but it was "greatly admired especially by Sir K. Clark and Sir M. Bone (which rather is, I believe an unusual honour)." With the second aerodrome painting, not finished until 1946, Sir Muirhead Bone "was so impressed that he asked the Secretary to write a special letter of commendation to me!" (*Ibid.*, postmarked 1 Dec 1945)

Although Alan had not been well represented in many War Artists' exhibitions during the war, he nevertheless was pleased to

"have 10 drawings in the War Artists show at Burlington House [*13 October–25 November 1945*] but they are not particularly well hung – or well chosen. It's quite a lot to have though isn't it? It's a tedious show, in my opinion." (*Ibid.*, undated)

Chapter 6

The post-war years

EVEN BEFORE HIS final release from the RAF, Alan was thinking of his career: "I'm going over to Ealing on Monday and expect to do one or two evenings there next session. It will help financially. The College is coming back in September" (Sorrell & Tanner 1944–7, undated ?June 1945). However, he later says: "I can't think how I shall fit in eventually. I feel so much time has passed and so much has happened that I'm a bit out of sympathy with the whole institution" (*ibid.*, 10 Apr. 1945). Then on Christmas Eve 1945:

> "I am writing from Knutsford *(Mrs. Gaskell's 'Cranford')* ... Yes it is a very nice job: as I have an absolutely free hand and need not feel myself bound by exact 'proportions' or things like that. Its an ideal job in a way because it links up 'Art' and present day demands very well and I think it may be the fore-runner of a lot of similar commissions."

These were landscapes commissioned by the architect Sir Geoffrey Jellicoe explaining part of a planning scheme for Knutsford, Cheshire. Jellicoe, who was awarded the Prix de Rome 1923, was an English architect, town planner, landscape architect, garden designer and author who was liaising with Alan regarding the development of overspill housing estates created to accommodate families from Manchester in the aftermath of the war.

In April 1946 Alan wrote:

> "I have just got back from Warwick – at least I got back this afternoon – and since then I have done the 2 rough sketches of the castle and shall deliver them to-morrow. They have turned out rather well. There were very few possible views of the Castle – it is not open to visitors, but I think I've got 2 interesting views, one with the river. I have received some more information from the G.W.C. so shall be able to get on with those now."

and

> "I've got this Warwick drawing to do now by May 1st so I shall have no time before then." (*ibid.*, ?Wednesday, postmarked 1946)

FIG. 37. Alan viewing the exterior and interior of the Daws Heath Chapel (1946)
(SORRELL FAMILY COLLECTION)

Another important consideration for Alan was his pending divorce from Irene and his future life together with Elizabeth. Elizabeth wrote that "in my daydreams I do confess that I weave little pictures of us living in a cottage in the country and you painting happily without any restrictions, and children romping madly in the fields." Alan replied that "it would be absurd for you to give your time to cooking and things like that and I hope we'll be able to get someone to do the work." Regarding their home, he wrote that he wanted to "steer clear of the subject of 'building' of any kind with your father [*George Tanner had a building business*] because I have the most strong and bitter feelings about speculative building". Later he wrote:

> "I have some exciting and important news for you about a possible future abode for us. It is that wooden chapel in Dawes Heath. I made enquiries and found it is for sale freehold for £675 – it can be converted for £200 more. Here it is in plan. I am viewing it Saturday and have seen the bank about possible loan and White about surveying it." (Sorrell & Tanner 1944–7, postmark illegible, 1946)

In 1939 he had described Dawes Heath romantically as

> "a district of close and sometimes impenetrable woodland that has existed from immemorial times. Long ago it provided fuel for London in the shape of charcoal, and now the trees are systematically cut every seven years, and sawn and split for stakes and chestnut fencing. On these occasions the woodmen make little encampments and their technique and tools are both picturesque and surprising in this age of mechanization, and, shall we say, corrugation? These chestnut woods have a peculiar and suggestive air of melancholy darkness, and the casual passer-by will naturally assume that they are completely deserted except for the woodmen during the septennial clearings, but he will be wrong, and if he will follow the narrow lanes that wind through them he will come upon lonely houses virtually lost in the woods. These houses are usually surrounded by small prim orchards which throw the nearby woodland into yet deeper gloom. The people who chose

to live this strange secluded life on the very edge of the large town are primitive, and famous for their strict religiosity and rigid sectarianism, and strange tales could be told of the odd instances of antique customs, and superstitions which still survive there". (Sorrell 1939b, 35)

Again he wrote to Elizabeth about the house:

"I have been inside this morning: there is no gas, but is outside and can easily be brought in. Electricity is out of the question for the time being – it is about 300 yards away and may be brought along at any time, though that may mean a year or two years! Then there is only a pump inside for water, so you see I am not concealing anything from you. The price is £650, not £675. Altogether it should come to less than £1000." (Sorrell & Tanner 1944–7, undated)

By July 1946 Alan had bought it and by the early February 1947 it was finished even though there had been problems in the building due to post-war restrictions on wood allowance. The builders

"can't get the timber yet and in any case the Ministry has cut us down to .500 for a standard instead of allowing .772. No extra for shelves, I fear. And no upstairs!". (Sorrell & Tanner 1944–7, postmarked ?Dec 1946)

Meanwhile, by September 1946 Elizabeth, Audrey (Elizabeth's sister) and her mother decided to weave some rugs, cushion covers, etc. Alan wrote: "I'm glad you are getting hold of a loom, how big are the rugs likely to be?" Elizabeth replied:

"I must tell you about the looms. We went up to the art school on Saturday – and were confronted with a room about the size of your mother's kitchen absolutely packed from floor to ceiling with bits and pieces of all sorts of things - including bits of looms! … we managed to sort out a weaving loom and an upright rug loom and a small hand frame for weaving … Whoopee!! I've woven one cushion cover on the hand frame!" (*Ibid.*, undated)

Although Sandersons provided wallpaper with her designs, my mother's motto was "don't buy what you can make."

Alan's divorce was finalised on 5 November 1946, much to the delight of Alan's and Elizabeth's respective families, enabling them to marry on 29 March 1947. After their honeymoon at the Queen's Hotel, Ambleside, in the Lake District where the RCA had been relocated during the war whilst Elizabeth had been a student, they began their married life, and initially were solvent. This in part being due to Alan returning to the RCA after he was demobbed, although "old Helps" said: "Why have you come back, you're making your way now, and you don't want to do teaching!" Emotionally rather than financially that was true: "I feel so much time has passed and so much has happened that I'm a bit out of sympathy with the whole institution." Later remarking: "The term is dragging itself out in a perfectly agonising way" (Sorrell & Tanner 1944–7, postmarked 10 Apr. 1945).

In 1948, Sir Robin Darwin became the New Principal and implemented drastic changes which Alan commented on in 1954. He wrote how, in the 1930s, Henry Moore

> "had been present at what was perhaps, an important occasion in his life, the dinner given to him by the staff of the Royal College of Art to express our regret at his resignation from that institution."

Adding that Moore had for some years been

> "making many disciples, but his developing personality became too strong for the civil servants who from their grey offices ultimately control the teaching of art in England, and though William Rotheinstein loyally supported him, it became clear that he must resign." (Sorrell *c.* 1962, 40)

Later, and less ceremoniously, Gilbert Spencer recounts his own dismissal:

> "Mr Wedgewood, a cousin of Darwin's, who had succeeded Lord Hambleden, was in the Chair, but he said nothing and made no impression on me. Away to the west sat Darwin casting his shadow like the setting sun, over my future. It was left to Sir Charles Tennyson from the wings in a kind of echo voice to tell me that I had been retired. That was all. In less than five minutes I had left the room." (Spencer 1974, 143)

Interestingly Darwin had previously been the head of art at Eton where he himself had been educated, and he was supposedly the model character for John Steed in the iconic 1960s television series *The Avengers*. He used to turn up at the RCA in a chauffeur driven Rolls-Royce wearing a bowler hat and carrying an umbrella. A striking contrast to Henry Moore's, Gilbert Spencer's and my father's backgrounds!

Regarding his own dismissal, Alan remembered how a Marx Brothers' film had influenced him as a child:

> "Groucho Marx rebuffed a cringing employee who was asking for his wages with the words 'What, would you be a wage-slave?' … for ever after that, whenever I accepted employment which offered me a regular weekly, monthly or quarterly

FIG. 38. Marriage of Alan & Elizabeth Sorrell on 29 March 1947
(SORRELL FAMILY COLLECTION)

EARLY LIFE AND EDUCATION 57

Fig. 39.

Left: a. Elizabeth nursing Richard in the kitchen (1948)

Right: b. the Sorrell family in the studio at Thors Mead (*c.* 1963), 19.7 × 31.7 cm (Sketchbook W, ASA)

(SORRELL FAMILY COLLECTION)

increment, I remembered those pregnant words … In spite of being keen and anxious to please, these salaried posts always became greasy poles down which I slid into the cold waters of unemployment. Finally, and this time after an acrimonious correspondence with the Principal of an august institution, I was courteously asked whether I would prefer to be dismissed, or resign. I chose the former, with glee, and since then have worked happily on my own, without a thought of security or Groucho Marx." (Sorrell *c.* 1962, 2)

By September 1948 Richard was born, followed by Mark in January 1952 and myself in August 1955. Alan and Elizabeth were happy but financial demands were paramount and although he had some sporadic teaching posts after the RCA, he decided to take note of my mother's encouragement and observation: first to be self-employed, and secondly to re-establish contacts with the archaeological world and the *Illustrated London News*.

In 1951 the then Ministry of Works for Scotland (now Historic Environment Scotland) commissioned Alan to produce a reconstruction drawing of "Jarlshof late Iron Age settlement". Elizabeth and Alan travelled to Shetland; Richard celebrated his 3rd birthday there (see Chapter 9). Alan had been suffering with an ulcerated leg due to poor medical advice in Essex, after having had a varicose vein unsuccessfully treated. In Shetland, a travelling nurse looked at the ulcerated leg, by which time the hole was the size of an old penny, and plugged it with a swab of gentian violet. It healed and Alan's leg was saved, but later it would lead to his fatal thrombosis.

* * *

Up till now I have been concentrating on my father's artistic and emotional development: his Prix de Rome; the Southend library commissions; the War; even the commercial art and childhood expeditions with my grandfather. All this developed in Alan the aptitude and vision necessary to work alongside archaeologists in artistically visualising our heritage. Alan was valued, needed and able to "earn some money to live" (Sorrell & Tanner 1944–47, undated, ?1944) but he was, as he said, "an artist, and not an archaeologist: this, of course, was never a secret, but I shall feel happier now that I have come clean about it" (Mark Sorrell 1981, 20).

For the 1951 Festival of Britain exhibition Alan had two commissions. First, to paint a decorative mural of British sailing boats to go behind the Nelson Bar of the exhibition ship of *H.M.S. Campania* which was to tour the British Isles. This light-hearted mural is now in the collection of the National Maritime Museum. Secondly, for the Dome of Discovery, whose overall plan was devised by the popular archaeologist Jacquetta Hawkes, Alan made four reconstructions of the Royal Palaces of Ur, Mohenjo Daro, Knossos and Jericho in association with three archaeologists: Leonard Woolley, Mortimer Wheeler and Kathleen Kenyon respectively (Fig. 41a & b). This established Alan as the leading artist of the time in visualising archaeological civilisations. In sad contrast, Alan had not been short-listed for the associated touring Arts Council exhibition *60 Paintings for 51*, which supposedly represented the most talented of British artists of the day. Many of Alan's friends including Ceri Richards, Gilbert Spencer, John Nash, Carel Weight and Charles Mahoney had been selected. Alan was hurt and realised the course his career was taking.

Elizabeth contended that Alan was more intense and intellectual than the present day painter, where the "happy accident" abounds and the camera compensates for the intellect. This is obvious on reading Alan's remarks in Rome and later in Greece. In Rome, Alan had bought a photograph of the

FIG. 40. *Working Boats from Around the British Isles* (1951) detail. Produced for the Nelson Bar on *HMS Campania*, the 1951 Festival of Britain exhibition ship which toured the British Isles. Oil on 5 panels, 122 × 914.4 cm
(COLLECTION OF NATIONAL MARITIME MUSEUM, IMAGE COURTESY OF LISS LLEWELLYN FINE ART)

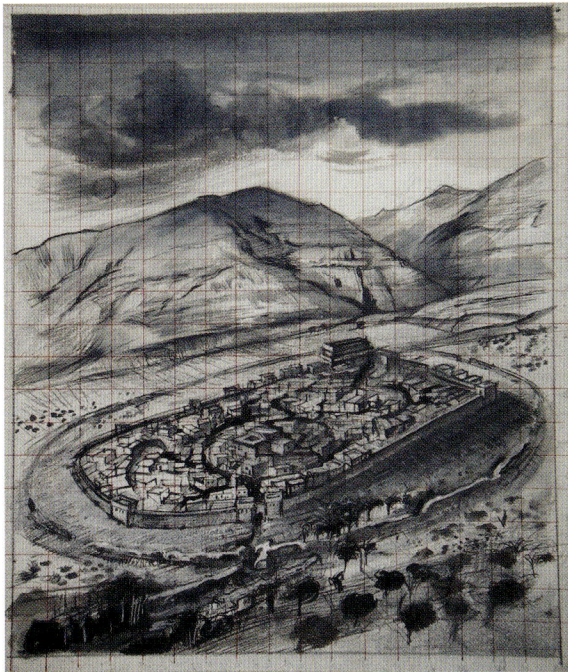

Left to right:
FIG. 41. a. Knossos and b. Bronze Age Jericho, working drawings (1951). Commissioned for the Dome of Discovery in the 1951 Festival of Britain to represent the work of the British School at Athens and then British School of Archaeology in Jerusalem (now the Kenyon Institute), the latter being produced with the cooperation of Professor Kathleen Kenyon. Pencil (ASA)

School of Athens to

> "try to analyse its design. There must be a conscious scheme, an organisation of all these separate yet cunningly unified groups and figures, it would be disappointing if he had to say 'Here is instinct, a tremendous instinct for spatial design, a happy accident, by a man with an aptitude for doing the right thing.' But of course its nothing of the sort, he quickly decided, it's the peak of scientific picture making plus a super sensibility to natural appearances." (Sorrell *c.* 1938, 62)

He would make

> "a careful tracing of the photograph and then cast about for the guiding lines of the picture. He found that the vanishing lines of the architecture converged to a point between the two middle figures, dead in the centre of the picture, and not only the architecture, but the edges of figures and objects, pointing arms and flying draperies vanished to this focal point with a precision that instantly belied the happy accident theory." (*Ibid.*, 64)

Once analysed, Alan

> "squared up the tracing and from it drew the outlines very carefully in pen and ink on a rather larger canvas which he took backwards and forwards to the Vatican till the painting was completed." (*Ibid.*)

On examining Alan's later works, such as his drawing of the *Raising of the Lintels at Stonehenge* there is a definite complicated underlying geometric structure overlooked by the general viewer. It is not surprising his dislike of the "illustrative" label compounded by his fury when, as in the Bible, they were bled off the page. I remember innocently asking why was he annoyed and did it matter? His reply was always the same "It ruins the composition". Alan was thorough and any shortcomings he endeavoured to rectify. In Rome, aware of his ignorance of human anatomy, he had employed models and then "went to the library and found a book on the subject, and sat down to study mechanics – in relation to figure drawing". (Sorrell *c.* 1938, 79).

He later remarked that:

> "the artist, is in fact, a highly practical, passionately, conscientious person, who must realise all the facets of a form and he cannot permit the glossing over of truth with technicalities. Think of Andrea Mantegna, for instance, minutely exact as a draughtsman, with a vivid sense of form, a scholar, and an impeccable craftsman. He is the archetype of the artist, who is capable of supplying the final visual statement which brings to life the learned treatise of the scholar." (Sorrell *c.* 1962, 54)

Alan was in sympathy with such attitudes but out of stride with many of his contemporaries, which may explain his continual quest to find artists he empathised with, even if it meant reading their autobiographies. These included Holman Hunt, Benjamin Robert Haydon and Edward Lear.

Together, Alan and Elizabeth maintained and re-inforced their strong beliefs, feeling at times isolated as if on a desert island. Although regularly exhibiting at the RA Summer Exhibitions, the RWS, as well as other exhibitions around the country, Alan remained a neglected outsider. He deeply felt his lack of recognition from the art world, which he justly deserved. Being too honest he did not "play the game" correctly! I remember being at the Royal Academy and he said to me: "Just look at them all rubbing their hands in front of potential patrons". Not surprising then that Andrew Lambirth wrote in *The Spectator* on 18 January 2014 that Alan was "a remarkable, oddly original and unduly neglected artist".

The year 1951 also marked the death of Edith at 84, who died pleased that Alan was happily married with a child and his career

FIG. 42a. *Raising of the Sarsens, Stonehenge* (*c.* 1965). Finished drawing. Pen & ink, 17 × 20.5 cm Produced for the book *Prehistoric Britain* by Barbara Green and Alan Sorrell published by Lutterworth Press 1968 (ASA)

EARLY LIFE AND EDUCATION 61

developing. Alan was very close to Edith and twice a year, in June and at Christmas, would, without fail, put a wreath on her grave. Before they were married, Alan wrote a touching vignette to Elizabeth to thank her and her mother for sending oddments and wools to his mother: "I helped her to cut out some rabbits last night" (Sorrell & Tanner 1944–7, 14 Oct. 1945).

Apart from his archaeological work, Alan would continue to paint murals, including a commission completed in 1951 for St Peter's Church, Bexhill-on-Sea. Alan had been recommended by E. W. Tristram (see Chapter 2) and, ironically, commissioned by and met the same George Bell, Bishop of Chichester mentioned earlier (see Chapter 5). Other murals included one commissioned by the company that made the salty beef extract *Bovril*, and *The Seasons*, a personal favourite, completed in 1954 for Warwick Oken Secondary Modern, now Myton School. It measures 52 ft long × 9 ft high (15.84 × 2.74 m) and is painted in oil straight onto the prepared wall. This is in a busy thoroughfare of a large school and was still intact and appreciated 60 years on. More recently a new head deemed it of no educational value to his pupils and had it covered over with opaque Perspex. An ex-pupil and teacher from the school, Mr Raymond West, has campaigned for it to be seen again, with huge local support. I have recently managed to have it listed by Historic England as a Grade II monument, with the support of the 20th Century Society.

Alan sought other kinds of commissioned work, including two group Senior Common Room conversation pieces for Magdalen College, Oxford. The first included C. S. Lewis and his classicist friend Colin Hardie, whom Alan had known since Rome. By now, Alan was as an artist a regular contributor of archaeological drawings for the *ILN* who also commissioned him to be a visual correspondent abroad (see Chapter 7). In 1954, he was sent to Greece and Istanbul, after he had read with concern many letters that "expressed that the walls were falling down … Fortunately Sir Bruce Ingram suggested I should make some archaeological studies for the I.L.N. in Greece and Turkey" (Sorrell *c*. 1962, 2). Then again Sir Bruce Ingram seemed "the man most likely to help me

FIG. 42b. *The Raising of the Sarsens* with geometric structural lines added by Julia Sorrell to indicate the underlying form within the composition. Alan reworked the original version produced for the Ministry of Works by simplifying the composition to increase the drama in this carefully worked out drawing. The structure of much of his work can be analysed in a similar way (ASA)

FIG. 43. Mural over the north arch, St Peters Church, Bexhill-on-Sea (1951). The figures from left to right are St Paul, St Peter, and then two local saints Wilfred and Richard. Oil on plaster
(IMAGE COURTESY OF DR ANDREW GORSUCH)

FIG. 44. *The Seasons* (1954). Myton School Warwick. Oil on plaster
(IMAGE COURTESY OF LISS LLEWELLYN FINE ART)

FIG. 45. *Conversation Piece: The Senior Common Room at Magdalen College, Oxford. Winter, 1954*. Second from the left leaning forward is the classicist Colin Hardie, Alan's friend from the British School at Rome. Far right is C. S. Lewis. Oil, 57 × 69 cm
(WITH KIND PERMISSION OF THE PRESIDENT AND FELLOWS OF MAGDALEN COLLEGE)

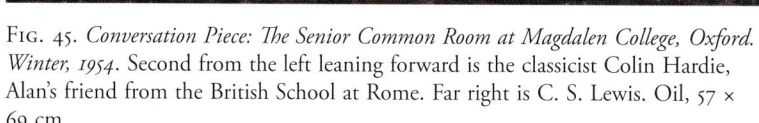

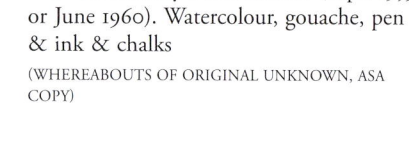

FIG. 46. Hinkley Point interior (Sept. 1959 or June 1960). Watercolour, gouache, pen & ink & chalks
(WHEREABOUTS OF ORIGINAL UNKNOWN, ASA COPY)

EARLY LIFE AND EDUCATION 63

FIG. 47. *Planting of the Trees* (1971). Watercolour, gouache, ink and chalks, *c.* 55 × 69 cm
(PRIVATE COLLECTION, © ESTATE OF ALAN SORRELL)

FIG. 48. *The Stone Men* (1961). The fragility of civilisation was a repeated theme in Alan's work, see Figs 27 & 76. Gouache, ink, watercolour and chalks on paper, *c.* 55 × 69 cm
(COLLECTION OF MARK SORRELL © ESTATE OF ALAN SORRELL)

FIG. 49. *The Spoilers* (detail) (1958). Oil on board, 123 × 243 cm
(SOUTHEND MUSEUMS SERVICE)

in getting to Nubia" (Sorrell 1974) to make a pictorial record of the villages before they were destroyed and the monuments moved in preparation for the building of the Aswan Dam in 1962, a dream of the then President Nasser. Alan approached Hinkley Point regarding a visual recording of the construction of the first atomic power station; likewise Southend District Council commissioned a series of paintings on the theme of the "Changing Face of Southend".

Another important part of Alan's post-war life was his attitude to the preservation of the local landscape and environment, which he visually expressed in many paintings. In June 1945 he had written:

> "For God's Sake don't vote Tory – unless you really admire Beaverbrook and want everything to be at the mercy of untrammelled private enterprise. Surely you believe in planning; even if some regulations are irksome. I don't want to see the speculative builder, for instance spoiling what's left of England (and making a fortune at the same time)." (Sorrell & Tanner 1944–7, 23 June 1945)

Although many of his attitudes were conservative (with a small 'c'), Alan would never be swayed on his beliefs. My mother recounted how early one evening Alan, baby Richard and herself were in the studio when a brick came through the window, narrowly missing Richard! Why? Because Alan advised everyone in the local council elections to vote Labour which had promised to protect the Green Belt. Being supposedly "safe seats", the Conservatives were disregarding the voters' wishes. Labour won, Conservatives were dumbfounded, and the land was safe for a while. As a child I remember Alan's relentlessness, whether shouting at workmen not to cut down a tree (by shouting, he did not stammer!) and then quickly getting a preservation order established: or our taking petitions to all the houses in the neighbourhood, which gave residents a voice to counteract the encroaching "concrete jungle". If, today, you walk down Dawes Heath Road, Thundersley, Essex, and see all the woods and fields there, remember Alan's efforts where he succeeded as an individual as well as an active member of the Campaign for the Protection of Rural England. Then the protection of the environment was not as prominent as it is today.

Alan expressed these sentiments in many paintings including *The Planting of the Trees*. This artistically successful and romantic painting encapsulates Alan's feelings. He wrote that this subject matter

> "is something I have thought about for years, but only lately put on paper. The trees were drawn from real trees, the earth from lumps of garden clay and the form of the hills was suggested by the stratification of coal. I made a cotton garment and draped it on a small lay-figure: soaked in water it

set in folds appropriate for the action of the figure – whose hands and feet were mirror reflections of my own". (Sorrell 1972, 47)

Alan was keen for his work to visually convey his values. Other examples include *The Stone-Men* and *The Falling Tower* (Fig. 27, above) where his concerns are the destruction of civilisation, or in *A Land Fit for Heroes* (Fig. 8, above) the pointlessness of war. In *The Spoilers*, Alan expressed his feelings regarding a local building development he had failed to prevent. We as children were involved in these campaigns, and used to audibly hiss the builder's name "Wigginssssssss" from our car window on driving past such a development! The last, unfinished painting, *The Assault*, Alan left on his easel showed diggers ripping up trees for the sake of a new supermarket. He once commented "Yes I'd like to do more drawings of trees: I don't want to get the reputation of being a man who can do such 'clever constructional stuff' certainly not" (Sorrell & Tanner 1944–47, postmarked 2 Mar. 1945) Yet, in contradiction, around the same time he wrote about *Watch Office, RAF, Station* (1944):

> "It is very architectonic in design and I don't mean it is full of buildings, though as a matter of fact it is of an architectural subject, the watch office at the aerodrome. It's most carefully balanced and full of unexpected rhythms and extremely sinister and full of foreboding. I'm rather proud of it, you know how vain I am. Of course I do base my designs on the principle of opposing forces, I mean that objects must be buttressed or held in position by other solid objects, so that the whole design becomes structural and in fact architectonic. It's a principle neglected by modern people and that largely accounts for much of their looseness and weakness. All the old Italians – who had so much to do with building – were conscious of it, and it gives a compactness and genuine finish to their work. I had a lot to do with architects and architecture in Italy and this influence has never left me." (Sorrell & Tanner 1944–7, ?Aug. 1944)

He was referred to by RCA students as "Old Angles", and maybe his interest in the architectural and his geometric structure of his drawings expressed his analytical, "problem solving" mentality, whilst the drawing of trees, stormy clouds, and charging horses, his romantic spirit? He felt

> "'Activity' expresses very well the character of south-east Essex – not brooding woodlands, not gentle hills, but watchful alertness, angular active forms, scudding clouds and an easterly breeze." (Sorrell 1934)

* * *

FIG. 50. *The Assault* (1974). This remained uncompleted on his easel at the time of his death, and was a protest against the building of a new supermarket nearby. Gouache, watercolour, pen & ink & chalks, *c.* 55 × 69 cm
(COLLECTION OF JULIA SORRELL © ESTATE OF ALAN SORRELL)

FIG. 51. *Watch Office, RAF Station* (1944). Produced while Alan was at RAF Squire's Gate, it depicts a critical moment in the life of an aerodrome when the squadrons return from missions, and it probably reflects his experience working on aerodromes in East Anglia. The watch office is signalling to an aircraft the strength and direction of the wind, and the runway that it is safe to land on. The number 34 indicates that the runway points 340° north: perhaps fire crew and ambulances are ready and waiting at the end of that runway in the case of a stricken aircraft, or the other runways are blocked by damaged aircraft. Pastel on paper pasted on card, 35 × 54.7 cm
(LAING ART GALLERY, NEWCASTLE-UPON-TYNE, IMAGE COURTESY OF THE BRIDGEMAN ART LIBRARY © ESTATE OF ALAN SORRELL)

What was he like at home? In Rome he:

> "had always been what is called 'tidy' in his dress, and at this time he always wore a necktie, parted his hair in the proper place, and kept his trousers creased by putting them under the mattress at night. Surrounded by untidy people, he was driven by a very fury of neatness and contrariness."
> (Sorrell *c.* 1938, 58)

This formal attire probably originated from his commercial art days and initially Alan would work at his desk at home wearing a suit, which wore away rubbing against the table. Gradually Elizabeth introduced casual clothing. An instance Richard remembered was him sitting in his high chair when a pair of sandals came through the hatch into the kitchen from the studio with an accompanying voice, "waste of money". After a while the sandals were retrieved and worn! Another time, when Elizabeth's brother, George, and Alan were sitting in the studio on a very hot summer's day, a suited accountant plus briefcase arrived: "Show him in". Elizabeth was at a loss – there was Alan in string vest and pants and there was the accountant. She showed him in and retreated to the kitchen laughing, although she admitted that her husband's attire had gone from one extreme to the other.

By the time I was a teenager he had two matching outfits my mother had bought him, one dark blue and one dark pink, the top being like a sailor's shirt complemented with a silk cravat around his neck. I was acutely embarrassed when my parents had lunch with me in my London college canteen, with my father in his pink outfit and my mother wearing one of her very tall hats, as she believed the height would compensate for her small chin. My father leant across the table and said "Don't worry, all children are embarrassed by their parents". He "lived" in these outfits and whenever my mother went shopping he would deliberately walk up the lane ahead of the car, directing her onto the road with exaggerated hand-signals in synchronisation with vigorous leg movements. The neighbours opposite would crane their necks to view such a spectacle from behind the net curtains, then speedily retreat. He was, however, always dressed conventionally for business meetings and private views.

In 1964 disaster struck when my mother woke up barely able to move. She had developed rheumatoid arthritis and, at that time, any possible cures were still in their infancy. This was too much for Alan and it is the only time I remember him crying. He was holding my mother's hand in the kitchen and saying: "This is the worst thing that has ever happened". My mother was stoically trying to peel vegetables. However, Alan dressed my mother, brushed her hair, cooked, in fact helped in any possible way during any flare-ups of the disease, as well as continuing with his own work. They kept going. Alan's absurd sense of humour became paramount. So now, when taking my mother her breakfast, there was a card with UTBH ("untouched by hand") covering her pills, or he would write a "doctor's health card" to make her laugh, and so gradually they were able to cope. Over the years, Alan's sense of humour had helped to buffer him against all the pain and suffering he had endured since his childhood.

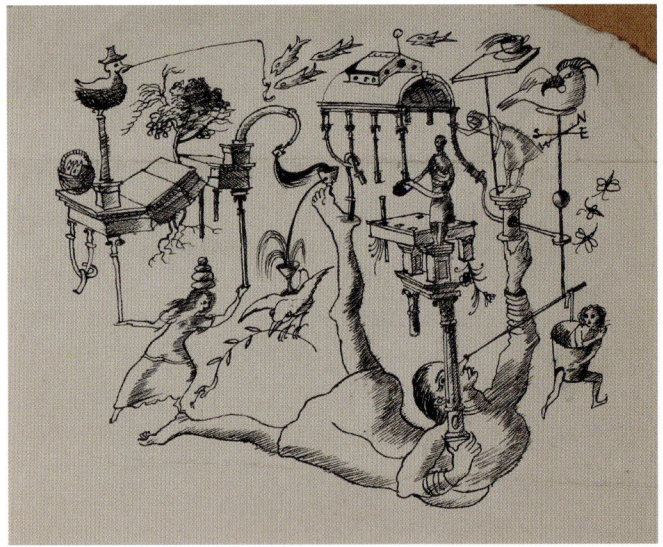

He would also tell absurd stories, like why he was "the Man who created Roman Britain", or how he had had to find his head at the Crimea when it had been shot off, while pointing to marks on his neck where he had retrieved and nailed it back on! I believed them all. Sometimes visitors, like archaeologists, unaware of this humorous trait in such a seemingly serious man, would be justly confused: for instance, when Alan disappeared into the kitchen, to be found kneeling down and whispering in Strüdel's (our miniature dachshund) ear asking if his Babykins wanted to go to the "beautiful excretorium" before carefully carrying him outside, they would look on bemused.

Otherwise Alan was serious and hard-working and would seemingly sit permanently working at his desk from morning till well after I had gone to bed. Alan wrote the following in Greece, but it is succinct:

> "I worked all through the day, for to leave a drawing is to risk the loss of that quality of it 'being in one jet' as my old professor once put it. Cohesion, continuity, unity, any of these words will do, but I prefer 'one jet' with its mental picture of a fireman's hose and the invincible curve of its streaming beauty." (Sorrell c. 1962, 207)

He tended to get up by 7.30 am, read *The Times*, take my mother her breakfast, answer his letters and then sit on one side of the studio/living room

FIG. 52.
Left: a. Birthday card for Elizabeth Sorrell (*c.* 1970)
(COLLECTION OF JULIA SORRELL © ESTATE OF ALAN SORRELL)

Right: b. Doodle (late 1940s). Pen & ink
(ASA)

EARLY LIFE AND EDUCATION 69

FIG. 53. *The Evening Meal in the Triclinium* (*c.* 1960). Pen & ink, 27 × 22 cm. Produced for the book *Roman Britain* by Aileen Fox and Alan Sorrell published by Lutterworth Press 1961
(ASA)

FIG. 54. Alan holding an aerial view of Roman Colchester (1973)
(SORRELL FAMILY COLLECTION)

working at his ex-army table, which was eventually replaced by a desk. His table was covered with information, books, plans, correspondence, plus inks, chalks, watercolours etc. There Alan would visualise our ancient civilisations while, behind the table, was an easel on which stood an imaginative painting awaiting completion. My mother would conjecture just how much work had been created in that studio! During his working day, Alan would get up and stretch his legs by pacing across the nearby fields and then return to his desk. The studio was so strategically placed in the middle of the house that we, as children, would run continuously through it. Amidst this pandemonium, Alan would raise his head, often with a white stripe on his lip where he had put his gouache paint-brush in his mouth, smile and then carry on working. My mother would worry about the noise and suggested building a shed in the garden. Alan was furious and explained he loved to be in the thick of it: instead of realising her thoughtfulness, thought he was being excluded. He loved the bustling atmosphere – like Mark and I crawling along the hall on our stomachs in accompaniment to Sibelius's *Finlandia* and, with the clash of cymbals, jumping into the studio screaming. Or sitting and drawing, with my father taking an interest "Why are you painting their faces orange?" he asked when I was about eight. "I only have a pink crayon, and faces are more orange than pink." "I see," he replied. Mark and I played the piano, Richard drew, I drew and embroidered, we read and did our homework there. Being lazy, I cajoled the others into doing my homework for me and my father helped with history! An added advantage of having the studio

FIG. 55. Sketchbook studies of Elizabeth for Fig. 53 (*c.* 1960). Pencil (ASA)

placed centrally in the house was that Alan would ask one of us, including my mother, to stop and pose for a while. I remember sitting while Alan drew me – often having to wear some drape, which would reappear in the drawing he was working on.

My mother was, as discussed earlier, also an artist in her own right. She was a watercolourist, producing work of the highest quality, which she regularly sold at the RA Summer Exhibitions and the RWS. Her *Ferns in the Conservatory* painted in 1945 was bought by the Tate. Elizabeth sat and worked on the other side of the studio with groups "set up" on her table. Although my parents actually got someone in to help with the housework, having three children was demanding and there was always a lot to be done. In any event, the women who came were not really any good and my mother would often tidy beforehand and was always concerned they had their coffee breaks. One woman would steal sugar, leaving a trail of it through the house, next day bringing us a huge bunch of flowers from her garden. My father tried to help, but from early in the marriage he was under pressure to produce the work. Once some archaeologists arrived too early for an appointment, only to find my parents washing the floor.

My mother was determined to maintain her career although becoming increasingly disabled by rheumatoid arthritis. My brothers and I remember her table and her neatly stretched white paper with her watercolours all ready and, whenever she had the odd moment, she could gradually fill the paper, systematically working and completing each painting one at a time. Alan and Elizabeth would work together for hours in the studio, sometimes not talking as they were deep in concentration. Their approach to painting was different in many ways and, of course, at times they may have argued but their fundamental beliefs were the same and they were happy together.

My mother wanted us to be surrounded by beautiful things and not to feel poor, as she believed this made one jealous. Whenever she sold a painting she would buy a little ornament, very cheaply, from a local antique shop and over the years the house gradually filled with "knick-knacks". Each ornament she tended to use in a painting so it "would pay for itself". She also bought silver cutlery so we eventually had enough to use daily and my father was determined we went to private school and have advantages he had not had. This involved excessive hard work and in his diary he continuously made financial calculations. Sometimes he was down to £2 in the one bank account but we children were totally unaware of this. For years we had no fridge, washing machine, in fact any gadgets including radio and television. Alan's work began to appear more and more on the television and so it was decided to rent one.

My father loved watching adventure and drama, and particularly enjoyed westerns like *Stage Coach*. When there was a sad scene, he would take out his revolting handkerchief and pass it to my mother to wipe away a tear. Although he was widely read, to relax he read swash-buckling stories such as C. S. Forester's *Hornblower* series. Likewise, he enjoyed creating a sense of drama in his work, with battle scenes, rearing horses, stormy clouds and so on, reflecting his turbulent life, a sense of drama and apprehension adding to his adventurous spirit. Before going to Istanbul he confessed to a professor at a luncheon in Athens:

> "my fear of being arrested as a spy whilst drawing the Byzantine fortifications. I hoped for a firm and hearty reassurance, but to my consternation the Professor, with a great laugh said 'Of course you will, dear boy – of course they'll arrest you – it's a military zone, you know'. Then, he added, with great kindness 'But don't worry they probably won't shoot on sight.' My host, perhaps noticed the wild look in my eyes, for he re-filled my glass at this point, and guided the conversation into another channel." (Sorrell *c.* 1962, 133)

So you can imagine Alan's consternation when drawing the walls of Istanbul:

> "Immersed in the difficulties of comprising several miles of space and air, and the forms contained therein, into the two dimensions of my sheet of paper, and bothered by the constant threatening breeze that tried to tear paper from board, and hat from my head, I was astonished to hear a voice in my ear, which seemed to boom like a cannon above the whistling of the wind. I looked round, and there was a man, enormous against the sun. He wore a military peaked cap, and had a soldierly appearance. He appeared to be in a good temper, but here at last, surely was the army, stern and implacable, doing its duty. He had approached me with stealthy and commendable skill: no doubt, the rest of the patrol was close at hand, probably

FIG. 56. *Ferns in the Conservatory* by Elizabeth Tanner (1946). Watercolour & gouache, 56 × 37.5 cm
(PRESENTED BY THE TRUSTEES OF THE CHANTREY BEQUEST 1949. © TATE, LONDON 2017)

FIG. 57. Alan, Elizabeth holding Strüdel, and Julia in the studio (*c.* 1970). On the easel is a reconstruction drawing of Orford Castle in progress
(SORRELL FAMILY COLLECTION)

covering me with tommy guns. I whipped out my special permit, handed it to him, and sat back to watch its effect. It was instantaneous and electrical: he drew himself up, assumed an expression of super military gravity, handed the permit back to me, saluted, and descended the rubble slope with such precipitation that I feared he may suffer a fall. I last saw him striding away, then suddenly disappear behind a fold in the land, or into what might equally well have been a deep hole. I noticed that he carried a leather pouch which flapped against his thigh as he walked." (*Ibid.*, 164)

When travelling to Nubia, Alan had worries after talking to a friend at the British Museum who

"asked me whether I knew anything of Horned Vipers. I said 'No', and he then explained that they were small snakes which frequented sandy wastes (Nubia was a sandy waste) and sprang at one with the speed and force of a whiplash. Here my friend made a sudden darting movement of his hand which nearly shot me out of my chair. He said their bite was fatal, and added with ghastly bonhomie 'Of course, you can cut your foot off, but its no good, you won't have time to finish the job.' I smiled bleakly, and said I would try to avoid Horned Vipers in their sandy lairs, until I heard that cobras lie in wait on the green river bank. My friend now made a horrible undulating movement with both his hands, and said in a bored tone 'they slide out of the long grass. Don't go near it, and avoid heaps of stones, cobras live in them.' It seemed that whichever way I turned, I should be in mortal peril. I was told that 'Gippy Tummy' (could that really mean 'Egyptian Tummy'?) was inevitable, but a patent medicine which had been famous since the Indian Mutiny, was strongly recommended as a palliative. I was urged to wash fruit in a well known disinfectant, and this advice was reinforced by an anecdote, chilling and macabre: He told me of a steamer crammed with Arab refugees whose only food was a supply of tainted grapes. He, in command, had a small bottle of Blue Dettol, in which he washed his grapes, and survived, spick and span. As for the refugees, a thumbs-down gesture was the appropriate conclusion to the tale." (Sorrell *c.* 1974, 7)

These were compounded when the *ILN*

"wrote to say that they were insuring my life for a very large sum. I could only point out that if I left my bones in the desert (and I strongly discounted the likelihood of this happening) she [*Elizabeth*] would be a wealthy widow. However, this elementary brand of humour did not appeal to my wife or my three small children, so I promised I would be very careful, and left it at that; there was nothing more to be said." (*Ibid.*)

Alan imagined himself like a character in an exciting film, as when in Egypt, his confiscated drawing materials were being returned to the Cataract Hotel by "a car travelling very fast, nearly colliding with the departing truck, and my various possessions were flung out rather than delivered in a non-stop U-turn act quite in the American gangster film manner" (*ibid.*, 168).

Alan later had to practise diplomacy to successfully secure the release of his 52 paintings back to Britain as time was speedily evaporating for him to catch his plane home. He explained that he had

> "entered into a contract with Sir Bruce Ingram to bring these drawings to him. Their publication in 'The Illustrated London News' will bring much valuable publicity and goodwill towards the U.A.R. in England. It will be one more step in our march towards understanding and friendship."

This was a firing of the heavy guns a little too soon, but nevertheless it made considerable impact, and the Under-Secretary tried another tack: "We can have coloured photographs taken of all your drawings, as good as the originals" (Sorrell *c.* 1974, 187).

My father had a penchant for hats – whether in Rome where, having stopped at Gibraltar for four hours he decided it was necessary to buy a souvenir: "one panama, an absolute necessity, and the perfect souvenir. So he bought one, and though, of course, it would have to hang on the hat-stand in the hall instead of reclining in dustless ease in the cabinet, it was, he felt sure, otherwise quite ideal" (Sorrell *c.* 1938, 239), or in Egypt, where he commented how "I had better luck in my search for a hat, and bought a wide brimmed linen one, which carried with it, I thought, a faint aroma of elephant guns and safari" (Sorrell 1974, 23). At home, as a joke, Alan wore a similar hat to the one described in Italy where he met "in the Via Panzani the padrone was a thin bent old gentleman who wore a black velvet jacket and a cap with a tassel" (Sorrell *c.* 1938, 169). Hats are often important additions for someone who is fundamentally shy, as they help to express a personality one can shield behind. Alan would normally go to sites either wearing a navy blue beret or an unkempt trilby.

Fig. 58.
Left: a. Alan on horseback (third from right) wearing a Panama hat (1929)

Right: b. Alan wearing his bush hat purchased in Aswan (1962)

(SORRELL FAMILY COLLECTION)

This brings me to another story. Alan was terrified of heights due to his clumsiness and lack of co-ordination. Whilst working at Hinkley Point he was doing a drawing from a 250 ft (*c.* 76 m) high crane which, with help, he had climbed whilst carrying all his drawing materials and wearing his trilby. Alan had excellent concentration, whether it be at the top of a crane or at the walls of Istanbul: "That day the conditions were trying, but the scene was so exciting, objectively and subjectively, that I soon became lost in it and forgot wind, sun, dust, and the easy chance of becoming yet another casualty by falling down into the dark street below me" (Sorrell *c.* 1962, 163). At Hinkley Point he was oblivious to everyone else working on the site having left, it being a half working day. Once he had finished his drawing, Alan had to descend unaided together with all his equipment. Halfway down a gust of wind blew his trilby off and, on trying to seize it, he nearly lost his footing. Fortunately he made it

FIG. 59. Alan in his blue beret sketching at Stonehenge (1958)
(SORRELL FAMILY COLLECTION)

FIG. 60. Hinkley Point: view of No 1 & No 2 Reactors from the Goliath Crane (Sept. 1959). The Goliath Crane was 250 ft (76 m) high and capable of lifting 400 tons
(WHEREABOUTS OF ORIGINAL UNKNOWN, ASA COPY)

and did not lose his hat! Similarly, at home, the ceilings were very high with suspended lights. Every time a light bulb needed replacing, the pattern was that Alan would bring in and set up the ladder while all four of us held it steady as he ascended with shaking legs. The glass cover was removed, and washed, the bulb changed and cover refitted. Alan then slowly descended and the job was completed until the next time.

Alan enjoyed a sense of occasion, as on his departure from Athens which "had a certain pomp and circumstance. No cannonades or flags, only the American Sixth Fleet which escorted the ship in the most faithful way, for many miles" (Sorrell *c.* 1962, 136) On his return to Aswan on the Government launch *Sheikh el-Beled*, Alan instructed

> "Abdin to: 'Hoist the flags fore and aft'. Startled though he must have been, he grasped the idea, and passed on the order. The crew, reacting more rapidly than I should have thought possible, found the ensigns and hoisted them fore and aft. There was something missing, the tuck of drums or the blare of trumpets. Never mind, sound the klaxon – and it was sounded. So we entered the port of Aswan with flags streaming in the breeze, and the klaxon giving its message for all to hear. The crew were delighted, Abdin,

Fig. 61. *Rock-Cut Tombs at Toshka, Nubia* (1962). Watercolour, pen & ink, 34.9 × 51.43 cm
(SOUTHEND MUSEUMS SERVICE)

FIG. 62. *Walls of Theodosius, Istanbul* (1954). Watercolour, chalks & pen & ink, 26.4 × 34.3 cm
(COLLECTION OF JULIA SORRELL © ESTATE OF ALAN SORRELL)

a little scared, and I had satisfied a lifelong ambition, hitherto thwarted. Why the hoisting of two small flags and sound of a highly unreliable klaxon horn should satisfy such a small schoolboy ambition, is something better left to the maunderings of a psychologist." (Sorrell *c.* 1974, 163)

Alan also craved attention, the feeling of importance and of being valued. Whilst drawing Toshka in Nubia, he was approached by "two white robed turbaned men, one with a gold tooth which winked and shone. It was the village headman and his aide, bearing a round tray with delicate porcelain cup, saucer and tea pot." (Sorrell *c.* 1974, 166). In Istanbul he admitted:

"After making the drawing of the Tower of Phrantzes, and encouraged by the fact that I had not been arrested as a spy, I went on to draw the ancient fortifications from every conceivable angle. To my chagrin, nobody seemed to notice my activities or care about them if they did. Reasonably sure now that it was safe to draw anything anywhere, I began to luxuriate in a tender feeling of neglect. I would have resented bitterly interruptions, noisiness and the looking over the shoulder, but to be ignored and left in peace was far more hurtful for the artist is vain with the vanity of the actor who needs an audience above all things. His work is, in essence, a 'showing off' and how can he 'show off' if there is no one to see? By painting self-portraits he can always have an appreciative audience of one, but that is not enough, and to have the potential admiring audience pass by on the other side of the road is most frustrating. Nothing pleases him, interest is impertinence, non-interest is incredible dullness, he should be left to himself to be miserable in his own chosen fashion." (Sorrell *c.* 1962, 166)

He so often missed opportunities, like on the *Sheikh el-Beled* which he shared with a party of Americans from Aswan to Abu Simbel, led by a Mrs. Lallie Gates-Lloyd. Her husband, with whom Alan sipped martinis on the deck in the evenings, was deputy head of the CIA. Lallie, a character out of the *Philadelphia Story*, had founded museums of modern art in Philadelphia and Washington, and wanted to buy Alan's drawings. Having no idea of who they really were, Alan told Lallie they were destined for the *ILN*. Lallie obviously enjoyed this artist's company: "Alan, you are the most amusing Englishman I have ever met – and you have such beautiful manners." Lallie said dreamily "We must fly away, Alan, to the Mountains of Moon" (Sorrell *c.* 1974, 32).

* * *

Alan began in Rome as a timid, shy young man full of inadequacies, whether related to his background and class, lack of money, low self-esteem, being gauche with women, unconfident or his accursed stammer. At that time, although Alan did not like brown paper parcels, he nevertheless thought them preferable than looking "too obviously an artist, and so he clothed his easel and canvases with this secondary dislike" (Sorrell *c.* 1938, 136). Gradually Alan developed strategies to cope and hide his inadequacies, if not overcome them. By the time he went to Egypt in 1962 he was no longer ashamed of being an artist: "I draped myself with my drawing-case [*with his name boldly written on it*], my suitcase, and my folding-chair and sunshade-case" (Sorrell *c.* 1974, 47). Later on his helper Abdin "carrying my yellow striped umbrella (open of course) over his shoulder walked slowly across and onto the shore" (*ibid.*, 129).

Alan maintained his beliefs about art, however unpopular: "for my preference is for a keen sighted opinion of the visual happenings (which is drawing) and not for a mechanistic dehumanised recorder of two dimensional pattern, which is photography" (*ibid.*, 6) Elizabeth and Alan worked in isolation and, removed from current fashionable trends of the day, maintained their own standards and integrity. They would write articles reiterating their beliefs in a positive, unflinching manner.

As children we were nurtured and never excluded from the adult world, whether it be private views or people, whoever they were, coming to the house, where we all ate together in the studio with my mother making surplus amounts of food. Some days archaeologists visited, other days it was

FIG. 63. Alan Sorrell, by Elizabeth Sorrell (*c.* 1970). Pencil on paper, 24.3 × 19.4 cm
(COLLECTION OF JULIA SORRELL © ESTATE OF ALAN SORRELL)

television producers or artists, and so on. Once Richard, a typical teenager, was in the front garden and a coach stopped and a loudhailer talked about Alan Sorrell living there. Richard ran into the house very red-faced.

Whenever possible, Alan tried to combine holidays with the visiting of sites for yet another reconstruction drawing. We all squashed into the old Volkswagen Beetle with all the individual work we were doing. Often, we would get to the end of the road only to return as one of us children had forgotten something important. Strüdel would sit on my father's shoulder making "nose paintings" on the window whilst Elizabeth drove: "You know he is a great abstract painter, perhaps we should exhibit his work at the RA" Alan would say.

Alan Sorrell was a complicated man but a sincere, good, and honest artist and a kind, thoughtful and loving husband and father. His contribution to art and archaeology was enormous and should not be underrated and forgotten. For me, I have found the journey through these pages and reminiscences with my father very cathartic. I hope you, the reader, have also enjoyed this synopsis of Alan Sorrell's full and eventful life and gained a greater insight into his character.

FIG. 64.
Left: a. *Harlech Castle, Gwynedd, about the year 1290* (1957). Pen & ink, pastel, ink washes & gouache, 38.5 × 54.4 cm

Below: b. *Conway Castle, Gwynedd, about the year 1290* (1957). Pen & ink, pastel, ink washes & gouache, 38.5 × 54.4 cm
(IMAGES COURTESY OF CADW)

Part Two

A LIFE DETERMINED

Mark Sorrell

To Tish

Chapter 7

Portrait of my father

A DOZEN OR SO CAMERAS are grouped together, this quite often happens, with people managing them, pointing them at an object – a transient royal, say, or rare winter migrant. Even allowing for differences of filters and lenses and for human skill, I think we can agree that in texture they will produce images which look similar. The camera is an instrument for registering, not interpreting, intensities of light and shade.

Persuade a similar number of competent artists to occupy a like situation – this almost never happens outside the life room – and if the bird has not flown meanwhile or even if it has, you would expect much more varied results. Why should this be? It is because, self-evidently, an artist focuses not only his or her powers of observation, of training and the appreciation of formal qualities, but half consciously infuses the subject with the exposures of a lifetime of influences, discriminations, insights, prejudices, enthusiasms; engaging, in pursuit of essential truth, his or her composite self.

I don't say this to revive the familiar artist *v.* photographer fixture, a pet hobbyhorse of my father's though it was – and understandably so, for what seemed to him the false values of photography threatened his career at every point - but rather to explain the approach we have taken in this book. Some 35 years ago, in *Reconstructing the Past* (Mark Sorrell 1981), asked to make and introduce a compilation of my father's reconstruction drawings, I more or less limited myself to investigating his working methods. I was too young, too close to him, I felt constrained; I did not have the sympathetic detachment which maybe only time gives to round out that account biographically, more searchingly, more rewardingly. So I welcome (for myself) the opportunity to look at him and his work afresh.

It is my contention that the reconstruction drawings which my father produced more numerously than any other genre or type – and he was prolific – are his finest achievement. At times he downplayed them, they were his "bread and butter work"; but no one who actually saw him leaning over his drawing board surrounded by open books and plans, pen or watercolour brush in hand, could doubt his intensity.

FIG. 65.

Top: a. *Tintern Abbey, Gwent as it might have appeared before its dissolution* (1959). Pen & ink, pastel, ink washes & gouache, 38.5 × 54.4 cm
(IMAGE COURTESY OF CADW)

Bottom: b. *Jedburgh Abbey, Borders, late 14th century* (1957). Pen & ink, watercolour & gouache, 56.5 × 72 cm
(HISTORIC ENVIRONMENT SCOTLAND)

He had great nervous energy always; his hand, drawing or writing, moved deftly, with assurance. Oddly, away from his work, he was awkward, unbalanced. His stammer, the most public manifestation of his social unease, was not oppressive – it worsened at moments of tension or confrontation – but even disregarding it, in speech he was witty but abrupt, never fluent. Physically he could be inept. He many times asked my mother, who moved naturally and easily, to teach him to dance, but her best efforts failed. He could not catch a ball, he fumbled it; in a father this seemed strange. In my childhood memories, the two games at which he excelled (at Christmas time when work stopped and tables for entertaining were joined together the length of the studio) were draughts, he with his "huffing" and, surprisingly, ping-pong (table tennis). (I see that Evelyn Gibbs, a fellow artist, in a diary entry of 1930 (Lucas 2001, 40), mentions playing ping-pong with him when they were students in Rome.) He liked family seaside holidays and going in the sea; but his only stroke was on his back. He propelled himself backwards through the water alarmingly, explosively, people scattering before him.

Things crowd in and I hardly know in what order to put them. I see him with us on the floor, on his hands and knees, appearing around the edge of the hanging table cloth, barking like a dog. Perhaps I remember this because it was unusual for him to be child-like. I see him with guests at lunch, at which we were always included, with a well-judged story keeping them in fits of laughter.

I almost hear the conversations, unfortunately nearly always flippant, which I had with him, standing by his worktable. His jokes were complex and ran for years, some even pre-dating us: one of the experiences of growing up was to join in with them. To understand them properly you had to know him. Knowing, for example, that he was completely uninterested in sport gave piquancy to his pretence to be following with close attention the flat-racing rivalry of Lester Piggott and Scobie Breasley. (Visitors, when the subject was raised, would ask innocently: Was he a racing man?) At a pause in the conversation he'd profess a sudden concern for Piggott. Was something troubling the champion? Was he ailing or sick? How was he doing this season? The table of winners in the unexamined sports columns of *The Times* would provide the answer; I'd fetch it. If well, he'd use some antiquated word of triumph drawn, by the sound of it, from the Victorian pages of *Boy's Own Paper*, equivalent to throwing one's cap in the air; if badly, he'd put on a long face, shake his head and say: "I feared something was amiss. The poor boy! I shall send Lester a telegram: 'Play up! play up! and play the game!'"

That's a line from a once famous, much-anthologised poem by Henry Newbolt celebrating public school heroics. His mind was stocked with tags from other poems of this kind: Longfellow's *Excelsior* and *Hiawatha*, Macaulay's *Horatius*, Tennyson:

"Spanish ships of war at sea! We have sighted fifty-three!"

and

"Cannon to right of them,
Cannon to left of them"

comprising the broken bread and meat of his schooldays. All of them lived on for him for mock heroic use;[1] but the Newbolt, with its heavy rhythms and exaggerated manliness, was a particular favourite. It was laughable certainly, it was grotesque – he who was himself heroic and steadfast and intelligent and emotional, would never have expressed himself like this – but I did use to wonder why it had made such a deep impression. Now it occurs to me that he must first have heard it in his own childhood before World War One, and that he associated it with the unthinking, flag-flapping, chapel-going conventionalities of the adults who surrounded him, with seriously fat, self-satisfied provincial public men:

> "The river of death has brimmed his banks,
> And England's far, and Honour a name,
> But the voice of a schoolboy rallies the ranks
> [at which point he'd break into a fake cockney falsetto]
> Ploy up! ploy up! and ploy the goime!"

Or he would quote

> "The sand of the desert is sodden red,
> Red with the wreck of a square that broke…"

then pause gravely and say "Or should it be dessert? The sand of the dessert?" My brother Richard, influenced by this kind of thing, wrote a clever parody of the poem beginning "There's a breathless moth in the clothes tonight." What became of it, I do not know.

Years later I came home from university brimful of enthusiasm for Yeats's poetry, only to have my father recall, as if it were yesterday, a radio broadcast, I suppose from the 1930s, of the lofty-voiced Yeats spouting verse as from a pub with his jolly beer mug thump-thump-thumping on the bar. Even after so many years the falseness of tone, the sheer awfulness of it, made him wince, and I saw how that reaction had shaped a package for dismissal. (Although I did persuade him to read Yeats's plays: he took the book to bed with him and out of this study came the idea for his imaginative drawing *Castle in the Wood*).

He liked the grand gesture, panache, Churchillian bravura, brass bands playing military music (but not what they represented), the extravagance of the baroque. He delighted in tales of the unselfconscious eccentricity of admired artists – Stanley Spencer with his boyish fringe pushing through town a perambulator full of his oil painting materials; or the same artist, so it was said, riding the swings of the recreation ground which his cramped lodgings overlooked, so as to catch on the upswing a glimpse of his latest panel propped up; or Holman Hunt, in his search for authenticity, with loaded gun on his shoulder and scapegoat carried on a donkey's back, toiling through the sands of the Middle East. Such things were glorious, they made him snort with laughter; but not what was not genuine or effete. As an embattled professional he had little time for the poseur. To dress and behave artily – the rakeish hat, the bold sketching positions taken up in public with nothing to show for it, the ostentatious display of (inevitably) immaculate painting equipment – were linked in his mind with the amateur.

The trivial vexing surface of life, how to compose oneself in public, was a problem which he could delve under but never quite solve. Delving under was what drawing was all about. The "stealthy consideration of angles" was part of his armoury (Sorrell c. 1962, 115);[2] not for nothing was he known as "Old Angles" to a generation of students to whom he taught life drawing at the Royal College of Art. But even in the act of drawing the problem at times became acute. Twice in his later career, in Greece and Istanbul in 1954, in Egypt and Nubia in 1962, he undertook extended trips abroad, in order to make complete drawings out of doors of human structures and landscapes threatened with destruction. The Nubian journey especially, when he lived for several weeks alone with a Nubian crew on a small boat travelling romantically beyond

FIG. 66. Alan Sorrell drawing at Armenna, Nubia (1962)
(PHOTOGRAPH BY BRUCE TRIGGER, SORRELL FAMILY COLLECTION)

FIG. 67. Armenna, Nubia: excavation of a Coptic house, Pennsylvania-Yale expedition (1962). Watercolour, chalk & ink, 34.9 × 51.43 cm
(SOUTHEND MUSEUMS SERVICE)

the bounds of what he would have regarded as civilisation, grew in his mind to be a triumph of self-realisation. In England too it was second nature for him to make preparatory studies in public places of landscapes, buildings, trees; and at such times I have seen him so keenly engaged, eye and hand working together, that he seemed out of reach.

But the wrong kind of consciousness had constantly to be batted away. His life was turmoiled with anxieties large and small: perceived slights in words or any emotional uncertainty nearly drove him distracted. He was vain and could not bear to be ignored; but it did not take much to overstep the limit and intrude. To feel (while he was drawing out of doors) the stealthy approach of a stranger, to have to endure the impromptu viewing and innocuous comment which demands acknowledgement, might be all it took to inhibit him. He was not like Edward Lear, whose work he loved, or Alan's younger contemporary, the painter John Ward, artists who, with calm self-absorption, chose to draw scenes of spontaneous activity, making the moment live. In places which he knew he would not revisit, when it seemed important to get down some form of record of the people, of ephemeral life – and even in Nubia he never carried a camera, indeed to the best of my knowledge, he never owned one – he would try and fail and abandon the attempt and regret his failure. Nor could he recall that vitality retrospectively. His figures would become wraiths, fleeting, veiled, imposed thinly; humanity, he would decide ruefully, was not his métier (Sorrell *c.* 1962, 215).[3]

So the figure studies in his sketchbooks, for later inclusion in drawings or paintings, are almost always of models, or of us or our mother – unclothed or in scraps of material as costume drapes – but most often of himself, usually in the nude, grown slightly podgy (it is remarkable how many ancient Native Britons and chilly Romans descending into the bath seemed to bear a resemblance to Alan Sorrell) seen in the wide wall-fixed mirror

Fig. 68.
Left: a. Hirsute Mesolithic hunter wearing stag antler frontlet, from *Prehistoric Britain* (1968). Pen & ink, 15.7 × 21 cm
(ASA)

Right: b. *Abu Simbel: experimental drilling in the Great Temple* (1962). Watercolour, ink & gouache, 34.9 × 51.43 cm
(SOUTHEND MUSEUMS SERVICE)

(in combination with other mirrors) in the studio – the mirror into whose depths, at party-time, one looked across the round table loaded with plates and dishes of food. It was only when people remained within a mental frame, busy with their own work and so not bothering him, like the Swedish engineers extracting core samples inside the Great Temple at Abu Simbel[4] that he would persist in drawing them away from home. Then he would be proud of his achievement and of his effort to include them.

As a young man, a student in Italy, he had gone to extremes to avoid the dreadful identification stamp of "artist". He has left record of how, in Rome, preparing for excursions from the British School, he would wrap up in brown paper and string his bulky oil painting box, folding easel, brushes and canvas-covered pieces of plywood, and sally forth burdened with a multiplicity of oddly shaped fraying parcels (Sorrell c. 1938, 135). It is not clear what he wanted to be taken for; concealment and unshowiness were his object. And my mother told me how, in the early days of their marriage, any attempt on her part which might even casually align him with bohemianism, with barefoot Augustus John (though he spoke admiringly of John's amazing drawings) by forcing him into a practical smock for oil painting, was bound to fail. Although in time he did come to accept a workmanlike pair of blue dungarees, into the pockets of which he could stick his brushes tips upward, and took off his jacket and sometimes his shirt.

The philosophical tangle of what he was about and wanted to become, the fog of received critical theory in which, like river shipping at night, he had floundered throughout his student days, was resolved for him at least temporarily, on the point of leaving Rome (1930), by an insight, a distillation which he wrote out in capital letters: "ART IS AN EXPRESSION OF ORDER" (Sorrell c. 1938, 295). But I think this could be better put: "Art is a means of ordering the self."

Nearly 40 years later, my mother's parents, who were elderly and in poor health, came permanently to live with us. At a distance they had been present all through our childhoods in visits to and fro, as had my mother's brother and sister and their families; we had life stories to share, knew something about one another, where we were, what we were doing. But there were no aunts or uncles on my father's side. His only sibling, Doris, had died shockingly in 1917, his father as far back as 1910 (see Chapter 2). He used to say a generation was missing in his family; part of what he meant was that his father and sister had both died young.

Surviving physical mementoes of them were slight. There was a pathetic cross and beads of that long-lost sister, kept in a box along with scraps of card on which she had painted flowers in blue watercolour; and sometimes – when we were looking for something else – he would turn up in the plan chest one of Ernest Sorrell's pastels, mostly unframed, in purples and greens of trees and water, and pause over it (giving it a burst of Fixative spray) and say "That's my father's".

I was curious to know more. In a wartime notebook of his, *c.* 1940, I had seen an extract in his handwriting, of a herald's visitation of Essex dated 1634 with a Sorrell family tree of that date and the villages they had lived in: Stebbing, Terling, Great Waltham. It's not too much to say that this was my father's foundation myth. As children we were taken into the churchyard of the last-named village to be shown my brother's forename, and my mother's, on a 17th century headstone. Not far away, on a side road, standing on its own among cornfields, was Hyde Hall, an Elizabethan half-timbered manor house with tall chimneys, the front defended by the remains of a moat choked with bulrushes and flags, a little pagoda-roofed summer house perched over it. The place had a neglected look but was lived in; and my father, telling us that it had been, far back, the family home, made several attempts to buy or even rent it, without success. I remember standing on the gravel approach, by hedgelines beginning to be scorched by Dutch Elm disease, and hearing him enthuse to my mother: Wouldn't it be marvellous if the children could grow up here? There'd be no need to worry about traffic.

But when I pressed him, trying to discover his side of the family by working backwards from his parents, he put me off only half-jokingly with words to the effect that "It isn't worth your effort. I'm the first person for centuries of any significance in my family". In his Rome memoir, written *c.* 1938 – which is, apart from anything else, a young man's honest attempt at self-analysis – he several times berates himself for his (inherited) "small tradesman's ways" (Sorrell *c.* 1938, 28, 222); and includes the rebuke of a hearty wine-bibbing artist visiting the School who, seeing my father's "pale serious face", exclaims: "We don't want any little missionaries or Jesus Christs here" (*ibid.*, 66). On another occasion a student kindly asks him, "Why didn't he join the Sallies [Salvation Army] and be done with it?" (*ibid.*, 123).

He used to make light of his relations, except his mother and father, saying there was not an ounce of ability in any of them. As for literary flair, he cited for me the example of an aunt or great-aunt who, asked to complete the little rhyme

> "There was an old woman
> Lived under a hill.
> If she's not gone
> She lives there …"

replied, after a great deal of hesitation, "Yet?"

His father's father, he used to tell us disparagingly, as if he espoused the social values of a Jane Austen novel, was an "Italian warehouseman" or grocer. It was my father's uncle, the solemn William, who, looking back over a gap, saw finer familial possibilities. We heard that William had come home from New Zealand, about the turn of the last century, intent on digging about in old records in pursuit of a crock of gold which was said to be lying buried "in chancery" at the far end of this illusion. If history would only bend as it should, he would find a connection with those 17th century mid-Essex yeoman farmers and gentlemen who had married into the likes of the Everards; and further off, more dreamily, with medieval knights.

Unfortunately, the final tile could not be laid. Shaping his face to express his frustration like one sucking on a lemon (because he believed unquestioningly in the truth of the claim), my father explained that his uncle had been prevented from forging the link by an ancient fire in the Waltham church papers. The story could not be proved, he said, laying emphasis on the word. So uncle William was unable to inherit a fortune. The crock was a pot egg. Nevertheless William continued to sit on it, and to spread his feathers. He had his notepaper embossed with that family's crest, a peacock on a ducal coronet, all proper; and he had a signet ring made with the device, the impress of which we were able to handle delicately on a blob of red sealing wax which was kept at home wrapped in tissue paper; and, as Richard has pointed out, young Alan signed his early art school drawings with the same monogram (Llewellyn & Sorrell, 2013, 19).[5]

William was a photographer. His greatest business and social coup was a commission to photograph the then Princess of Wales, the future Queen Mary, cradling one of her babies after its christening; it formed the frontispiece to an issue of *The Illustrated London News* (26 August 1905); the original hung on our vestry wall. Building on this tenuous link, William had a throwaway printed subtly combining commerce with improving advice on how to photograph sitters of all degrees and qualities to best advantage. In it he described himself as an artist.

Ernest, my father's father, a jeweller and watchmaker, actually aspired to be an artist and was one in his free time. William was a Congregationalist lay preacher, an unenlightened man who, dressed all in black on Sundays and with a large Bible under his arm, made the home when the children were growing up miserable with talk of hellfire. Ernest was more modest and engaging. Father and son would seem to have been close. There's a photograph of them together on board a pleasure steamer off Southend (Fig. 3). Alan, who must have been about two and still wears frilly clothes, sits below his standing father, and seems to be calling out and throwing up one arm, the left one, in pure joy. I do not believe I've seen another photograph of him of any age looking so unreserved.

One of the few childhood memories Alan shared with us was of accompanying his father on sketching expeditions to Hadleigh Castle and elsewhere and of picking up stones which he carried home reverently wrapped in a handkerchief. His earliest known signed drawing, dated 1909, shows a yacht on the estuary in full sail. When, in the next year, his father died with bewildering suddenness, bereft and in a diminished household Alan may have resolved – of course this is speculation – to be like him and take his place; specifically to be the artist that Ernest never was. Much later, looking at Ernest's drawings with critical awareness, he saw their shortcomings but in them too he saw his father.

The family web which Alan discouraged me from exploring has, since his death, been thoroughly mapped, back to 1700, by others[6] – research which reveals the flimsiness of his uncle's wishful thinking. Not a ducal coronet to be seen from here to the horizon; not a strawberry, far less a strawberry mark, hiding underneath a nettle. The first Anglicised Sorrell of this newfound family, so a new myth (maybe) has it, was no conquering knight in antique helm, one of Duke William's men, wading ashore to do battle with King

FIG. 69. *Bishop's Palace, St David's, as it might have appeared* c. *1530* (1958), the final drawing. Watercolour, pen & ink, chalks and gouache, 41 × 57 cm
(IMAGE COURTESY OF CADW)

Harold, but a hustled migrant, a French Huguenot who arrived hundreds of years later on shipboard stowed away in a barrel of apples rather like Jim in *Treasure Island*. I like this story, its anxiety and desperate shifts; I'm not sure my father would have. I remember hearing him refer once or twice to Huguenots in the family, but I'm certain he knew nothing of this.[7]

More pertinent and interesting however, is that generations of these forebears now faintly delineated, who settled in the poorer parts of east London – the connection with Essex goes no further back than to Ernest who moved to the coast probably for health reasons[8] – were craftsmen. They were copperplate engravers, silk block printers, steel pen makers, map makers, pattern designers. Ernest too was a craftsman, and craftsman-like qualities of precision were what my father, who inherited these traits, always extolled. Here he is *c.* 1962 giving his definition of an artist:

> "Archaeologists, who are generally serious-minded men with a habit of logical thought, methodical and competent in all their scholarly processes, are liable to regard the artist as an undependable erratic sort of fellow, hazy in his mental outlook and liable to fits of temperament, all of which make him unsuitable as a collaborator. This remarkably romantic but ill-informed assessment is of course due to the fact that archaeologists do not, normally, know much about artists. They are not hostile, but alien to them ... The artist is, in fact, a highly practical, extravagantly conscientious person, *who must realise all the facets of a form*, and who cannot permit the glossing over of truth with technicalities. Think of Andrea Mantegna, for instance, minutely exact as a draughtsman, with a vivid sense of form, a scholar and an impeccable craftsman. He is the arch type of the artist who is capable of supplying the final visual statement which brings to life the learned treatise of the scholar. Mantegna, were he living today, would be delighted at this new fashionable interest in the past; he might even prefer it to contemporary paintings whose abrasive surfaces would certainly annoy him, whatever message they might convey to the initiated." (Sorrell *c.* 1962, 54) [My italics]

This, written at a time when he realised that people were primarily associating him as an artist with his reconstruction drawings, amounts to a mini self-portrait in words. I have only one caveat: my father was indeed a scholar, but not in any limiting or specialist sense. Equipped with acute artistic sensibility, his scrupulous intelligence enabled him to cross disciplines.[9] One archaeologist has commented to me that what, for her, characterised working with Alan Sorrell was his meticulousness within the bounds set for him. He was recognisably one with the student he once was, whom he describes, in Rome, as settling down to work "in his rather oppressively honest enquiring way" (Sorrell *c.* 1938, 31).

As a student, my father was a figurative would-be narrative painter. Roger

Fry and his acolyte Clive Bell had clouded the waters for him intellectually in the 1920s by aggressively championing post-impressionism at the expense of the masters of the European visual tradition; notoriously, Fry's advocacy had included feeling able to reconfigure Rembrandt, no less, as a "mere illustrator".[10] As a student Alan supped anxiously at this table and had his digestion upset; but he was never tempted into abstraction. Instead (like painful religious sectaries of old) when the painter Ceri Richards, whom he had known and liked at College, followed the new light it broke their friendship; and I heard him more than once lamenting the loss to art, as he saw it, of Victor Pasmore's incomprehensible conversion, comparing his harmonious "this" before, with negligible "that" after.

The context gives edge to a revealing statement to be found in one of his courtship letters to my mother, written just after the war:

> "The reason I don't experiment is that I consider myself to be merely an illustrator (Giotto also was an illustrator!). I mean it doesn't seem to matter what the tone of my voice is (to alter the metaphor) so long as I can be understood. Of course, it's easy to pick holes in such a theory & prove it to be a fallible one but I mean I am not likely to spend years experimenting with, say, impressionistic colour so called or in anatomical dissection or with 'abstract forms.'" (Sorrell & Tanner 1944–7, *c.* 21 April 1946) [11]

John Ward recalled that in the 1930s (Ward 2006, 18), when my father was on the teaching staff of the College and Ward was a student there, they found common ground and congeniality in a shared love of Pre-Raphaelite drawings and early "French" paintings (I think he means Flemish: Van Eyck, Bosch and especially Brueghel, an important influence[12]). Sorrell was, he writes, "obstinately his own man". And at their first meeting in Rome in 1929, Aileen Fox (Henderson, as she then was) remembered him as "a difficult young man, with a slight stammer, diffident yet determined" (Fox 2000, 50).[13]

Those two years in Rome had given him time to look inwards and about him, freed from commercial pressures. According to Fox (*ibid.*), during the whole time she was there he "worked on a large canvas with the rustic figures of a young man and a girl sitting in an Essex cornfield, painted in the manner of Stanley Spencer" (probably his *Annunciation*). In the archive of the British School at Rome is a photograph, the only visual record of it which I know of, of another wonderfully awkward expressive drawing of his, extended over several sheets of paper as his exploration outgrew the original sheet. It is of a god-like creator or originator, long-gowned, right foot and right hand extended, intently planting trees in a stony landscape, a bundle of more young trees clasped to him. It's an adventurous drawing with the powerful single figure dominating the composition.

He seems, after leaving Rome, to have sold this work in its chrysalis state, keeping not even a photograph to remind him of it,[14] as if he had made a conscious decision to turn aside from its line of development. However, the image stayed in his mind: years later the sympathetic body shape, the directional focus of hand and foot, wholly impractical as it is – as any intending tree planter would soon discover! – would re-emerge almost unchanged in his *The Planting of the Trees* (1971) (see Fig. 47).

Perhaps this turning aside was a kind of emotional withdrawal. He continued to make "imaginative compositions", as he called them, throughout his life; indeed they were central to his idea of himself as a creative artist. However, as time went on, the scale of the figures they contained tended to diminish and expression to be transferred insensibly to the world they inhabited or which sometimes replaced them: to his romantic treatment of carved stone, wave-worn or overgrown, shaping itself into craggy human features; of trees single and entwined, sinister or benign; of shaky ruined structures.

Such drawings, which he might return to over months, began in a dreamlike image; but their execution proceeded by way of numerous studies from life. My mother, near the start of their relationship, encouraged him to work in a freer way, and in an undated letter (Sorrell & Tanner 1944–7, early Dec. 1945), mentioning a drawing of thatchers which he is about to begin, he comments: "I'm going to do it without models as you suggested and it will be interesting to see what happens"; adding, a few days later, "With all my years of careful study (more or less!) I ought to be able to let myself go oughtn't I?"

But he did not, really. Instead, it was my mother's method which changed, as she fell under his influence, from free-ranging if stilted flights to direct observation and patient accumulation. What he said of his own work could soon equally well be applied to hers:

FIG. 70. *Planting of the Trees*, British School at Rome drawing (*c.* 1930) (PRESENT WHEREABOUTS UNKNOWN, IMAGE COURTESY OF THE BRITISH SCHOOL AT ROME)

"I always find it necessary to have information about every detail and incident in a work, and it is not by any means a source of pride but often of keen regret that I cannot improvise. Thus every individual leaf and all the curious bends of the tree-trunks require[d] as much study as the figures themselves." (Sorrell 1939b, 36)

These were controls which, like a mapmaker, he laid over an imagination which was wayward, hidden, indirect. It was hard enough, even without these constraints, to be a narrative painter: to embody in solid form the nuances for which a writer has the luxury of words.

As a follower, centuries after their time, of Giotto and Piero della Francesca, it was inevitable that he should have begun with Christian stories used allusively and for decorative effect. Such stories have besides the advantage of familiarity, especially when the title is a handle: so, "a young man and a girl sitting in an Essex cornfield", when entitled *Annunciation*, takes on a quite specific meaning: it becomes the angel Gabriel whispering in the ear of the Virgin Mary. But being one for whom truth was important, he couldn't long continue with what he didn't believe in. Then too, both before and while training at College, he had supported himself by working as a commercial artist, an experience which disciplined him to meet deadlines but provoked in him a lifelong anxiety about superficial "charm", as he called it, of client-pleasing commercial facility in his work.[15] A good drawing was effortful and to be wrestled with in the act of creation; "charm" (that loaded word!) was oily and devious in intent, untruthful and therefore despicable. And yet if the finished drawing, however earnestly meant, looked laboured, not being, as it were, in one jet, it was a failure. A work of art, he would say, enjoying the mixed metaphor of one of his earliest tutors, should appear "like an arrow shot from a gun".

Nonconformism of the most dreary kind had shaped his childhood. Simply, unaffectedly, it continued to be important to his mother, who lived to be very old; but not, except in the broadest sense, to him. Religion played almost no part in our lives growing up: we were left to come to it or not as the need moved us, were not christened or baptised and never entered a church except to look at medieval effigies and misericords and stained glass windows, things which, precociously, we delighted in. Our chapel with its high light-filled windows, an agreeable studio space, was secular and stood among the fields.

But he would not permit carelessness about religion. He sharply scolded me once for sliding a Bible across the floor. I, being rough with books generally, could not see what I had done wrong: it was not as if it had gone far. And he seemed almost to choke on his words as he explained that that was not how you should treat *that* one.

In *The Long Journey* (1936), a transitional work, he subtly combines two events in a single sophisticated composition: the fatal fall of a young man from an apple tree and his reception, still in his work clothes, in the dark wood of the afterworld. His first sketch had simply shown a man, or soul of a man, arms trailing as he "crosses the river" (to use the parlance of chapel) – in this case a bridge over a ragged trench – into a wood which is featureless, all but impenetrable. But he must have found this image too personal and obscure, for he worked and reworked it. By the fifth sketch (as he tells us in a rare analysis),[16] he has thought his way into something more visually satisfying. Now he shows the death on the left hand with the fallen man surrounded by weeping women; and, on the right hand, beyond the bridge, the moment of delivery as he is greeted with handshakes and embraces. The eye finds a winding narrative path – on which, midway, the man's head is laid – which commences at the door of his house, passes the apple tree and extends over the bridge into eternity.

At least in this picture he offers the consolation of an afterlife. Many of his later imaginative compositions are maelstroms of ruin and catastrophe continuing in this world. These were the private visions of a reconstruction artist. At best we see in them laughable reversions to primitive life, charades of lit fires and washing lines occupying empty space behind magnificent propped facades, the rest of the building having fallen. It is as if he is showing us total collapse, the heart-stopping end of everything familiar, balanced and secure. Human life is still there, but it's clinging by its fingertips. It's as if a giant meteor has struck.

Confiding in my mother, in letters soon after their wartime meeting, he spoke often of being haunted by a horror of death, felt he had already grown old (he was 41), that achievement had passed him by. I came to some understanding of this vein of anxiety in him when I was a teenager. I remember a peculiar recurring experience of mine, of feeling detached in the midst of reality, as if standing in an echo chamber; of seeing the world, whichever way I looked, clearly but distantly as if through a tunnel; a sweaty waking nightmare. My father, watching me once, told me to "Snap out of it"; but when I described to him these marginalised states which were so unnerving:

> "vanishings,
> Blank misgivings of a creature
> Moving about in worlds not realised"

he began to speak of his own experience, long ago, of panic fear. He (and my mother joining the conversation) thought it derived from a primordial wood fear (it always happened in woods) but I think this was giving dignity to it, depersonalising and intellectualising something which had disturbed him horribly. He could not tell me what triggered it, only that the experience seemed significant. It seemed to arise in him, always out of doors, without obvious stimulus, in a still atmosphere, as if something undefined but terrible was about to happen. I now find reference to this, plainly set down, in his Rome memoir, and link it in my mind to the turbulent losses of his childhood, unconsciously expressed in his imaginative work:

> "No wire, not expected, School perhaps closed – so he runs on. It's panic fear, the same as on two separate occasions years ago. Once in a wood at dusk; a steep wooded path, and very silent. The trees are black, and there's somebody or something behind each bush, and the hanging, slowly swaying branch is a horror, he must run till he drops, and he reaches light and space at last with frothing lips and shaking limbs. Again: a deserted wood-enclosed road in Wales, with ever so many furtive trickling rivulets, drip, drip, dripping, and a white gate creaking, and a great yellow moon behind the trees …" (Sorrell *c.* 1938, 248)

It is the authentic voice of gothic horror, a surge of bubbles from deep suppressed fears.

Narratives without words are tricky things. He liked words and the act of writing. He used to say that if you put a pen in his hand, to write, you set him free, that he flowed – and the appearance of his manuscripts, which are not heavily marked with corrections, bears this out. He wrote three unpublished discursive book-length autobiographical manuscripts, from which Julia and I have quoted extensively in this text; numerous letters; and several published books where his words accompany series of his reconstruction drawings: *Living History* (1965), *Roman London* (1969), *British Castles* (1973) and *Roman Towns in Britain* (1976). These were the issue of many a winter's night, written first in longhand on foolscap sheets or in school exercise books, usually as he knelt, shut away from us, at the little davenport with its sloping top in the vestry.

He revered an English tradition of drawing as exemplified by Samuel Palmer, Blake, Cotman, Turner, Edward Lear, the early Millais and Holman Hunt, Charles Keene and the like; artists who, most of them, were nourished by a powerful literary tradition. Where sometimes, to my mind, in his imaginative compositions he falls short, is precisely in his attempting to convey ideas visually. Perhaps this was what Sir William Rothenstein, his mentor and encourager at the Royal College of Art, foresaw and tried to warn him of. In a cancelled passage in his early memoir, my father interprets his advice thus:

> "Rothenstein said a very true thing to me when I was a student, 'You should work more, and not think so much'. He meant that the artist's

hand and eye have always got to be much more skilful and acute than the rest of his physical make-up; that it's no good having grandiose ideas for pictures, or even a passionate imaginativeness, until they, the hand and eye, are absolutely in harmony, and the hand is the joyous slave of the eye: you attain freedom, in fact, in which to express your ideas." (Sorrell *c.* 1938, 69)

But was this what Rothenstein meant? Did he not simply mean that seeing as a painter should take precedence over any intellectual musings?

The sense of something unstated, imperfectly conveyed, is well illustrated in an imaginative drawing of his dated September 1931, entitled *The Postman*. It was exhibited, with his Icelandic drawings, at the Walker Galleries in London in 1935. In 1973 John Ward, having visited a retrospective exhibition of my father's work held at Reading, mentioned it in a private letter:

> "I loved the early ones. I remember hearing about the Icelandic ones when I was a student (and at that time the only other artist connected with Iceland was Wm Morris) and a drawing which I've always longed to see since I recall the description so clearly is of a postman on [a] bicycle riding against the wind & rain. It's curious how this has been something of a symbol of your work. I've always thought of you working against the grain of fashion, strong and boney and sparse."[17]

It's true that Ward never saw this drawing (it was not exhibited at Reading either), but it is striking how widely his interpretation of it diverges from anything Alan could have intended. It is impossible to read this drawing as being emblematic of an artist's lonely struggle! There is, rather, a real darkness in the shrouded figure, face and hands hidden, riding purposefully away from the viewer on an old-fashioned bicycle. It is not actually raining – in fact the cornfields beyond him, with their stooks, are bathed in sunshine

FIG. 71.
Left: a. *The Long Journey* (1936). Pen, ink & gouache, 37 × 52.3 cm

Right: b. *The Postman* (1931). Ink, gouache & pastel, 53 × 37 cm
(IMAGES COURTESY OF LISS LLEWELLYN FINE ART)

– but the atmosphere is oppressive. We might even go so far as to imagine that, hunched over and contained within himself, the man is hugging a guilty secret. But more than that who can say?

Well, as it happens, for most of 1940 my father lived in wartime London while bombs rained down and, unlike Henry Moore with his shelter drawings, turned to words, and wrote underground a number of short stories which, in their rawness and neurotic touches, are unlike anything he ever wrote again. One of them, *A Simple Story*, set in Victorian or Edwardian Shropshire, may be based on a true incident. It concerns the doomed romance of a girl living in England, whose man has gone to Australia to make his fortune, intending to return and marry her. Their nemesis in the story is a tangential, apparently inconsequential person, the village postman, a "pale-faced little chap, who always had such awful chilblains". He intercepts the first letter from Australia and opens it, hoping to find money; and then stops each subsequent one, not even opening them, to hide the original crime. As a letter becomes due, the girl waits trustingly, but increasingly despondent, for the postman to appear on the lane:

> "There she'd stand & watch him come down the hill on his bicycle, but he never stopped but started pedalling away & said 'Nothing to night mam' over his shoulder, never anything else."[18]

She dies broken-hearted, thinking she has been abandoned. Her lover comes home from Australia just too late; and only then is the evil agency of the postman revealed.

The Postman would make an excellent illustration of this story; but to have it standing alone, as Alan did, without the text (which it preceded by nine years), is like putting the cart before the horse. It does not go properly.

Or, to take another example of a disconnection, where a subject has needed to be melted imaginatively before it can be reconstituted, we might consider a composition from later in his career entitled *The Archaeologist in Nubia* (1965). A man in European clothes, standing awkwardly in a small boat, is being helped to land at the entrance to a rock-cut temple. The setting is eerie, with harsh shapes of rock, lurid skies and, to one side, clusters of peculiar tilting domed buildings in the desert. Actually, the drawing represents the exterior of the temple at Abu Oda on the Nile, together with some 13th century Muslim tombs half a mile (0.8 km) away which my father shoehorned into the picture for dramatic (or exotic) effect. He made sketches on the spot in 1962 and invented the painting at home. Everything structural in it, hills, temple, tombs and all, was engulfed soon after by the rising waters of Lake Nasser.

The facts as labels are not important, they can be trawled out of his writings; what matters is whether the drawing works on its own terms. It would help if the human figures were larger in scale, so that the trembling inefficient steps of the archaeologist on the gangplank could be seen in contrast to the "cat-like sureness" of the Nubians. It would help if my father's dread of heights, expressed at home by him on the top of wobbling stepladders and us hanging onto them, and his legs, were known. If the drawing had been called *Artist in Nubia*, it would not have been a greater departure from essential truth than his concertina-ing of the landscape; for though the European depicted was Dr John Harris, a mild-mannered epigraphist from Oxford (as my father tells us in the MS account of his Nubian travels), he shared with Harris his alarm at the narrow planks which, in Nubia, were the only means of egress from boat to shore. My father's fearful plank-walking became a favourite party set-piece around the lunch table at home as he exaggerated the height, the depth, the dark waters curdling far below:

FIG. 72. *The Archaeologist in Nubia* (1965). Watercolour & pastel, 53.34 × 78.74 cm
(SOUTHEND MUSEUMS SERVICE)

> "At that moment I noticed the plank, a very narrow, bendy plank, and the only way onboard. Ever since I read *Treasure Island* at an early and impressionable age, I have disliked the idea of walking the plank, but I had studied the problem, and I knew there were two ways of doing it – the gay dash or the shuffle. Garlanded as I was with my suitcase, drawing-case and folding-chair case, I chose the latter, and was glad of Osiris' outstretched hand at the other end. Lallie and the others seemed wonderfully unconcerned, but that may have been because their luggage was carried for them." (Sorrell *c.* 1974, 24)

But even this is not the crux of the matter. That surely lies in the contrast between the confident crewmen in their white *gallabiyas* – fishermen and expert boat-handlers at ease in this environment – and the dark-clothed, intrusive, physically incapable foreigner. And beyond this is the realisation that the livelihoods, the very homes and the weird moon-like landscape which the riverine Nubians inhabited, would soon, all of them, disappear because far-removed government men had decided that they should.

The drawing is the poorer without this explanation. But that is not how

FIG. 73. *Artist in the Campagna* (*c.* 1931). Pencil, ink & watercolour, 39.5 × 57 cm
(IMAGE COURTESY OF LISS LLEWELLYN FINE ART)

FIG. 74. *The Enormous Head* (1967). Gouache, watercolour, pastel & ink, 50.8 × 68.58 cm
(PRIVATE COLLECTION)

it should be; and that is why I believe that his reconstructions have their force. There, where his imagination was channelled and directed, where every possibility in a scene had to be weighed and recreated – the whole landscape in every detail revived – he is unequalled.

We have seen that he came to that distinctive work by an indirect route. According to an autobiographical note scribbled in one of his sketchbooks,[19] he became interested in archaeology "soon after leaving Rome". His references to "history book themes" (Sorrell 1942, 87) and "historical stuff" (Sorrell & Tanner 1944–7, *c.* 15 March 1946) in the 1930s and 1940s in regard to the reconstruction work on which he was then engaged, are indicative of a certain reserve; but the artist who, apparently, depicts himself in *Artist in the Campagna* (?1931) contemplating, outside Rome, a heap of fragments, the relics of a past civilisation, is not far removed from the imagist who created *The Enormous Head* (1967); and there are clear connections between the observer who sees iron huts joined to the garden front of an elegant country house in *Officers' Mess, RAF Station* (1943) (how he would have loathed and abominated this barbarism!)[20] and the reconstructionist who shows us Anglo-Saxon squatters inhabiting the ruins of a Roman villa (1964).

The peculiar historicising tendency of his mind comes out in riffs like the following, apropos of nothing, in love letters to my mother:

> "I've heard of Ashford, Kent, of course, where Napoleon lived after Waterloo. He became a prominent figure on the local council, leader of the Boy Scouts and Church Warden. Once a year he threw open the grounds of his house to the public: all the flower beds were designed on the plans of his battles and it was noticeable that he always took pleasure in picking the geraniums wh[ich] symbolised the British redcoats, of course. He died quite recently and was given a Viking funeral on the river Cuckmere, wh[ich] caused trouble because the smoke and flames disturbed a swan's nest." (Sorrell & Tanner 1944–7, *c.* 14 Oct. 1945)

FIG. 75. *Officers' Mess, RAF Station* (1943) Ink & watercolour
(WAR ARTISTS' ADVISORY COMMITTEE PURCHASE PASSED TO THE AIR MINISTRY, CURRENT WHEREABOUTS OF ORIGINAL UNKNOWN, ASA COPY)

FIG. 76. Anglo-Saxon squatters occupying an abandoned Roman villa, from *Saxon England* (1964). Pen & ink, ink washes, 18.4 × 42 cm
(ASA)

As children he told us all, at different times, the extraordinary story of his participation in the Charge of the Light Brigade (1854). Riding gallantly amid the roaring and yells of battle, he was quite unfazed when a cannonball carried off his head. Dismounting and feeling around, he found it again and, although naturally inconvenienced, rejoined the charge, passing through the terrified Russian gunners holding it aloft; and so returned. "O the blood, the blood!" he exclaimed, and we could well imagine. In Scutari hospital, Florence Nightingale herself skilfully reattached head to trunk; unfortunately in the dimness of her lamplight putting it on backwards. It meant that, going on parade, he had difficulty obeying simple instructions like "Eyes Front"; but in time thanks to the intervention of Lord Raglan all was amended. Dear Florence's stitchery was so fine, he told us, that to this day you could hardly see the join – and I remember staring amazed at his neck, creased and stubbly from shaving, as he pointed to it, not seeing a join and not knowing what to think.[21]

Conviction lay in the detail, an abundance of it.[22] When, in his doodles, controls are relaxed and he allows himself freedom to invent, everything is interconnected and balanced like a conjuring trick, a tower of acrobats effortlessly suspended (Fig. 52b). Again and again in his writings he returns to the importance of the informed imagination:

> "Since true imagination springs from a hypersensitive appreciation of fact, it becomes evident that, without a deep study of fact, the artist will find himself empty of inspiration, and *then* it is that he turns to fantasy; since he is too indolent to study the strangeness of actuality, he will invent peculiar forms and impossible situations. Naturally they will not carry conviction ..." (Sorrell 1940e, 131)

Again:

> "I have gone into this question of 'learning' the subject at some length, because it seems to me that it is impossible to produce any worthwhile picture without the understanding which springs from knowledge. It is not by any means a vague appreciation of 'atmosphere' that is required, but an intense study of each object, each square yard of land, sea and sky, and then perhaps, when your pencil goes to paper, or your brush to the canvas, it will be handled with, at any rate, some degree of certainty and conviction." (Sorrell 1942, 88)

Towards the end of 1940, continuing air-raids over London forced the College to close temporarily and he found himself out of employment. It was then that he made a life-determining choice: not to seek a soft civilian job but to volunteer, as a non-combatant ranker, for "special duties" in the RAF. Immediately he was carried into a different world, was liberated in two senses: from a marriage which had become so wretchedly unhappy

FIG. 77. *Caerlaverock Castle, Dumfries, its likely appearance in the 15th century* (1959). Pen & ink, watercolour & gouache, 56.5 × 72.0 cm
(HISTORIC ENVIRONMENT SCOTLAND)

that, going home at night, he would hesitate and pass the door many times before bracing himself to enter; and from the deadening routine of teaching at the College four days a week. A "stodgy lot" (Sorrell & Tanner 1944–7, *c*. 21 Jan. 1946) was how he described his colleagues when, after the war, he returned briefly and with reluctance to their ranks before his dismissal by Robin Darwin launched him fortuitously on his full time career as an artist.

Before the war (he told my mother), he had all but lost faith in himself, felt the sources of inspiration dying in him (Sorrell & Tanner 1944–7, *c*. 11 Aug. 1944). In bleak hutted camps in wartime, his spirits revived. Caught up in events larger than himself, he was living history more immediately, perhaps, than at any time since his early childhood when he had watched through a telescope a great naval pageant – the ships of the Grand Fleet, 40 miles (64 km) of them, anchored like a fantasma at the mouth of the Thames.[23]

He was a man with no soldierly instincts: "Somehow, Corporal Sorrell, I can't see you sweating the squad", Cyril Fox joked.[24] He described to us his revulsion at basic training, the twist you were supposed to give when you thrust a bayonet into the guts of a stuffed sack and the shout accompanying it. He had no illusions about war, past or present. He saw the medieval castle for what it was, a "stern and barbarous" structure designed to intimidate, and made appealing to us only because time and neglect and nature's overgrowing have softened it (Sorrell 1973a, 5). Hadrian's Wall in its prime, he tells us "must have been an engineering eye-sore ... We can only enjoy the Wall because it *is* ruined and ineffective for its original purpose".[25] My brother Richard reminds me that, looking with him at a famous Paul Nash watercolour of the Battle of Britain, a decorative marvel with its arabesques of smoke trails filling the summer sky, my father's comment was laconic: "Very pretty."

His own war drawings were a personal record, neither propagandist nor celebratory. Indeed he seems deliberately to have sought out military buildings and hardware which were aesthetically unpleasing (perhaps this was not difficult), because he saw in them and in the cropped and tortured landscapes surrounding airfields, emblems of brutality to be investigated. Stray comments in his letters confirm that he saw such buildings embedding the surrounding violence – a similar transference from the psychological to the atmospheric as that which informs his imaginative work. To my mother, on his *Watch Office, RAF Station* (1944) (Fig. 50): "It's most carefully balanced and full of unexpected rhythms and extremely sinister and full of foreboding, a bit like this [sketch]" (Sorrell & Tanner 1944–7, *c.* 23 Aug. 1944).

FIG. 78. *Cricieth Castle, Gwynedd, late 13th century* (1961). Pen & ink, pastel, ink washes & gouache, 38.5 × 54.4 cm
(IMAGE COURTESY OF CADW)

To E. C. Gregory, secretary to the War Artists' Advisory Committee on his *Machine Gun Range and Rifle Range, RAF Station* (1944):

> "I have just finished a drawing of a rifle range. I must confess that I am v[ery] pleased with it, wh[ich] may be because it's got a feeling of murder blood & sudden death in it! V[ery] cheerful – but honestly I think you will like it."[26]

Yet, volunteering in 1940, having lived through months of ferocious bombing in London, he was insistent in his desire to serve his country in any capacity which might contribute to the war effort. In particular, he saw the relevance of the interpretative skills he had developed as a reconstruction artist. Writing to the Secretary of State for Air, he enclosed a photograph of an aerial panorama (probably Roman Caerleon) recently completed, on which he had worked with Cyril Fox and V. E. Nash-Williams, saying:

> "This drawing was built up from written information, the Ordnance Survey map of the district, & the plans of the excavated section of the site, & my own sketches & photographs of the landscape."

And:

> "I am *not* trying to interest you in pictures or 'Works of Art' but in a type of drawing which I think must have an application to bomber targets. I believe such drawings could amplify & partly take the place of the models which I understand are sometimes made. The saving in time & cost will be obvious."[27]

FIG. 79. *Machine Gun Range and Rifle Range, RAF Station* (1944). Ink, gouache & watercolour, 32.4 × 55.4 cm
(IMAGE COURTESY OF THE POTTERIES MUSEUM & ART GALLERY, STOKE-ON-TRENT)

This offer coincided with the recruitment of a team of professional artists and designers to a secret unit which he joined, based first at the Royal Aircraft Establishment at Farnborough and then at RAF Medmenham. There they were put to work not to make drawings but models of exacting detail, based on contoured maps and timed aerial photographs, where interpretation was the key, where imagination had little or no play. Constance Babington Smith describes the Model-Making Section located in the cellars at Medmenham which was, for a short time, the focus of my father's energies, as:

> "one of Medmenham's most secret departments ... The work of the model makers, which contributed vitally to the planning of innumerable operations all through the war, was far from a merely mechanical task ... The Model Section was full of the whirr of electric fret-saws and the tapping of hammers as the contours that had been traced from greatly enlarged maps were cut out of hardboard one after another, and then mounted and nailed into position. Next, after being smoothed by electric chisel, the land form was given an unbroken surface with a special plastic substance, and after this had set an enormously enlarged photograph, damped to make it supple, was pushed gently into place ... Finally the model was painted ... and the model makers set in place with tweezers the Lilliputian buildings and trees and fences ... Anything over three feet high was shown three-dimensionally, and if you stooped down and looked along the surface of the model you could see exactly what the Commandos were going to encounter ..." (Smith 1961, 160)

Years later we find him entering a plea for the contouring of archaeological site plans:

> "Think how limited is the validity of a plan of, say Harlech Castle: who could imagine the dramatic character of its topography without detailed contouring and sections from sea level to the tops of the towers?" (Mark Sorrell 1981, 22)

and to us as children, without ever mentioning Medmenham, he spoke of his patient work as a modeller and how you could estimate a building's height in an air reconnaissance photograph from its shadow length. So the rigours of one discipline nourished the fruits of another. A later posting, as a camouflage officer seated at a desk in the Strand, where, on large scale plans, he made

> "... landing grounds fade out from human ken
> 'Neath magic touch",[28]

was equally productive. Having put his marks on paper, he would be flown over the site to observe from the air how effectively, with different paints and textures, the camoufleurs had carried out his pen-and-ink suggestions for extending imaginary woods and fields, hedge patterns and rural roads over raw concrete. He helped to plan military airfields, including one at Framlingham (1942) (see Chapter 5),[29] dispersing their buildings; and later still was commissioned to paint large aerial panoramas of them which, with their skyscapes and command of perspective, show a marked advance on his pre-war reconstructions for the National Museum of Wales.

But without doubt the best decision which he took in the war years was to unhitch himself from a failed relationship and go forward with another in love and confidence, which gave him the security to produce his best work. Thankfully he did.

FIG. 80. *Caerleon: Bird's Eye View of the Roman Legionary Fortress* (1939). Watercolour, pen & ink, gouache. 69 × 93.5 cm
(AMGUEDDFA CYMRU – NATIONAL MUSEUM WALES)

Notes

1. Lionel Elvin (an old schoolfriend) to AS, 11 July 1965 (ASA, correspondence), re-establishing contact after 50 years, remembered "a very stirring rendering you did, at the age of ten or so I suppose, of de Montfort's last stand at Evesham. I was in your class then at the Chalkwell school."
2. "Thus a stealthy consideration of angles will lead one into space far more naturally and easily than a straightforward trying for it, and an equally stealthy consideration of two dimensional patterns is likely to achieve a realisation of solid form far more satisfactory than a head-on attempt to express the third dimension". See also Sorrell c. 1938, 49: "It's no good beginning recklessly, with fiery enthusiasm, but if you analyse shapes, and estimate angles, and get interested in small things the drawing will grow of itself. You must, of course, be vividly aware of the whole, but the only way to truly express it is through this ant-like assemblage of its tiny details". ES to AS 1 April 1962 (ASA, Nubia letters file), relaying artists' talk at an annual lunch at the RWS: "[Wilfred] Fairclough and others were talking to me and he said in a loud ringing voice which must have been heard everywhere: 'Alan Sorrell taught me more about life drawing in ten minutes than others did in years ... absolutely wonderful.' 'I'll tell him you said so,' I said. 'Yes do, although I've already told him so myself,' he replied.'"
3. "the close and affectionate study of humanity is, perhaps, not my métier."
4. AS to ES, Abu Simbel, 21 Feb. 1962 (ASA, Nubia letters file): "Today I've spent in a quite extraordinary way, in one of the side-chapels of the temple, making a drawing of some Swedes drilling to find out the structure of the rock ... It's turned out very well, & of course, it really is an absolutely unique thing ..."
5. A soft focus interview of 1939 shows him in thrall to these ideas (Mories 1939, 84–5).
6. Particularly by Maggie Johns, whose findings, both privately communicated and posted on Ancestry.com, I am drawing on here.
7. An undoubted reference to our common ancestor may be seen in my father's cheerful mural of coastal shipping, painted for the Festival of Britain (1951) and recently purchased by the National Maritime Museum, in the shape of a small figure, on the lower edge where two panels join, lifting the lid of a barrel from which he is emerging. But I have it on good authority that this blow-in was added post-1974 during restoration work. He was not part of the original design.
8. In a speech, opening a local art exhibition in the 1960s, Alan described himself as "one who is almost a Southender (I arrived here at the age of 2) ..." (AS handwritten notes, Richard Sorrell)
9. Mark Sorrell (1981, 20): "As you probably know, I am an artist, and not an archaeologist ... There are certain advantages in being an outsider. For instance, I do not know too much ... I can see the wood without being too keenly aware of the trees."
10. See an interesting discussion of this by Anthony Blunt in his introduction to *Seurat* (Blunt and Fry 1965, 5–8).
11. In Horton (1955, 18) we find the same phrase: "For Sorrell the subject has always been a *sine qua non* –a necessary and indeed imperative stimulus to picture-making. He has not been afraid of being stigmatised as a mere illustrator. A fervent admirer of the great Italian narrative painters &c ...".
12. He specifies "Flemish" in a letter of condolence to my mother, Dec. 1974 (ASA, correspondence).
13. Dykes (1980, 6) quotes her as describing him as "a dark thin young man with a stammer, diffident yet determined".
14. *Planting of the Trees*, with other works, was shown in a joint exhibition with Donovan Hebden at Southend Art School (*Southend Standard,* 19 Oct. 1933, 16). It was probably sold at this time.

15 This attitude included a rude dismissal of places deemed by all to be obviously picturesque, for example Venice in 1954: "Venice is beautiful & must be wonderful for everybody except the creative artist! If I were old & bored, with tons of money & no interest in anything this would be the place." (AS to ES, Venice, 25–26 July 1954, ASA.)
16 Sorrell 1939b, 36.
17 ASA, JW to AS, 24 Oct. [1973].
18 From the handwritten version of *A Simple Story* (1940, ASA, red spiral exercise book). At its end is this note: "Written during the air raids on London at night, Sep 1940. There is a German plane near & the guns are firing."
19 ASA, Sketchbook G, 18.
20 To point the contrast he added, between the original sketch (ASA, Sketchbook V) and the final drawing, a classical statue on a plinth. The air station was Bradwell Bay, Essex.
21 His interest in the Crimea was stirred in his own childhood: "I can vividly recall my mother telling me, when I was a boy, about events which now seem legendary. She told me of a certain Sergeant-Major O'Connor and Mrs O'Connor whom she knew as a girl. The Sergeant-Major had served in the Crimea, and his wife had been maid to Lady Cardigan, whose husband led the Charge of the Light Brigade, and who lived in grand style on his steam yacht anchored off shore. Mrs O'Connor did not think much of Florence Nightingale, whom she described as 'A very interfering lady'…". (Sorrell c. 1974, 83).
22 An elaborate short fiction of my father's, *The Lost Land of Torresedo*, illustrated with "an Imaginative Reconstruction in Colour", and supposedly based on an 18th-century document recently found in a "narrow-necked antique vase", was published in *Lilliput* (March 1949, 74–9). He was delighted when a reader wrote in to ask, if Torresedo existed, where it was to be found on the map.
23 July 1909. His emotions surrounding these events are powerfully recalled in his short story *The Shadow* (alternative title *The Gun*), written in 1940.
24 ASA, CF to AS undated, "New Year's Eve" (Dec. 1944).
25 AS letter to *The Times*, 31 Dec. 1970, 11e.
26 IWM 1940–6, AS to E. C. Gregory undated, late 1944.
27 Draft letters in pencil, red spiral exercise book (1940), ASA.
28 From *Lament for Cam* [Camouflage], some mock-heroic wartime verses of his over which I have heard him chuckle (ASA, undated typescript, probably 1944).
29 See AS to G. Elmslie Owen, War Artists' Commission, 3 May 1943 (IWM 1940–6) concerning a proposal for drawings: "I should like to make the drawings at Framlingham, because I sited the hutments and devised the camouflage scheme there, & it is a typical wartime aerodrome."

Chapter 8

Beginnings and the National Museum of Wales

SORRELL WAS BROUGHT UP in "the sprawling brick acres" of Southend (Sorrell 1939b, 35); his first wife, his exact contemporary, in industrial Leicester, a place which, in later years when he was out of that marriage, he remembered without affection ("a dull Midlands town"). Southend's sprawl was not only formless, it had no visible ancient core. The town owed its existence, or at least its vitality, to the construction, some 70 years before his birth, of a famously long pier for excursion steamers, and soon after that of a day-tripper's railway from London. At the needy start of his career, looking homeward for commissions, he approached Southend's town council with an offer to make mural decorations, with the pier and its surroundings as their subject; which, he assured them, would be "genuine historical paintings of the only history we can know – that of our own time" (Sorrell 1942, 88). They encouraged him but, somewhat to his disappointment as he confessed, directed him to themes more firmly rooted in the past: *Admiral Blake's Fleet Refitting at Leigh* (1933) (see Fig. 21); *The Foundation of Prittlewell Priory by Cluniac monks c. 1100 A.D.* (1935); *The Building of Prittlewell Church Tower* (1936); and *The Arrival of the First Mail Coach at Southend* (1937). He was still working on this series when, in 1936, he had occasion to stay with Irene's people in Leicester.

There he was bored. Tiresome conventionalities always brought out the mischief in my father. If with humour he failed to lighten the atmosphere, his usual way of coping with his restlessness was to walk off rapidly in any direction away from the house. The tactic in Leicester soon led him to a more interesting scene. On a site beside the Jewry Wall (a huge piece of exposed Roman masonry) the authorities had demolished a factory, intending to build public baths; but among its footings more Roman remains had been discovered. Archaeologists were at work in these holes in the ground, directed by Kathleen Kenyon – "formidable", Aileen Fox called her (Fox 2000, 108) – watched over from above by cloth-capped workers under a lowering pall of smoke.

Alan joined the watchers: "It was purely the visual side then", he explained later.[1] (He had been friendly with classical scholars and archaeologists in Rome, friendships which endured, but I cannot find that he expressed, at that time, any interest in their work.) He made some slight notes in a sketchbook which he developed into a drawing. Kenyon saw it, and seeing in it possibilities for publicity (and, probably, for the prolongation of the time the town would allow her for her investigations) beyond anything which Sorrell had had it in mind to do, took it, with his permission, to show Bruce Ingram, editor of *The Illustrated London News*.

That once famous paper had been one of the first in England, alongside such forgotten rags as *The Illustrated Police News*, to enrich newsprint with illustration. First published in 1842, it had survived the vagaries of fashion, the transition at the end of the 19th century from steel engraving to photography and, under Ingram's editorship, which began in 1900 and lasted extraordinarily until his death in 1963, would even for a time compete with live television. Lavishly illustrated, it was a paper for the fashionable lounge, for the Victorian and Edwardian equivalent of the coffee table. As a student in Rome, sitting in the midst of Mussolini's dictatorship, my father recalled that:

> "'The Illustrated London News' was the most eagerly awaited journal of the week and that arrived on Sunday mornings. From so far away the actions of Mr Baldwin and Mr Ramsay MacDonald possessed abrupt puppet-like absurdity, whilst 'Heavy snowfall in London' or 'Floods in the Midlands' might have had to do with moon weather, so remote did it all seem. King George and Queen Mary became foreign potentates ... " (Sorrell *c*. 1938, 122)

In addition to its social and political documentation, the stately *ILN*

FIG. 81. Excavations beside the Jewry Wall, Leicester (1936). *Illustrated London News*
(DESTROYED IN WW2, ASA COPY)

carried articles on music, theatre, gardening, books, auction house sales and so on, and always found space for archaeology. Bruce Ingram's interest in the last-named had been fired by childhood holidays taken with his parents in Egypt, in the course of one of which it was his proud boast (Bacon 1976, 12) that he had "stood on the shoulders of Rameses at Abu Simbel". In 1922, when Tutankhamun's tomb was discovered in the Valley of the Kings, Ingram had moved quickly to obtain, with *The Times*, exclusive reporting rights. Also, within days, he sent his historical reconstruction artist, Amédée Forestier, to Marseilles, to interview Lord Carnarvon on his way home, for first-hand details on which to base a drawing (*ILN* 23 Dec. 1922) of the moment following discovery, when Carnarvon and his daughter and Howard Carter had advanced by candlelight into the outer chamber. Over the next decade, the *ILN* published 22 features in colour and black-and-white on the developing story. This strong response enhanced the paper's reputation as a proving ground where working archaeologists gave a first account of their excavations;[2] and popularised the subject as never before (Bacon 1976, 177, 189).

Forestier had contributed to the *ILN* since 1882 (Smiles & Moser 2005, 76). I asked my father once who had been before him in this field, and the only name I recall his mentioning was Forestier's. He found an image of his to show me, of a Stone Age hunter; and spoke of him with respect. At his death in 1930, in a brief obituary, C. H. B. Quennell said:

> "To my certain knowledge, for the last 25 years there was hardly any discovery of archaeological importance which was not illustrated by [Forestier's] drawings in the pages of the *Illustrated London News*. Forestier was especially interested in prehistoric man and loved to bring him to life, not by fictitious imaginings but by the most careful reconstructions based on scientific research." (*The Times* 19 Nov. 1930, 19d)

But since that time no one had appeared to succeed him until Kenyon brought in my father's drawing. Ingram at once agreed to publish it; but he wanted another to stand beside it which should be a "restoration" from the same viewpoint of what could be inferred from the excavation – consisting, in Kenyon's opinion, of a basilica-and-forum complex at the heart of the Roman town. This "restoration", on which they collaborated, was Alan's first reconstruction drawing (*ILN* 13 Feb. 1937). Kenyon proposed that a copy of it "should be put up on the site, as that is so badly needed to help people to visualise the building."[3]

In an article accompanying the drawings, Kenyon acknowledged that much of the supposed basilica lay out of reach beneath a medieval church; and that that part of it which could be examined (the Jewry Wall itself) had some peculiar features; nevertheless she was confident that it was correctly so described. However, writing later to Alan, she revealed, alarmingly, the extent to which further work had hollowed out her conclusions:

> "The Bath in the middle of the Forum was a complete surprise, but of course the centre was originally open, and your drawing represents the first period. Actually further clearance has altered some of the details, but not the general idea. I didn't do anything more about the idea of a reconstruction of the whole, because I came to the conclusion that there were too many uncertain points, and it might turn out to be wasted effort until the excavations were completed. I still very much want to have it done, but I think it must wait until another year."[4]

It was never done. It is interesting to see Kenyon, a superbly skilful excavator, accounting for the anomalous presence of baths in the forum – well might she call them "a complete surprise" –not by changing her theory but by inventing another period to accommodate them, although forum and baths were built more or less simultaneously. And this position she held to. It would not be until the 1960s, when the actual forum was uncovered on a different block, that the Jewry Wall was reinterpreted. It is now supposed to be the wall of a gymnasium associated with Roman public baths. Plans for their 20th century successor were not proceeded with. The site was scheduled and remains open.

So Alan's drawing was premature; imaginative reconstruction in this case, through no fault of his own, had outrun the evidence. Nevertheless he was launched.[5] In the same letter Kenyon writes:

> "Dr Wheeler is anxious to get in touch with you with a view to having some reconstruction drawings done of Maiden Castle. He would of course supply all the details. He would like you to ring him up at the London Museum as soon as possible, tomorrow if you can, and arrange an appointment."

This was Mortimer Wheeler, whose discovery of a war cemetery at the eastern entrance of Maiden Castle had provided gruesome evidence of a Roman assault on the fortress in AD 43. My father embodied his findings in a fine aerial drawing (*ILN* 4 Dec. 1937). In the meantime, Cyril Fox at the National Museum of Wales, impressed by the Leicester reconstruction, had contacted him to make drawings. Kenyon, Wheeler, Fox, W. F. Grimes, Ian Richmond and others made up a small coterie of inter-war excavators, most of them colleagues and friends, who were intent on setting British archaeology on a much sounder base than theretofore, by establishing systematic methods of digging, recording and comparing.[6] What is noteworthy is that, in the process, they did not fight shy of Alan Sorrell, an avowed non-specialist who brought imaginative zest to his interpretations, but admired his work and actively encouraged him. Undoubtedly his

FIG. 82. Roman assault on the eastern entrance of Maiden Castle, Dorset (1937). *Illustrated London News*
(DESTROYED IN WW2, ASA COPY)

drawings helped them to gain public attention, which was necessary, but I think what they respected about him was that he brought to bear the intelligence of the visual, testing and challenging them to consider their work in ways which they had not expected.[7]

It was Mortimer Wheeler who famously stated the principle that archaeology, a scientific discipline, is also a romantic quest:

> "...the archaeological excavator is not digging up *things*, he is digging up *people*; however much he may analyse and tabulate and desiccate his discoveries in the laboratory, the ultimate appeal across the ages, whether the time-interval be 500 or 500,000 years, is from mind to mind, from man to sentient man...It is a truism of which I constantly find it necessary to remind the student and indeed myself: that the life of the past and the present are diverse but indivisible; that Archaeology, in so far as it is a science, is a science which must be extended into the living and must indeed itself be lived if it is to partake of a proper vitality." (Wheeler 1956, 17)

In the mid-1960s, in a contentious article, Reyner Banham described my father (specifically as represented by his reconstruction drawings), as "the last of the line of 'history painters' in the 18th century sense" (Banham 1966, 689). The article was an attack on Alan's weather moodiness, on what Banham stigmatised as the imposition of "one man's untrammelled Gothick imagination" on our conception of, for example, prehistoric Britain – an attack to which I shall return. What I want to fix on here is that Alan quite liked the phrase. Indeed, late in his career, he built on it (Mark Sorrell 1981, 20, 21) to associate what he was trying to achieve (in reconstruction drawings) with the mainstream of European visual art before the Impressionists. That older artistic tradition, dating back to the Renaissance had, he said, included innumerable "reconstructions" of the Crucifixion, had been replete with recreations of scenes of Biblical history of every kind, down to Holman Hunt's stagnant and hapless, "marvellous and passionately felt" *Scapegoat*; as well as of battles and sieges. This was his argument, but the connection, to my mind, is not properly made for, as Gombrich shows (1972, 380, 381), the history painters to whom (presumably) Banham was referring, who constructed pictures of historical incidents based on intensive antiquarian and historical research and had instructional (but not for the most part religious) designs on us, belonged to a later flowering than most of these: were indeed almost children of the French Revolution. As a category, in the 19th century, history painting included the good, the bad and the awful, to take titles almost at random: *The Boyhood of Raleigh; Curtius Leaping into the Gulf; Israel in Egypt; A Converted British Family Sheltering a Christian Missionary from the Persecution of the Druids*. And it is clear to me that, apart from some book illustrations, in his reconstruction drawings my father is not in this line at all. Some of his imaginative compositions are nearer the mark. His *Prince Charles Edward in the Highlands*, for instance, has a fiery enclave of plumes and staves all but lost in the encircling storm, amid mountains, wrecked trees and rushing river.[8] His recreation of *Agamemnon's Homecoming to Mycenae*, too, shows a torchlit, barbaric scene as full of foreboding as anything from *Macbeth*.

But archaeologists are not, most of the time, digging up named or famous people. They have to do with fragments of the past, recover things by signs and traces. The narrative thread for them is in anonymous day-to-day living, guided by remains of rooms and roads; with fragile objects dropped or hidden or buried ceremoniously; with hearths, pits, bones.

As far as I can see, Alan tried his utmost to make sense of this material. Function and probability were what mattered to him. That is the key. His approach was in no way pretentious. He did not take it upon himself either to ennoble like a history painter (history as pageant)[9] or demean, and did not at all consider himself to belong to a more advanced, lofty stage of civilisation. From scattered statements it is actually not too hard to synthesise what he thought he was about in his reconstructions:

1. The facts

"The visual apprehension of the artist, disciplined in the most rigorous manner by the facts assembled by the archaeologists, can make a valuable contribution to the search for the truth about the past" (Mark Sorrell 1981, 26)

2. Humanity

"… I would say that the [artist's] prime objective is to convince the spectator that these structures really did exist, that they were inhabited by live people who did not stand about to give scale to the buildings but were active and busy"[10]

"My approach involves thinking of history as a continuous process … People are alive and active round us now; they were just as alive and active round others in past times" [11]

3. Atmosphere

"… most important, that all this building and humanity existed in an envelope of atmosphere, under the moving sky, surrounded by hills maybe or woodland or some other kind of landscape or townscape"[12]

4. Artistic integrity

"Then, as I am an artist first of all, shapes and forms are important to me. So I try and see things as they were and build up interesting pictures. Strong imagination helps to define subjects clearly";[13]

"I, of course, am all for humanistic culture with its imponderables, rather than the precise formulation of factual information which is technology. But it must be stressed here that precision to a hair's breadth is an essential quality in all good art …" (Mark Sorrell 1981, 21)

Wheeler and Fox, who belonged to an older generation than my father, had been friends since the 1920s. In 1924, when Fox was hesitating between museum posts at Dublin and Cambridge, Wheeler, as the then Director of the National Museum of Wales, persuaded him to join him there instead as Keeper of Archaeology; a move which, two years later, led to Fox succeeding him in the top job (Scott-Fox 2002, 55–8). As an archaeologist, Wheeler admired Fox for his thoroughness and promptness of publication, but even more for his intense engagement with the cultures he was digging up. As an example of this, in *Archaeology from the Earth*, he quotes a typical exploratory passage from one of Fox's reports on a Bronze Age burial, commenting:

> "What matters to us here and now is not, of course, the particular episode which I have cited but the creative act of reasoned imagination that has gone to the making or remaking of it. Fox's interpretation may not be correct in all its details; in any event the objective facts upon which it is based are fully recorded, and the interpretation of them can be reshaped in the light of fuller knowledge. The great thing is that those facts are infused with a rational intelligence; they emerge from Fox's brain as three-dimensional entities ..." (Wheeler 1956, 18)

It is this creative focus of Fox's, so closely aligned to my father's way of thinking, which lights up their pre-war correspondence as they worked together, with V. E. Nash-Williams (his replacement as Keeper), on reconstruction drawings. Fox was an enthusiast, an encourager, an enabler. Alan completed nine commissioned drawings for the museum, three series of three in each, before the war's disruption made anything further impossible for a time. And I feel sure that it was the memory of this happy working partnership which helped him, after the end of the war, to decide that he could make his living full-time, as a freelance, from reconstruction drawings.[14]

In her late-written autobiography, Aileen Fox states that she and Alan had kept in touch after their Rome meeting; and that, now married to Cyril Fox, it was she who suggested that he would be a suitable artist to make reconstructions for the museum (Fox 2000, 102). Certainly she became a strong advocate for his work;[15] and in April 1937 she made contact, with Cyril Fox attaching a note (their letter or letters are now missing). In his reply, addressed to Sir Cyril, Alan is friendly but not familiar:

FIG. 83. Watercolour drawing of Cyril Fox (1946). Chalks, charcoal & watercolour
(IMAGE COURTESY OF GEORGE FOX)

> "I was glad to learn from Lady Fox's letter, & from your note, that you liked my Leicester forum drawings. I should welcome the opportunity of doing other archæological pictures. You mention the possibility of a 'reconstruction' being wanted for the Museum, & of course I should be

very pleased to do it for you. It is good of you to think of me in this connexion." (NMW 1937–c.60, c. 18 April 1937)

His teaching commitments gave only limited opportunities for a meeting, but Cyril Fox invited him to stay with them midweek in Cardiff, bringing with him the Leicester drawings (which were in monochrome) and another example of his work in colour. Then he could see the museum, and they could discuss sites, fees and so on.[16] Aileen Fox takes up the story:

> "It was May when he came and I took him for a walk up the Wenallt [woods above Rhiwbina] in the flush of new green leaves, bluebells and spring flowers. When I exclaimed on its beauty, he said he didn't really like it, it was too green, like lettuces, and he preferred more sombre tones. This is very evident in all his paintings with their strong dark skies and windswept landscape and was part of his perpetual attitude to life." (Dykes 1980, 13)

That has the ring of truth. I remember a starry-eyed visitor at our house remarking on "the green fields of England" and my father's provocative reply: "Yes, aren't they horrible? That acid green! Give me the desert, the burnt hillsides of Greece" ("Oh Alan, you can't be serious", etc).

The meeting was a success. Not only were three drawings of the Roman town of Caerwent, including a large bird's eye view (see Fig. 28) promptly decided on for a fee of £60, but the sample in colour which Alan had brought (*Icelandic Farm*; see Fig. 24), pleased so well that it was kept and, through Fox's good offices, purchased for the museum. In June, Alan paid a second visit and, with Nash-Williams, got down to work. He reported to Fox:

> "I travelled down to Cardiff on Friday evening as arranged and on the Saturday we went out to Caerwent & also Caerleon. I was able to get a good idea of the lie of the land at Caerwent & I made a drawing there of the surrounding hills which will form the background to the large drawing. I put in a considerable amount of work at the museum & have gone through Ashby's 'excavations' [1901, 1910] pretty thoroughly. With all this information & with the help of my numerous sketches the production of the drawings should not present any very great difficulty. I promised Mr Nash-Williams full sized preliminary pencil drawings in the first instance. These can be easily corrected & will make the final work both quicker & cleaner." (NMW 1937–1960, c. 29 June 1937)

Two of these preliminary "cartoons", for the smaller drawings in this set, have survived. Interestingly, early in the same year, the *Southend Standard* (reproduced in Llewellyn & Sorrell 2013, 118) carried a photograph of my father in profile, neatly dressed, pencil in hand, seated in front of a similar although half-sized study for the last of his "history book" murals then in progress. Another photograph, of a squared-up study for his imaginative composition *The Long Journey* (1936; see Fig. 71a), also exists (Sorrell 1939b, 36). In each case the working method is identical and the studies dauntingly precise. They even include – prefigured in shape, clothes and action – the diminutive human actors in the reconstruction scenes.

But it was not long before Alan grew dissatisfied with this over-tight way of working: experience taught him the merit of keeping reserves of spontaneity for the final painting. Elsewhere he writes:

> "I have found that preliminary studies can be too complete – I almost said 'too good'. One becomes anchored to a very complete study, and when this is transferred to the cartoon, the latter is likely to look what it is, a mere copy of something else ..." (Sorrell 1952b, 35)

Thus, in 1939, when he embarked on a third series for the museum, he began by sending Fox and Nash-Williams a small sketch for each drawing in which he was chiefly concerned with the scale of the various objects and the general layout; sent it again adjusted – with erasures in Chinese white – in the light of their observations; and only then began the preliminary study, commenting: "As you will see I am leaving more this time until the finished picture, as I think I am apt to lose rather than gain by putting too much into the first draft" (NMW 1937–c.60, c. 17 Sept., c. 16 Nov., c. 14 Dec. 1939).

Another matter to be faced at an early stage was how far working for a museum would compromise him as an artist. I think he was not alone in finding the historical sections of some museums rather tame; so there was a need for the defining of terms. A "certain exciting dramatic note" would, he believed, "be a highly desirable quality in these reconstructions." And he hoped to show that a reconstruction drawing could be a work of art; as such, vital and self-renewing, it would have "a far greater power of education and attraction than a possibly accurate drawing where form and design have perhaps not received such particular attention" (Dykes 1980, 13).[17] Here was another reason for him to be tireless in the pursuit of truth if it could be found.

Julia has shown how he prepared for the library murals at Southend by making drawings on the spot, studying in museums, questioning the experts. This process of immersion and familiarisation was exactly the one he followed with his reconstructions, including what he described later as his "usual cross-examination" of archaeologists,[18] at first in person and thereafter in notes jotted on and around sketches sent back and forth.

In the two surviving Caerwent "cartoons", made so very near the beginning of his career as a reconstruction artist, we can almost observe him feeling his way. Nash-Williams chose the subjects; but it was Alan who decided, for dramatic effect, on a high viewpoint, thereby immediately surrounding himself with problems.[19] By tilting up the Roman town, he opened space between the houses as they would be seen in a scale model, but also effortlessly carried the eye beyond the excavation site into untested areas. In the Caerwent drawings this was not such a problem as it later became, when he was so often asked to lay down smoke to screen districts where the information ran out, or alter his viewpoint to hide them.[20] The animators of computer models of ancient sites, employing a technology which Alan did not live to see, find themselves even more nakedly outrunning knowledge as they enter rooms and peer round unexplored corners without benefit of smoke, to the extent that they have been urged to "find techniques for displaying areas of fudged data within [their] models" (Miller & Richards 1995, 21).

Apart from this, looking down searchingly from above roof height could present structural challenges which might not otherwise have occurred to the archaeologist tentatively building from below. Questions such as whether, in a province far from Rome, Roman town houses might be shown with two or more storeys, were the obvious ones for an artist to ask; the answers harder to find.

I give a flavour of the comments written round the edges of one of these "cartoons" – the one showing some well-appointed houses in the south-western corner of Roman Caerwent during a raid. Nash-Williams's replies were in green ink; for ease of reference, I have put them within brackets:

> "I should like some information about the degree of regularity in the roofing & stonework. Were the roofing slabs all of one size or did they increase in the lower ones? ('Same size and regular.')
>
> Could you possibly send me a very small piece of the typical stone?
>
> Flames & smoke from cornfields set on fire by raiders. The running men belong to a sort of border militia & and are not supposed to be legionaries. ('Good.')
>
> Factory with two chimneys over furnaces. ('I am doubtful about the chimneys (see below). I shld play for safety & omit chimneys everywhere. But show some smoke cowls along the eaves of the bdgs instead.')
>
> This is the stoke hole to heat the adjoining hypocausts. I suppose there must have been a chimney. Also a woodyard with gate as excavated. ('Good! The chimneys, however, will I fear have to go ...')"

And in point of fact the form of Roman chimneys was still much in doubt though it would have been hard to question their existence (Lowther 1976, 35–48). It was a detail, of course, but one which was important visually (because chimneys break up the monotony of otherwise unvaried

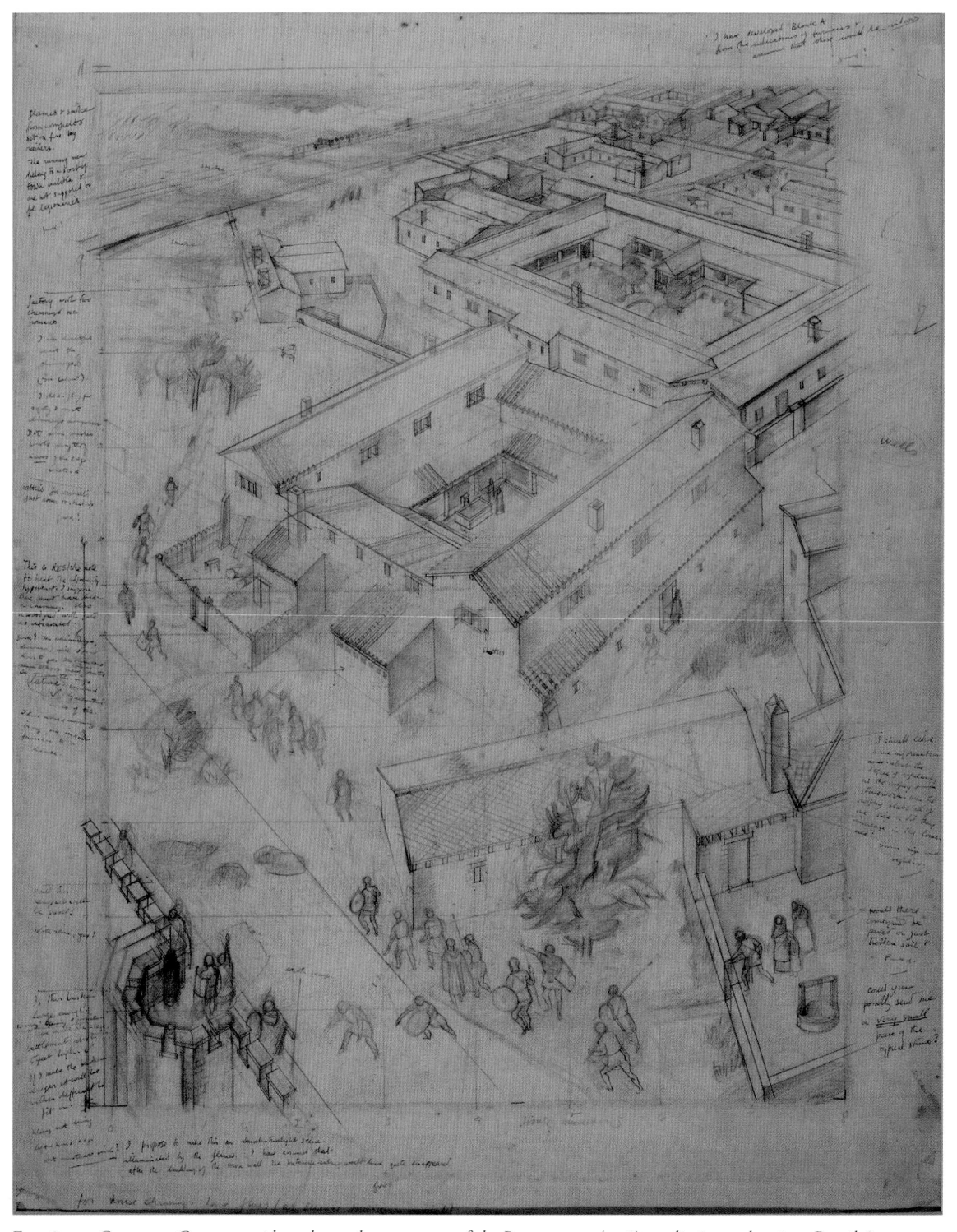

FIG. 84. a. *Caerwent, Gwent: a raid on the south-west corner of the Roman town* (1938), preliminary drawing. Pencil & crayon on tracing paper, 62 × 48 cm
(ASA);

Fig. 84 b. *Caerwent, Gwent: a raid on the south-west corner of the Roman town* (1938), final drawing. Pen & ink, gouache & watercolour, 65 × 45 cm
(AMGUEDDFA CYMRU – NATIONAL MUSEUM WALES)

rooflines, and what affects the eye matters and has always mattered) and also practically, because the hot gases rising from Roman underfloor and intra-wall heating systems must have had some means of escape. Thinking in terms of probability, Alan would have argued that you would not go to the expense of installing such a system only for it to deposit smuts in the rooms. It would be like having running water and letting your basements flood.

He sent off the "cartoons" in early October. Nash-Williams was temporarily absent, and Fox returned a quick response: "My dear Sorrell, I have just seen your drafts. Delightful! I am <u>very pleased</u> indeed with their promise. I like the drama you are introducing into the smaller drawings."[21]

At the first opportunity Nash-Williams replied:

> "You will find one or two comments scribbled in the margins, but these do not represent final views on the various points raised. Perhaps, however, we can have a chat about them when we meet in London. I may interpolate here that the principal difficulty that has been holding me up in regard to the drawings (which are, in my opinion, most admirable) is the question of chimneys for Roman houses. I have not so far been able to find definite evidence for such a feature, but possibly you have some information on this point."[22]

And, a few days later, responding to Alan's reply:

> "With regard to the question of the Caerwent chimneys, after reading what you say about the persistence of ancient house-types showing such features in Italy today, I should say that we shall be justified in including them in the drawings. I raised the point, because I had not been able to discover a chimney in any of the Roman building reconstructions that I had examined ... I should think the Quennells must have had something definite to go upon before they admitted the chimney to their reconstructions."[23]

No doubt hoping to soothe, he added that, in any case, the issue would not affect the general drawing "as the chimneys cannot bulk very large in it" – at which point Alan seems to have decided to omit them altogether. But I cannot imagine that Nash-Williams's answer pleased him. Drawing was for Alan, whatever else it might be, a rigorous work of analysis: it was how he interpreted the world. As a drawing instructor at the RCA, he would home in on any unresolved area in a student's work, ask what they meant by it, submit it to the geometry of angles; it was the same with his own. Similarly, with clouds, he would say that they should not be seen as an afterthought or convenient hood to pull down, but as a positive addition in a drawing, helping to create an ambient atmosphere by relieving and containing complex features on the ground. And smoke, in a panorama, was an obvious sign of habitation. (Incidentally, in a later extended discussion of his methods (quoted in Mark Sorrell 1981, 25), it is interesting to see him employing a phrase which is not immediately understandable: "... the reconstruction which is conceived as a work of art has that *super-realism, the realism of the dream*, which fixes for ever the image of the scene or incident or personage depicted" [My italics]. Knowing how he stored vivid phrases in his mind, sometimes from years back, I have no doubt that he connected this "super-reality" with a specific light effect, which he often used, and the mood which it induces: with that eerie penetrating distinctness you sometimes get on a stormy day.)[24]

He would study plans and mark them, likewise the excavation report if it was available; but here again, too often, would find himself struggling to give shape to what he was being presented with, as if smoke had been let in among the words.[25] And leading on from this:

> "I have often wondered whether archaeologists really do visualise their finds in the round ... A plan, neatly drawn and lettered, with various textures denoting periods of building can so easily be regarded as the final solution of the detective problem which constitutes every archaeological excavation ... So often their reports are tame records of 'finds', stopping short of the imaginative, or rather, intuitive effort to breathe life into dull bones, which one might assume was the true objective of all historical investigation." (Sorrell *c.* 1962, 53)

Of course the other side of this argument is that opinions change, new connections are found as new discoveries are made. Definitive answers cannot be given just by wishing for them. Can an archaeologist ever be said to be in possession of all the evidence? But perhaps what these different approaches reveal at their extremes is the dichotomy between science and art. Fox sought actively to lessen that division. So did W. F. Grimes who, recalling their exciting work together on Roman London, remembered "how searching Sorrell's questions could be in his pursuit of accuracy and how insistent he always was on getting details as near to the truth as possible" (Dykes 1980, 15).

At the risk of labouring the point, I should like to show how Alan did finally arrive at an uncontroversial representation of Roman chimneys. Soon after the war, after Fox's retirement which occurred just then, he revisited Cardiff with a commission from Aileen Fox to paint a portrait of the distinguished archaeologist with his family, a "Conversation Piece" (Fox 2000, 109). He wanted at the same time to explore the possibility of obtaining further reconstruction drawing commissions, having, for six years since mid-1940, been entirely removed from all such work. Nash-Williams, whose life had been similarly dislocated, responded in due course, suggesting the Roman villa at Llantwit Major which he had begun to open up in 1938.

He wrote:

> "The Villa is of courtyard type, with the residential ranges occupying two sides of the courtyard, servants' quarters the third side, and granges and workshops, the fourth. There are also ditches and banks around the site, and one can of course imagine such things as a garden, orchard, etc. The whole place seems to me to invite a picture ..."

And my father, replying in a similar spirit (although, with an eye to business, he had demanded and got his fee increased to 50 guineas), said: "it sounds just like old times!"[26]

They conferred about how they should proceed. Alan proposed a preliminary meeting in London, but Nash-Williams, thinking back to their earlier campaigns, asked whether he would not prefer to visit the site first "so as to get the setting before tackling the building. That, I remember, was your *modus operandi* for Caerleon and Caerwent";[27] and Alan agreed. In due course sketches were in the post. In a letter accompanying an early one, Alan writes:

> "I have put a lot of queries in the margin, & probably other points will occur to you. I hope you will be quite ruthless in yr. criticism as I am sure that is the best way to get satisfactory results. This should make a good picture, I think, & there are possibilities of getting a lot of interest into the surrounding countryside ..."[28]

Nash-Williams at Llantwit was one of the first excavators to identify some "attractive stone finials that adorned the roofs of the buildings as shown (in the pencilled notes) on the villa-plan";[29] decorative features for which he listed parallels recovered elsewhere (Lowther 1976, 40). These found their place in the drawing; and also I notice, although I have found no discussion of the point, three stone chimney stacks, two of which smoke discreetly. This drawing was one which pleased my father very much; indeed it feels substantial as if these buildings truly sat as depicted in the landscape, occupying that air and space. Nash-Williams's dating of the villa has since been adjusted; had there been an opportunity, my father would have amended the drawing to incorporate these changes as in other instances he did as knowledge moved forward.

His post-war work for the National Museum of Wales became intermittent – he had, in any case, too many other calls on his time – but it did include two further town scenes of Roman Caerwent, which were brought to completion shortly before Nash-Williams's death. It is interesting to compare these with their pre-war predecessors and to observe an increase of technical assurance and their warmth of tone. However, their gestation was painful. It began well enough, in December 1953, with Alan replying

FIG. 85. *Llantwit Major Roman Villa, South Glamorgan* (1949). Gouache, watercolour, pen & ink, 61 × 76.5 cm
(AMGUEDDFA CYMRU – NATIONAL MUSEUM WALES)

to the commissioning letter and relating how his own life was developing:

> "I have had an interesting time lately: in the summer from July to October I was busy on an enormous decoration at a new school at Warwick [Myton School, see Fig. 44] & now I am doing a painting at Magdalen College of the dons having their port & biscuits. I am doing various drawings too so I can't complain. We are all well – we have 2 little boys now. I hope you & your family are flourishing ..."[30]

One of these Caerwent drawings shows a Romano-Celtic temple complex in a block adjacent to the forum. In their first discussions they had settled on a high but acute viewpoint which would isolate this group of buildings; and a surviving pencil sketch shows how it would have been arranged, with some lines of perspective added. But at an early stage Alan's love of a wooded horizon, a helicopter's eye view, intervened; and, although he feared he was exceeding his instructions, he asked permission to include, beyond the temple, nearly a quarter of the town plus the town wall. Nash-Williams found no difficulty in agreeing to this, as follows:

> "The important thing, if possible (but it may *not* be!), is to bring out the idea of the chessboard lay-out of the town in squarish building-blocks. For this purpose, houses can be conjectured and inserted (in one or two stories) in the unexcavated spaces, as deemed necessary. One point of detail: most of the *private* houses at Caerwent had roofs of hexagonal stone roofing-slabs (of Old Red Sandstone). But it will be quite all right to use tiled roofs in cases where you think it specially desirable from a pictorial point of view. The public buildings had better all have tiled roofs."[31]

As 1954 advanced, they exchanged the usual analytical letters and lettered sketches until communication began to be hampered by outside pressures: by Alan's awareness that he would be spending much of the summer abroad, in Turkey and Greece, where Bruce Ingram was sending him to make, among other things, preparatory drawings at several excavation sites for future reconstructions. For his part, at Caerleon, Nash-Williams had his hands full directing a rescue dig.

As a template for the Romano-Celtic temple at Caerwent, Nash-Williams had supplied a German reconstruction of a temple of similar type – I think the model reproduced in a Wheeler article (Wheeler 1928, 304 fig. 2) and again in R. G. Collingwood's *Roman Britain* (1932, fig. 56). In this, the outer walls are of columns supporting a lean-to roof, which covers a walkway surrounding the sanctuary or central holy place. But at Caerwent there are unexplained external buttresses to these outer walls and some internal strengthening too. Studying these, Alan wrote, just before he went away:

> "The only point really is that I think the *side* walls of the temple shd. be solid & *not* with isolated columns as in the German illustration you lent me, that's really all, & I am proceeding with the drawing like that – I'm sure it's right, but I did not like to diverge too much from the illustration without telling you. But I will go ahead now ..."[32]

To which Nash-Williams replied:

> "I am still not clear why you feel that the side walls of the temple should be carried up solid, instead of being shown as sleeper walls carrying full-length columns, as they almost certainly did. I fear that it would not be safe to depart so drastically from the German reconstruction, unless there was infallible evidence for such a departure. I shall be very interested to know what the difficulty is ..."[33]

The summer followed. Back home in November 1954, invigorated after a memorable journey, Sorrell sent another sketch. He had by now conceded the argument for columns (although, to my eye, some strategically placed foliage in the final drawing hints at his reservations):

> "The intervals [between the columns supporting the side walls] will be *slightly larger* than the others, & I am now *disregarding* the internal

buttresses – & the external ones too, & bringing them just up to the levels of the low wall, though I'm still wondering what their function cd. be! One other point –- & this was raised with those earlier [pre-war] drawings I did for you – what about chimneys in the houses' roofs. Do you think they had any? I can't imagine just holes to let the smoke out. There's a lot of *roof* in these drawings …"[34]

Already in this correspondence, nearly two decades after the question had first been raised, Nash-Williams had agreed that, where there was evidence of hypocausts, smoke cowls capping the wall flues could be shown. They were to be small and cylindrical with conical tops, with square vents below, all in one piece and made of tile. The use of tile would explain why, when they fell and smashed in the last days of Roman Britain and became mingled with thousands of broken roof tiles, their excavated fragments should not have been more frequently identified as such.[35] But Alan's concern now was with Roman town buildings, assumed by the excavator to be houses, which were without hypocausts. How would they have been heated in English (and Welsh) winters in the chilly north and west? Months passed, the question was left hanging and, waiting for it to be taken up and resolved, Alan pushed on with other work, putting the drawings aside until it was. Finally his pleas rose almost to anguish:

> "Regarding the chimneys: it's the building without hypocausts, furnaces & wall flues that I'm thinking of cf. the long buildings alongside the temple. I'm sure they did not have furnaces etc. but I do feel they must have had some heating arrangements, & therefore (I suppose) chimneys, holes-in-the-roof, or something like that [sketch with three options] … I can see the difficulty if there is no structural evidence for fireplaces & so on … P.S. The priest's house is an example of what I mean. No evidence I suppose of wall flues etc, but surely it must have been heated somehow. I just can't imagine a brazier only!"[36]

This provoked a swift and, I'm sure, welcome response:

> "I think that it will be quite legitimate to show chimneys on the Caerleon [sic] houses in the way that you suggest – similarly on the Priest's house. One would have expected the latter to have had a hypocaust-system, but apparently the excavators found none. The only thing to do, therefore, is, as you suggest, to show chimneys, placed, I should say, at the summit of the roof. I cannot find that any of the authorities face up to the problem of smoke-dispersal from ordinary Roman buildings. Perhaps, therefore, we had better not make our chimneys too obtrusive!"[37]

Much later, Alan would comment rather gloomily on the "colonial-type dullness" of Roman Britain:

> "The skyline must have been dull too, with no chimneys to break the long horizontals – very like those dreadful contemporary housing estates which

130　ALAN SORRELL: THE MAN WHO CREATED ROMAN BRITAIN

are now ruining the outskirts of our towns and villages. Such skylines demand clouds above them; perhaps the foamy shapes of cumulus clouds are means by which some sort of artistic unity can be achieved ..." (Mark Sorrell 1981, 25)

But this verdict contradicts his practice. Sanctioned by Nash-Williams, in this drawing of Roman Caerwent he did for the first time introduce small Sorrell-generated smoke boxes with louvred sides sitting on the roof ridge. Subsequently he spread the type, apparently designed and made to his own specifications, to the rooftops of other towns of recreated Roman Britain – to Wroxeter and St Albans and London's Cripplegate Fort among others – in a token creative act which stubborn logic seemed to justify.

But chronologically I have run a little too far forward. Now I should like to go back a bit. Cyril Fox had little direct input into my father's drawings of Roman Wales. At about the time that these two of Caerwent were nearing completion (1955) he wrote a friendly letter, lamenting the distance which, post-war, their respective homes had put between them since the Fox family had moved, following his retirement, from Cardiff to Exeter, and my father from London to isolation in Essex:

> "Dear Alan,
>
> How nice to hear from you! There is no artist of my acquaintance with your grasp of the historical process & vivid power of recreating the past. And I have always regretted the perversity which led you to dig yourself in at Thundersley – just because a barbarous God thought it a nice place. Why, it's on the periphery of Britain! ..."[38]

Pre-war, while he was still in a position of influence, Fox had been keen to commission for the museum as many Sorrell reconstructions as possible. No sooner was one set completed than he was pressing for another. In June 1939 he wrote: "Both Nash-Williams and I look forward ultimately to having a very wonderful and extensive series from your able mind and brush."[39]

And a month later:

> "Nash-Williams and I feel that, at the moment, we have exhausted the importance of Roman Britain, since we have six drawings by you; and there is the whole field of prehistory to be attacked! There are two or three of the great chambered tombs in Wales which have been completely excavated, and we feel that a drawing of one of these would be a very fine thing. I finished a year ago the complete excavation of a round barrow of very elaborate construction – here again is a fit subject for your scholarly and imaginative pen. Thirdly, Nash-Williams has investigated one of our great hill-forts – Llanmelin. I can imagine nothing more exciting than a drawing of such. Will you come down sometime before the summer is over, stay with us, and let me drive you round to look at these places? ..."[40]

FIG. 86.

Top: a. Caerwent, Gwent: preliminary drawing of Romano-Celtic temple complex (1955). Pencil, ink & gouache, watercolour, 29.5 × 47.5 cm
(IMAGE COURTESY OF LISS LLEWELLYN FINE ART)

Bottom: b. *Caerwent: Romano-Celtic Temple Complex*, the final drawing (1955). Watercolour, pen & ink, chalks/charcoal & gouache, 70 × 91.5 cm
(AMGUEDDFA CYMRU – NATIONAL MUSEUM WALES)

FIG. 87. *Roman London: The Cripplegate Fort* (1966). Mural for the City of London Police Headquarters. Pen & ink, gouache, watercolour & chalks, 71.12 × 120.65 cm (WHEREABOUTS OF ORIGINAL UNKNOWN, ASA COPY)

Years later he would express regret, a mark of his regard, that circumstances had made it impossible for him to go further and fill the archaeological section of the museum with Alan's reconstruction paintings.[41] Already, in August 1939, the times were not propitious; and within days of their conference at the prehistoric sites, Britain was at war. Alan, living and working in London, was determined to honour his commitment to Fox, although he expected at any moment to be put to military camouflage work. With cynical detachment he noted on all sides – in particular, I suspect, among his colleagues at the College – eruptions of civilian self-importance: "Tin helmets have broken out here, like the measles, & everybody looks extremely tough!" (NMW 1937–*c*.1960, *c*. 18 Sept. 1939).

But there was a lull, indeed the College remained open until the autumn of 1940; and, uninterrupted, the reconstructions went ahead.

One of them is of Tinkinswood, a Neolithic chambered tomb near Barry in the Vale of Glamorgan. In the burial place, under a massive capstone, excavators at the beginning of the 20th century had discovered the remains of about 50 individuals, supposed to be members of the same tribe or village laid there at different times, together with flints, pots and animal bones. The drawing, which Sorrell and Fox planned together, would show an interment ceremony, the details of which owed much more to conjecture than to hard evidence.

Sorrell's first sketch underlies his second, which has been drawn over it and the "cartoon" stage is missing; but a sequence of changes, large and small, can be surmised from their correspondence:

[AS, *c*.18 Sept 1939] "Are the trees & the fence alright in the Tinkinswood sketch? Artistically they are important."

[CF, 10 Nov] "I went to Tinkinswood this morning and stood in the correct position. Here, then, the proportions of the great capstone were as shown in red. You must halve the approach, bringing (we suggest) the ritual-killing of the ox down towards the right bottom corner. We do not object to women and children, let them be grasping a sheep by the wool, and have a goat or two by a thong! Delete the oak palings – no evidence for this. It will enable you to show the return dry-walling, giving the line of the cairn on the left of the picture ... Don't forget the costume details including the knotted-string skirts! ... We have no evidence for shields; but a stone axe in a belt [sketch] is in order, also spears as you have them."

[AS, *c*. 17 Nov] "I am sending you, herewith, the corrected sketch ... Would the man sacrificing the ox *cut its throat*, or stab it in the back of the neck? Do you think the people in the foreground would be interested in the killing (as shewn) or awed by the funeral? – I suppose the *children* would, in any period of history, like the former ... I will remember about the various points of costume, especially the knotted skirts! ... This question of the *degree of awe* shewn by the onlookers is rather important but I suppose it is a very difficult point to decide?"

[CF, 28 Nov] "Both Nash-Williams and I agree that your sketch, in scale and general character, which is all that can be discussed at the present stage is excellent. So go ahead with the full-scale preliminary drawing! ... As for your particular points: – (a) Cut the ox's throat. (b) Children interested in Ox, adults in funeral! Very peaceful here."

[AS, *c*. 15 Dec] "I am sending you herewith a preliminary sketch of Tinkinswood ... This picture has of course far greater possibilities than the Roman ones – as a picture I mean –& I am greatly looking forward to doing it." [On a sheet enclosed with this letter are Alan's detailed suggestions, as follows; Fox's replies are in brackets] I have assumed that the roofslab was originally a more perfect rectangle than it is now, & I have drawn it so in order to give it the cornice-like effect you mentioned when we were on the site. The corner marked 'A' is the part I mean especially. ('Alright: but make edges irregular.') ... The group marked 'D' are supposed to be on the look out for enemies – this also gives me a chance to shew front views of costume. ('Agreed.'). Two women following the bier are tearing their hair – is that alright? ('Excellent.') The people would have straight blackish hair? ('Yes.')".

[CF, 16 Dec] "Nash-Williams and I have been studying your excellent detailed sketch. The whole thing is shaping up admirably ... But we feel that in the process of developing artistic balance and human interest, we have allowed ourselves to lose sight, in some degree, of what must have been very dignified and very serious ritual ... We suggest white-robed priests –*coarsely woven whitish-grey woollen* – with gold rings round their necks and on their arms, as the best means ... Priestly figures, rigid, on either side of procession (the procession, and women tearing their hair in the procession, and the stone removers, are *excellent*). Priestly figure superintending sacrifice with a boy by his side (boy on his left). Sacrifice up a little; show blade of bronze (yellow) knife. Attitude of sacrificer excellent ..."

[AS, 12 Jan 1940] "I am returning herewith the amended Tinkinswood drawings ... Although I realise that the period was long before Druids had been thought of, I imagine the priestly figures *would* approximate to the Druid type. I should like the acolyte to be *handing* the priest something – can you suggest a likely object? – a bowl for the ox's blood? ('Blood-bowl Ty Isaf type'). The priests will be dressed in whitey coloured garments & the people (dirty coloured skin & black hair) will be in dull earthy red, ochre & blue. ('dull earthy red & brown', AS's 'blue' deleted.) I hope the 'feeling' of the picture is more appropriate now, that was always the difficulty ... Would any parts of the tomb be whitened? ('No.') Some of the men would wear furs? ('Yes.')"

[CF, 17 Jan] "I do not know what the Druid type is, but I have no doubt that the Priests would approximate thereto! I dare not suggest a *metal* fillet, but I do not see why they should not have one to keep their hair tidy – a brown or ochre woven fabric tied in a knot at the back might do ... The people should be, as you suggest in your letter, in dull earthy red or ochre, clothes; I add brown, but we exclude *blue*! ... Some of the men certainly would wear furs, as you suggest, but not finished like Révillon Frères! A very good idea of yours for the acolyte to hold a blood-bowl; I have drawn the shape of it – a neolithic bowl – on another sheet." (Fig. 88c)

[CF, 18 Jan] "Grimes gave us a lecture last night on chambered tombs. He said all *angles were rounded*. [diagram showing left foreground] So please make angle at X in your drawing a continuous curve of small slabs rather than a quoined angle."

[AS, 2 Feb] "The Tinkinswood drawing is now about half finished & looks well, I think. Do you think any of the men would wear *hats*. I have no note of hats in my sketch book, but vaguely recollect seeing a photograph of one in yr. book – something like this [sketch], made of cloth, I suppose. I know this is only a detail, but such little things can help a picture very much. In the Roman pictures I had *too much* information and in these rather too little! ... The women – some of them – wore this sort of thing, I know [sketch], a sort of bandeau with a net over the top part."

FIG 88.

Clockwise from top right:

a. Tinkinswood, South Glamorgan: interment ceremony, first sketch (1939). Pencil & gouache
(IMAGE COURTESY OF LISS LLEWELLYN FINE ART)

b. outline drawing of a Neolithic bowl by Cyril Fox, from a letter (1940, see text). Pencil
(ASA)

c. *Tinkinswood, South Glamorgan: interment ceremony at the Neolithic chambered tomb.* The final drawing (1940). Gouache, ink, chalks & watercolour, 50.5 × 66 cm
(AMGUEDDFA CYMRU – NATIONAL MUSEUM WALES)

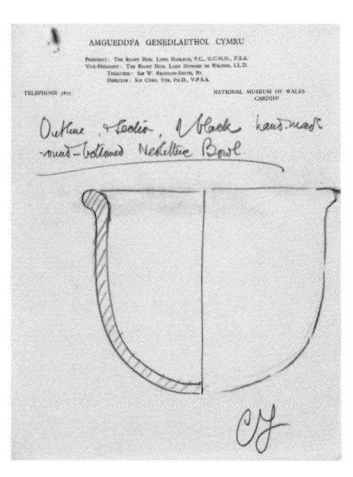

> [CF, 3 Feb] "Savory and I appreciate your difficulty – the absence of information about dress in the Neolithic times in Britain – but we must just accept it. I do not think we can accept either a hat or a woman's hairnet such as you sketch. I am afraid you must make both the men's and women's hair tousled and/or lank ..."
>
> [AS, 21 Feb] "I have just completed Tinkinswood & I will despatch it to you this week ..."
>
> [AS, 18 July, asking for temporary return of completed drawing] "I'm sorry to give you this trouble, but I am anxious to make some changes which I think will give the picture more truth."[42]

By which he means: not insights into the unknowable but greater lifelikeness in the modelling of the imagined figures he has at command, his aim being to convince.

> [AS, 27 July 1940, returning amended drawing] "You will notice I have redrawn practically all the figures. One of the difficulties is to know *when* to use a model & originally I tried to do without with a result not at all to my satisfaction. But I think it is now really greatly improved ..."[43]

During the war, Cyril Fox directed several "rescue" digs. Most archaeological activity was not, as might be supposed, at sites threatened or wrecked by enemy action but followed an unprecedented take-up of land for military and war-related purposes: for new factories, camps, airfields and battle training areas. Levelling the ground for an airfield, for example, meant obliterating all human features and undulations in a landscape. During the war there were over 16,000 such developments: for hard-pressed archaeologists the criterion for intervention was often the presence of a site identified as ancient on Ordnance Survey maps (O'Neil 1948, 21). The losses were incalculable, will be forever unknown, but there were discoveries too: as by Professor Grimes who, seconded to the Ministry of Works for the duration, famously brought to light an Iron Age "temple" ahead of the construction of a new runway at Heathrow in 1944 (Grimes 1948). Fox movingly recalled his feelings at one such site in Wales on the last full day of excavation:

> "the pair of bulldozers lining up at 5.45 p.m. in hungry anticipation; and his astonishment when, having busily packed everything into the car, he turned to look his last on the dumps and trenches in which six weeks of active life had been spent, [and] saw only an expanse of brown muddy soil like the rest of the future airfield, and the giants who had compassed this levelling within half an hour roaring off to pastures new." (*The Times*, 27 April 1949, 5)

Fox's last collaboration with Alan occurred during this period. On a remote upland in the Black Mountains, far from any scene of conflict or present

FIG. 89. *Maen Madoc, Powys: Dervacus's Son Inspecting his Father's Monument* (1940). Gouache, pen & ink, chalks & watercolour, 26.5 × 37.5 cm (AMGUEDDFA CYMRU – NATIONAL MUSEUM WALES)

disturbance, a stone had fallen. It was a tall pillar, known locally as *Maen Madoc* (Madoc's Stone) but commemorating a different unknown person of much earlier date. On it is carved in debased capitals, some of them upside down, some back to front, the Latin inscription: DERVACI FILIUS IUSTI IC IACIT (*Dervacus, Justus's son, lies here*). In June 1940, in the same month as a British army in retreat was being lifted off the beaches at Dunkirk, Fox was asked by the Ministry to re-erect this monument. He went further, investigating its situation, taking photographs, drawing plans, compiling a report. Then, on impulse, the material having been set up in proof, he sent the lot to Alan, saying:

> "I have just finished excavating a site of some interest. A famous inscribed stone *Sub-Roman*, circa 550 A.D., on a wild moorland in Breconshire (Fig. 1) at a height of 1400 feet, recently fell. H.M.O.W. asked me to supervise the work of erection. Now, I discovered (a) the original site of the monument, and (b) the 1st century Roman road on the edge of which it was placed! Fig. 3 and Fig. 4 show the *margins of the Roman stone paving* in five places ... The men are placed to show the scale of the road which is 16 feet broad. It is composed of small and large flattish boulders and pebbles, the larger being 12–20 inches in breadth. I think Fig. 3 is the best point of view. Now would you make a SKETCH (not a finished picture) *for me personally* showing the stone as it was in the 6th Century, with a little packhorse traffic on the road and two or three well dressed *Sub-Romans* (young gent in battered toga with a touch of aristocratic purple) looking at the recently erected monument to Father? The stone is a warm red sandstone: the moorland grey-green. The road material will be a bit grassy, traffic being in decay, and they removed a bit of the road to put the stone up and left the debris lying near!!"[44]

There was no discussion, in this case, between artist and archaeologist. The draft report (Fox 1940) and his letter, sent on 26 June, constituted Alan's evidence; he was working on the sketch around 18 July, and returned it complete within a few days. But there are several points of interest here. The clumsy lettering on the pillar, which is itself unshaped (so far removed from the stately monuments which the Romans erected when they held sway in Britain) is eloquent; as is the dedicator's decision to place it within the cobbles of a fading Roman road. The drawing depicts, in other words, a shadowy post-Roman world, heroic but fleeting, a world of impending

FIG. 90. *Via Appia* (1970). Pen & ink, ink washes, 26.8 × 21.4 cm Produced for the book *Imperial Rome* by Anthony Birley and Alan Sorrell published by Lutterworth Press 1970 (ASA)

catastrophe. But in the minds of these horsemen enough of the Roman heritage remained for them to recall that their forefathers commemorated the worthy dead in tombs raised beside highways – like those improbable ones crowding either side of the untarmacadamed *Via Appia* leading south from Rome along which my father and other students walked one moonlit night in 1930, a night which haunted his imagination (see also Fig. 20):

> "It was only when they had left the pale round Cecilia Metella tomb behind that they began to savour the lonely beauty of the night and scene. For a time they could hear distant town noises, but now it was only the baying of a dog, and once the far away jingling of carts, and the varying notes of their own footsteps as they walked, now on the stone Via Appia, and now, softly, on the grass borders ... The moon began to decline about two o'clock and it sank at last into the pale mist that came creeping gently round the ruins, making them huge and sinister and leaving the tops of the stone pines hanging like great bats flying on their secret nocturnal journeys ..." (Sorrell *c.* 1938, 291)[45]

So many lines and connections are suggested in one small drawing.

Fox liked it:

"Thank you very much for the charming drawing – with a touch of the sinister about it in keeping with its period & the harsh countryside. Pray tell me what fee I am to send you."[46]

To which Alan replied:

"It was a pleasure to commemorate Dervacus for you & of course there will be 'no charge' –that, I think, is the technical term! You & Aileen have shewed me so much kindness that I am glad to be able to do such little things for you – I hope there will be others later on." (ASA, *c.* 3 Aug. 1940)

Aileen Fox in her memoirs (Fox 2000, 102) remembered taking my father by car to visit the site above Ystradfellte. I am sure she did; but in January or February 1941, when he was already in uniform, he had still not seen it,[47] so this journey most probably took place years later, after the war. The drawing stands alone, a product of his informed imagination.

Notes

1 "Art in the service of archaeology" in *The Times Educational Supplement* 21 June 1968, 2079.
2 "All the discoveries of the 'diggers', admirably reproduced, find their way into the *Illustrated London News* …" (*The Times* 5 May 1950, 5c).
3 ASA, KK to AS, 19 Oct. (1937).
4 As note 3.
5 Kenyon and Alan worked on a reconstruction of Jericho for the Festival of Britain (Fig. 41b), a subject they revisited for the *ILN* (19 May 1956); and on Roman Sabratha (*ILN* 29 March 1952); and Alan consulted her for his drawings for an illustrated Bible (1969). In that context he wrote: "I have not forgotten that it was your kind help which set me going with reconstruction drawings – you may remember the Jewry Wall at Leicester!"(ASA, 21 Nov. 1967).
6 Wheeler 1956, *passim*; and see, for example, Cyril Fox: "British Archaeology when I began was ignorant of or indifferent to fundamentals …" (Scott-Fox 2002, 32)
7 W. F. Grimes to Elizabeth Sorrell in a letter of condolence, recalled that, since his first contact with Alan had been at the National Museum of Wales in the mid-1930s (in ASA, Grimes's earliest letter is dated 20 Aug. 1937): "I can probably claim to be his oldest co-worker in the archaeological field. I admired and respected him as an artist & enjoyed his gentle kindly humour as a man … you may like to remember that his work has lasting value & has given – & will give – continuing pleasure & enlightenment to a lot of people, by no means all of them archaeologists like me." (ASA, 24 Dec. 1974).
8 He noted with approval a review of this painting in *The Scotsman*: "Prince Charles Edward is none of your romantic adventurers. In fact he is almost non-existent, a mere flick of the brush in one of the wildest storms ever depicted since 'Mad' Martin was at his maddest" (ASA, 31 March 1956).
9 *Cf.* S. E. Rigold's introduction to *Living History*: "On the other hand, [Sorrell] has avoided that false, and all too common, historical-pageant verisimilitude, produced by posing figures in exaggerated postures and fashions; for living history is not the same as staged history." (Sorrell 1965, 8).
10 From typescript of speech given at a seminar at the Institute of Archaeology, London, March 1972, on the reconstruction of Roman buildings (ASA).

11   As note 1.
12   As note 10.
13   As note 1.
14   "You will be glad to hear that I wrote to Sir Cyril Fox and heard from him the other day. He and his wife are extraordinarily kind ..." Sorrell & Tanner 1944–7, early June 1945; "I'd like you to meet these people [the Foxes], they've helped me a lot in the past and I think they will again." *Ibid. c.* 6 Aug. 1946.
15   ASA, AF to AS, undated (early 1938) commenting on his aerial view of Caerwent: "I must tell you how much I like Caerwent – you have got that lovely watery atmosphere of the west in your greens and blues ... Obviously it is a picture in which it is going to be fun to walk about in (like Breughel's) [.] I haven't had time to fully explore it, because it has been sitting about in various peoples' rooms ... Everybody seems pleased with it – I hope you are, and enjoy doing it, rather than it being a dull duty for L.S.D. ..."
16   NMW 1937–*c*.60, CF to AS 19, 23 April 1937.
17   Quotations from an AS letter seen by Dykes in NMW and since mislaid; it must date from early summer 1937.
18   Sorrell (*c.* 1962, 116), describing Sinclair Hood at Emporio, Chios, 1954: "Always the first to march away to the sunbaked excavations, directing, digging and encouraging, he drove his team in the kindest and most relentless way. He impressed me as being continually wrestling with problems which were very nearly, but not quite insoluble ... Therefore, I postponed my usual cross-examination until a later date, and then, with the greatest kindness, he answered all my questions, and went to a great deal of trouble to help me out of the pitfalls into which I had fallen, or would have fallen, without him."
19   The four Southend panels (reproduced together in Llewellyn & Sorrell 2013, 54–5) also had a high viewpoint to which, in that case, their tall narrow shape, designed to fit between windows, predisposed him.
20   An early instance comes in a letter from Nash-Williams concerning the legionary fortress at Caerleon: "With regard to your query about the continuation of the road from the rear gate of the fortress, it is unfortunately impossible to decide definitively what happened to it, as there is no evidence. The best plan, therefore, would be, if possible, to fade it out (?by means of trees or shadows) beyond the point to which you have already carried it ..." (ASA, 20 March 1939).
21   ASA, CF to AS, 4 Oct. (1937).
22   ASA, N-W to AS, 23 Oct. 1937.
23   ASA, N-W to AS, 26 Oct. 1937. Alan and his first wife had just returned from a holiday in Italy. The reference is presumably to a diagrammatic drawing, *Exterior of Roman Villa*) in Quennell & Quennell (1924, fig. 84), which has four chimney stacks on the roof ridge.
24   *Cf.* a passage in Sorrell *c.* 1938, 97: "The new day was stormy, with great clouds moving majestically across the sky and promising rain ... The atmosphere was very clear and objects had the appearance of super-reality in that they seemed more definitely solid than usual, with an added quality of harshness which perhaps is inseparable from any form of intensity ..."
25   "... I must admit that I have often been intimidated by the extraordinary profusion of technical terms and a professional jargon which, for me at any rate, becomes a kind of smoke screen, obscuring rather than revealing the subject of the exercise." (Mark Sorrell 1981, 22).
26   NMW 1937–*c*.60, N-W to AS, 26 Oct. 1948; AS to N-W, undated, replying.
27   NMW 1937–*c*.60, N-W to AS, 10 March 1949.
28   NMW 1937–*c*.60, AS to N-W, 10 May 1949.

29 NMW 1937–c.60, N-W to AS, 9 April 1949.
30 NMW 1937–c.60, AS to N-W, 1 Dec. 1953.
31 NMW 1937–c.60, N-W to AS, 2 June 1954.
32 NMW 1937–c.60, AS to N-W, 2 July 1954.
33 NMW 1937–c.60, N-W to AS, 7 July 1954. The outer wall is now believed to have been solid: Brewer 1993, 46.
34 NMW 1937–c.60, AS to N-W undated ?Nov 1954.
35 NMW 1937–c.60, N-W to AS, 2, 15 June 1954; Lowther 1976, 37.
36 NMW 1937–c.60, AS to N-W, 2 April 1955.
37 NMW 1937–c.60, N-W to AS, 4 April 1955.
38 ASA, CF to AS, 1 Feb. ?1955. My father explained to us that the the name "Thundersley" meant "the upland pastures of Thor". The rector of the day, the Rev E. A. B. Maley, to whom much seemed portentous, put in print his observation that thunderstorms, approaching majestically along the valley of the Thames, habitually shattered all around his parish, but almost never over it (Maley 1937, 49). This was pleasing; and after lengthy discussion and dozens of failed choices, in 1947 our parents cheerfully decided to call our deconsecrated Peculiar People's chapel "Thor's Mead" – a quaintness which lived on (to my no small embarrassment at school) till house numbers came in.
39 ASA, CF to AS, 27 June 1939.
40 ASA, CF to AS, 20 July 1939.
41 ASA, CF to AS, undated ?1951: "Thank you for your card which – as all your work does – captures the spirit of a given period in the past more completely than any one else's I have ever seen – British or foreign. If I could have carried my Council & staff with me I would have had the most magnificent murals on the Arch[aeological] Gall[ery] walls, that would have added distinct[io]n to NMW for ever. I am so thankful, anyway, that I encouraged you at a time helpful to your development ..."
42 An example of his thoroughgoing nature. Another comes in a letter to my mother (Sorrell & Tanner 1944–7, c. 10 July 1945), telling her that he has just "coolly" turned down the offer of the principalship of an art college at £650 per annum, a post which would have enabled them to live comfortably: "Not really because of *you*, but because I really don't want to get involved in administrative work. I know I shd want to do it properly if I started and I have a horrible businesslike kink wh[ich] only wants a chance to swamp me." Her reply, by return of post, is characteristic: "Oh darling if ever we can marry, I'd rather live in poverty and feel you were free and happy and doing your own work, than live in a respectable house and you a teacher. I couldn't bear that ...".
43 ASA, Letters 10 Nov., 28 Nov., 16 Dec. 1939, 12 Jan., 17 Jan., 18 Jan., 3 Feb. 1940; NMW 1937–c.60, Letters 18 Sept, 17 Nov., 15 Dec. 1939, 2 Feb., 21 Feb., 18 July, 27 July 1940.
44 NMW 1937–c.60, CF to AS 26 June 1940.
45 Apart from *The Appian Way* (1932, see Fig. 19), he revisited the moonlit Via Appia in another historical context in his imaginative composition *Benvenuto Cellini Escaping from Rome* (1949; reproduced in Llewellyn & Sorrell 2013, 178); and again, reworking the 1949 drawing, in *Via Appia* (1972, Kent Education Committee).
46 ASA, CF to AS 30 July 1940.
47 NMW 1937–c.60, AS to CF undated, from RAF Farnborough shortly before being transferred to Medmenham: "I should like to go to the place, it must be fine, in a bleak sort of way".

Chapter 9

Jarlshof, Shetland: a work in progress

ALAN WORKED WITH John Hamilton on reconstruction drawings of Jarlshof (1949–51), Clickhimin (*ILN* 18 May 1957, 812–3), and Clickhimin again (illustrations for the 1967 guide book); they also together produced the book *Saxon England* published in 1970. One reason for the success of this long collaboration was a compatibility of temperament: they laughed at the same things:

> "Lerwick has also had a Viking Congress attended, as the local paper has it, by 'savants' and 'doyens'. I went to one of their meetings and discovered that Evelyn Waugh draws direct from life – down to the small boy who was violently sick at the end of the sixth row. The lecture was on Viking ships and the savants had obviously expended a good deal of time beforehand in formulating their questions – they were lavishly salted with nauticalities 'abaft', 'fore', 'aft', 'starboard', 'larboard' – and concerned possible Greek, Egyptian, Phoenician and Polynesian origins. To all these the Norwegian professor replied 'Alltså ho-ho-ho'. Only one question really baffled him concerning a ship's 'undercarriage' – but it was later discovered that the Philistine who posed it was a former R.A.F. type and was therefore excused." (ASA, JH to AS, 20 July 1950)

Another is that Hamilton, as the excavator, involved himself imaginatively at every stage in the development of the drawings. This was a true partnership with outstanding results.

Jarlshof and Clickhimin are in Shetland, and my father was charmed by the remoteness of their situation: the wide treeless landscape, the transparency of the water, the atmosphere rapidly changing from clarity to murk and back again as rain squalls drove across it. He wrote to my mother in 1949, during his first visit: "I'd love you to come here. It's much nicer than Iceland in all ways."[1] And in the following summer she did go, with their two-year-old son (Richard), some of whose earliest memories are of this place.

Each time Alan stayed at the Spiggie Hotel run by a Miss Burgess. Here are his first impressions from the summer of 1949:

> "Dolphins have been playing in this bay all the afternoon ... Spiggie is about 15 miles south of Lerwick, along a coast road, & I came here & went on to the excavations at a place called Jarlshof. I have been quite busy today, & I think I shall be doing 2 drawings. It is unbelievably quiet here ... I went out for a walk with the archaeologists (4 men!) to look at some old cottages, very like these Viking houses I am to draw. The people are very amiable, the women wear black clothes & black shawls. Outside each cottage is a great stack of peat & there are always some very clean looking sheep grazing near by. The cottage roofs are like a Samuel Palmer drawing, all covered with weeds & long grass. It is the kind of place that would grow on me tremendously I should think."[2]

The connection of old and new, of continuity in the midst of change, is, as I have tried to show, a theme running like a steel thread through my father's work. It informs his imaginative drawings; but he was also constantly searching out present examples for his reconstructions. Thus, to get the feel of the lie of a medieval thatched roof, he would draw the decaying farmhouse at Claydons, near our home on Daws Heath. It was, for him, what bound recorded and unrecorded history together. Hamilton too, in his published work, and in private letters, was intrigued by connections between the verbal, the visual and the found:

> "These boats [the Shetland yawl] are no longer made but two old examples lie down at the 'fisherman's' beach at Spiggie. We have also found the weight stones for a primitive 'steelyard balance' – known as the 'pundler' locally and one or two drawings exist in old books of this subject. Altogether, surrounded by living fossils this is a reconstructionist's paradise."[3]

The reference to boats relates to one of Sorrell's reconstruction drawings of the Viking settlement at Jarlshof, in the foreground of which they cluster, hauled up on a stony beach. Iron clinker nails at the excavation site had attested to their presence; their appearance had to be surmised from other sources. When the drawing (*ILN* 19 May 1951, 808–9) was already far advanced, Hamilton wrote:

> "At last I have completed a study of all the references to small boats in the Icelandic sagas. At that time the 'sexaering' [six-oared fishing boat] appears only very occasionally to have been provided with a sail. Mostly, it was used for a day's or night's fishing, the men rowing to and from the fishing banks or shoals. Therefore if you haven't finished the final sketch could you reduce the number of masts?"[4]

And when he saw a proof in advance of publication, he commented:

"It [the drawing] is really excellent. I was a little troubled about the boats – whether the prows should be higher – but as luck would have it, we discovered an inscribed slate obviously drawn by one Magnus Sorrell with small boats in the foreground and a young cow or bull in the background with a Scandinavian knot in its tail. The prows are cut away in the same fashion as the 'yawls'. So all is well."[5]

A glance at the Jarlshof site map – for it is with Iron Age Jarlshof that we shall be concerned in what follows – shows four periods of habitation which, even in their ground plans, are distinctively expressed: Bronze Age, Iron Age, Viking and a medieval farmhouse, whose high shattered walls dominate the scene. It was with the Viking settlement that they began in 1949, with three drawings – two exteriors and an interior – commissioned by the *Illustrated London News*. At an early stage Hamilton reported:

"everyone is highly delighted with the drawings. The Educational Authorities are extremely interested and threaten to make a film of the settlement. So, if on your next visit to Shetland you find us all parading about in tin helmets and waving blood drenched swords you will know what is afoot."[6]

Hamilton at this time was Assistant Inspector of the Scottish branch of the Ministry of Works, and was keen to persuade his department, as

FIG. 91. Alan Sorrell sketching in Shetland (1949)
(ASA)

FIG. 92. *Jarlshof, Shetland: the Viking settlement, boats drawn up* (1949). *Illustrated London News*
(WHEREABOUTS OF ORIGINAL UNKNOWN, ASA COPY)

the excavations continued, to take over the commissioning role and make further drawings possible. But there were delays. Some were internal: in one letter he mentions "the discussions and reorganisation following the Gowers Report", which had appeared in June 1950 and was meant to establish demarcation lines between the Ministry and the National Trust.[7] My father's diary too was crowded in 1950, with three murals to complete for the Festival of Britain: his other commitments that year included a notable drawing, with Grahame Clark, of the Mesolithic hunter-fisher site at Star Carr (*ILN* 3 Feb 1951, 172–3).

A new season commenced at Jarlshof. The archaeologists had now moved on to uncover the Iron Age settlement with its wheelhouses and broch tower, half of which had been eroded by the sea. Hamilton's advocacy continued. In May 1951 he wrote:

> "The weather here is bitterly cold with showers of driving sleet. However, the finds have been exceptionally good. Next month we hope to begin excavating out the courtyard surrounding the broch tower. This should be most spectacular and I hope it will be possible to have a reconstruction made. I have been trying to impress on the Ministry the desirability of having these drawings made for the department. If all goes well the Jarlshof broch project would be the first thus giving you an opportunity of coming to some arrangement for the future. Will keep you advised of developments."[8]

FIG. 93. Jarlshof: ground plan from official guide book (1953)
(HISTORIC ENVIRONMENT SCOTLAND)

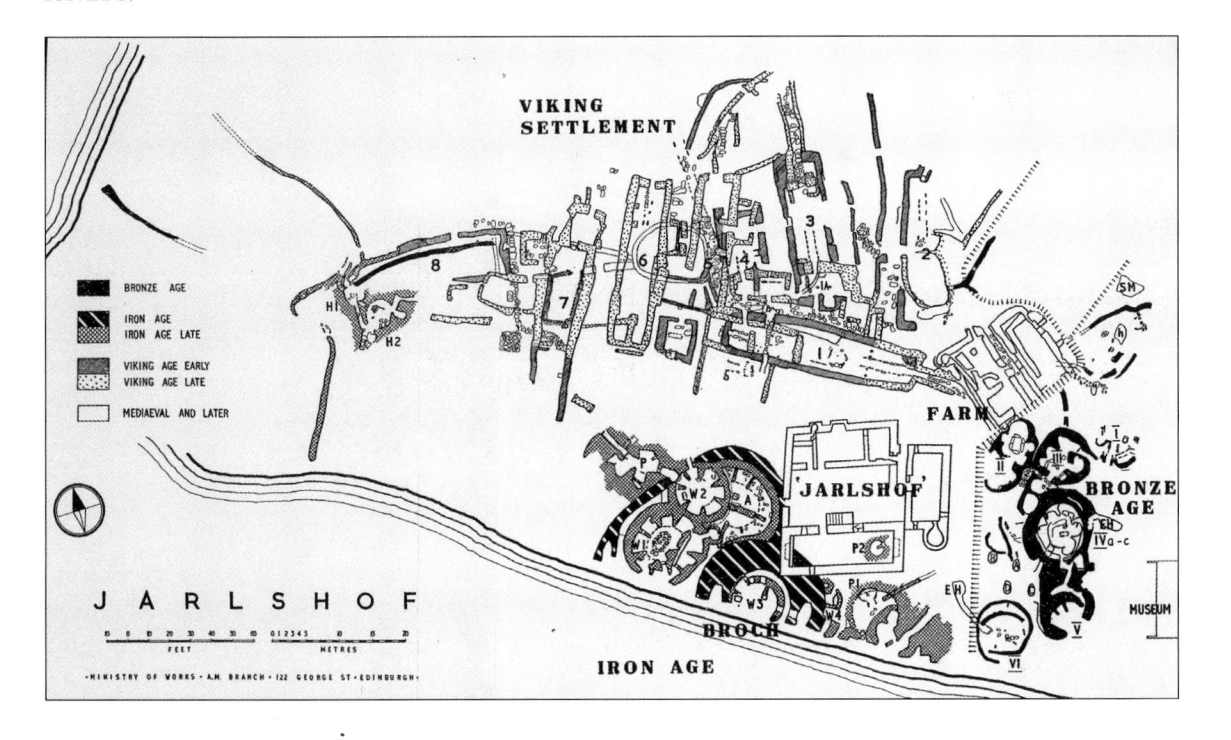

At Mousa, an island off the east coast of Shetland Mainland, a broch tower stands spectacularly alone in a stark landscape. It had been consolidated in the early 20th century to a height of about 40 ft (12.2 m); but at the same time traces of the beehive huts which once surrounded it had been cleared away. In other words, Mousa's splendid isolation is deceptive: careful, patient excavation at Jarlshof revealed what, at the other site, had been missed or disregarded. On 21 June 1951 Hamilton wrote to Alan:

> "I had hoped that it would have been possible to let you have a definite line on the earlier Iron Age village ere this. Unfortunately the structures are proving extremely obstinate and instead of a simple courtyard with well behaved inner pent roof we are running into a tangle of 3 to four periods – all very difficult when some 15ft of superimposed earth has to be removed before anything can be seen at all. I very much doubt whether we shall have the sequence worked out by the time I leave for Norway at the beginning of next month and a return session will be necessary in September." [Alan Sorrell Archive]

But when September came, Hamilton was able to report success in persuading the Ministry to commission Alan to make a reconstruction drawing of the Iron Age settlement; welcome news, which enabled artist and archaeologist soon to meet again at Jarlshof. This was Alan's first such commission from a government department – a forerunner and precedent which went unnoticed in London five years later (until Scotland reminded them of it) when the desirability of employing him to make reconstructions of English and Welsh subjects was being discussed.[9] The Scottish Office paid £35, which was £10 more than he would receive initially from London. Copyright in both cases was taken by the Crown. (Alan used to say, at home, that had he received a fraction of a farthing in royalties on every one of the thousands of postcards of his drawings which were to be sold at Ministry sites, and a share of the reproduction fees paid for their repeated use in books and on television, he would have been a wealthy man. He might not then have died in harness.)

On site, he made precise line and wash drawings of the cavernous interiors of the beehive huts excavated from the dunes. As he and Hamilton walked over the ground together, they will have

FIG. 94. Jarlshof: wheelhouse interiors (1951). Pen & ink, ink washes
(SKETCHBOOK F, ASA)

JARLSHOF, SHETLAND: A WORK IN PROGRESS 147

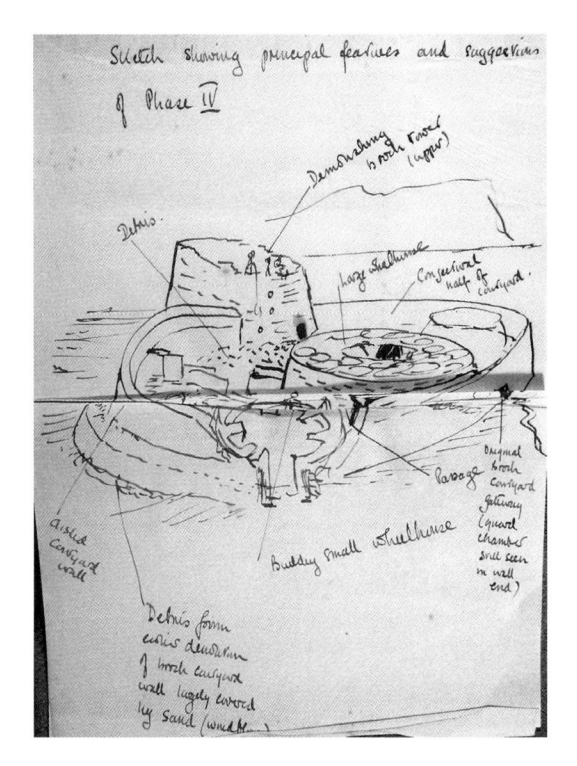

FIG. 95. Jarlshof: outline reconstruction sketch by John Hamilton (1951)
(PASTED INTO SKETCHBOOK F, ASA)

discussed their implications and also decided on a viewpoint. One, with the great massif of Sumburgh Head stretching away behind into the distance, was so fine it almost chose itself.

Hamilton had by this time rationalised the history of the Iron Age settlement into five phases. Phase IV was the one he selected for the drawing: "the most spectacular in the series from the visual point of view."[10] Among the notes which Alan received from him on his return to Essex was a "Sketch showing principal features and suggestions of Phase IV" which is, remarkably, the artist's drawing in embryo as conceived by the archaeologist. (In 1956 Hamilton would do the same for Clickhimin.[11]) It leaves vacant for the present the seaward (destroyed) half of the courtyard which would have later to be filled with conjectural buildings; but it includes a dynamic incident which was not finally used: the 'slighting' of the broch tower (after it had outlived its usefulness) by agriculturists, who throw down lumps of material for use in the dwellings below.[12]

Alan, as always when he had focus and a goal, was thorough and worked fast. Before the end of October he had produced a preliminary drawing (later squared up for enlargement) with all the discrete details, both gathered and supplied, already integrated into a harmonious composition. This marvellous leap towards realisation is the contribution which only he, as an artist, could make (Fig. 96a). Part of the way he does it is by heightening the broch tower to 50ft (15.2m) – which could be justified archaeologically – and by emphasising its dominance with verticals, including, in its opened-up interior, the motif of a ladder-like tier of apertures. (These he had sketched at Mousa, which he and Hamilton had visited by motor boat.[13]) The drawing is labelled with points A to H needing clarification.

Hamilton responds with 11 pages of notes and sketches. He comes immediately to the chief problem which the preliminary drawing had revealed:

> "The most difficult feature to visualise is the roofing on the 'beehives'. On the limited evidence at one's disposal I believe we can add a flat or truncated dome roof [sketch]. It is difficult to decide whether this should be based on a continuation of corbelling up to the central smoke vent [sketch] or whether to introduce a lighter timber roof with turf covering [sketches]. Whichever is chosen, the outside appearance will be approximately the same – because whether timber or stone – roof sods were probably put on against rain seepage etc."

He moves on systematically through other points:

> "D the porch to the small wheelhouse should be omitted and the above doorway entrance inserted [sketch]. The floor in front of the doorway is paved like a path and on either side the mounding sandblow is retained by walling consisting of upright irregular slabs or stones (2′ to 3′) [0.9–0.9 m] in diameter on top of which horizontal masonry is laid for 3 or 4 courses. A wooden door could be shown about 3ft in."

He adds imaginative touches which would have delighted my father's heart:

> "I notice on our monuments in Shetland and the islands that a grey lichen gets a firm hold on the outer stone faces [of walls]. I enclose a photograph of Mousa broch showing this lichen growth on the outer face. In colour this lichen is a light grey-green. We could, I think, remove the 'artificial' appearance of the main courtyard wall top by covering its slightly more broken contours with lichen and grass [sketch]."

And:

> "I wondered whether, instead of the boat on the horizon we couldn't show the peaks of Fair Isle with a beacon signal. If you don't like this idea just dismiss it."[14]

It was entirely typical of my father's nature, if he was not happy about something, to worry about it. As far as this drawing was concerned, it did not matter how the roofs of the beehive huts were supposed to be supported, their appearance in a seagull's eye view was unaffected, but he was concerned with accuracy and with load-bearing practicalities (although he was not a practical man). As a solution he seems have suggested (his letters are missing) an elevated inner ring of wooden posts. Hamilton, put on his mettle, replies with a flourish of scholarly justification:

> "Now as to the wheelhouse roofs. I am enclosing a volume of the Proceedings of the Soc. Antiquaries of Scotland 1903–4. You will find on p 180 Fig 6–7 pictures of what are probably descendants of our wheelhouses. They are of course smaller with an interior diameter of 7–8′ [2.1–2.4 m] against our 20′[6.4 m]. Nevertheless I think you will find them instructive. You might also compare Fig 11A p 188 for a similar structure in the Maritime Alps. There is some evidence to suggest that our wheelhouses may have been introduced from Iberia via Cornwall in the late Iron Age. I think the best solution is to leave only a small smoke vent in the roofs of our wheelhouses [sketch]. This, of course, will totally obscure any view of their interiors – negative from your artistic point of view but oh! so convenient from the archaeological. Will you concede this point?...Very many thanks for your most interesting suggestions concerning the [internal] form of roofs. It is certainly worth bearing these in mind in future excavation of such sites where it may be possible to locate and identify postholes. In the present case– and with the Hebridean and S French examples in mind – I think it better to give the houses a flat conical roof."[15]

FIG. 96.

Top: a. Jarlshof: preliminary drawing of broch and wheelhouse settlement (1951). Pen & ink & ink washes
(COLLECTION OF MARK SORRELL © ESTATE OF ALAN SORRELL)

Bottom: b. *Jarlshof Iron Age Settlement, as it might have appeared about AD 450* (1951). Pen & ink, watercolour & gouache. Size not recorded and original currently unavailable
(HISTORIC ENVIRONMENT SCOTLAND)

Other areas of the drawing where, presumably, my father was seeking help, next receive consideration:

> "I have been unable to get any photographs of sand dunes from our library but include a Forestry Commission pamphlet of sand dunes at Culbin. I trust this will be of use. In the immediate vicinity of the broch where

peat ash & other occupational refuse was thrown it might be expected that grass could grow in the close cropped Shetland way. Along the beach and at some distance from the broch there would be rough couch grass as on dunes [sketch]. *Costumes* This is difficult problem. Presence of weaving combs and spindle whorls & loomweights from Broch & Post-Broch sites suggests *woollen* clothing. No doubt leather capes or mantles. Suggest woollen skull caps, and 'kilts' (no tartan please!). Skin shoes. Woollen shirts with leather overcoats or jackets. At Jarlshof – remote site and presence of stone tools in abundance suggests primitive conditions. Figures should not therefore be too civilised in appearance [sketches]."

This was as much documentation as my father could hope to receive. He now went on confidently with the final drawing and posted it off towards the middle of December. I extract Hamilton's happy reply:

"My dear Sorrell, Just a few lines to express admiration and wonder – your drawing arrived today. It is superb! I think it is the most magnificent of all the Jarlshof drawings. And the tinting adds so much to the texture of the stones, the turf and the sand dunes! I simply cannot take my eyes off it. There are no additions or modifications to be made at all. Congratulations and many thanks – it is a tremendous sensation to see all the niggling archaeological detail & broken ends of an excavation interpreted into an artistic whole and the people brought to life again! ..."[16]

This drawing was produced at a stressful time in the Sorrell household, and in the latent pre-life of the present writer who, although due to arrive, delayed putting in an appearance. A coincidence maybe; but it is my favourite among my father's reconstruction drawings!

Notes

1. ASA, AS to ES undated, *c.* 18 Sept. 1949.
2. ASA, AS to ES undated *c.* 16 Sept. 1949.
3. ASA, JRCH to AS, undated fragmentary letter, probably 1950. See also his article "Viking Life in a Shetland Settlement" (*ILN* 19 May 1951, 806–9). A "Shetland Ness Yole" is included in the parade of British coastal craft in my father's maritime mural for the Festival of Britain (1951).
4. ASA, JRCH to AS 8 Jan. 1951.
5. ASA, JRCH to AS 8 May 1951.
6. ASA, JRCH to AS 16 Dec. 1949.
7. ASA, JRCH to AS 8 Dec. 1950; Thurley 193.
8. ASA, JRCH to AS 8 May 1951.
9. MoW 1956–74: WORK 14/2246, Memo, D. L. Macintyre, 17 July 1957.
10. ASA, JRCH to AS 10 Sept. 1951.
11. ASA, Sketchbook F, sketch affixed pp 8–9.
12. ASA, Pasted into sketchbook F between pp 2–3.
13. ASA, AS to ES undated *c.* 3 Oct. 1951.
14. ASA, JRCH to AS 31 Oct. 1951.
15. ASA, JRCH to AS undated (after 23 Nov. 1951).
16. ASA, JRCH to AS 17 Dec. 1951.

Chapter 10

Years of achievement

FOR 25 CROWDED YEARS after the war, until his death, Alan was in demand to produce reconstruction drawings. Other forms of representation continued to be important to him – topographical drawings for example, including three series whose significance for him lay in the "edginess" of their subjects, being threatened with or undergoing violent change: the walls of Constantinople (1954; see Fig. 62), the temples and villages of Nubia (1962; see Fig. 61), and every stage in the construction of a nuclear power station in Somerset's green acres (1957–65; see Figs 46 & 60). He also carried out schemes of mural decoration in church (see Fig. 43), school (see Fig. 44), factory canteen and other public buildings, and imaginative compositions, enjoying such changes of scale and application: indeed he said he would die artistically if he were not able to work in more than one direction.[1] But it was from the reconstructions that he gained a steady if precarious livelihood, enabling him – and my mother, who was just as busy with her paintings – to provide for us. In my childhood, he seemed constantly to be taking the train to London to meet archaeologists on one project or another; or, at the door, to be receiving parcels of books or a returned annotated sketch or tracing.

In 1945 Edward Bacon, who became a good friend, took charge of the archaeology section of the *Illustrated London News*. Bacon's journalistic flair and alertness to a breaking story put Alan, time and again, in place to be the first visual interpreter at famous excavation sites. Post-war, Alan's working credits for that paper are remarkable: he reconstructed the Mesolithic hunter-fisher settlement at Star Carr with Grahame Clark; the Carrawburgh Mithraeum with I. A. Richmond; the Walbrook Mithraeum with W. F. Grimes; Sabratha and Jericho with Kathleen Kenyon; the Agora at Athens with Homer Thompson; Nestor's palace at Pylos with Carl Blegen; the Greek city at Emporio on Chios with Sinclair Hood; Jarlshof and Clickhimin with John Hamilton; the fortress at Buhen in Nubia with W. B. Emery; Xunantunich in Mayan Honduras with Euan Mackie; Çatalhöyük with

FIG. 97. *Cheddar, Somerset: the Anglo-Saxon palace, period II, c. AD 930 to late 10th or early 11th century* (1963). Illustrated London News
(WHEREABOUTS OF ORIGINAL UNKNOWN, ASA COPY)

James Mellaart; the Anglo-Saxon palace at Cheddar with Philip Rahtz; remote Wharram Percy with J. G. Hurst.[2]

Equally remarkable in these years were the many reconstructions he made for the Ancient Monuments branch of the Ministry of Works, of weather-open sites in state care in England, Scotland and Wales (now managed separately by English Heritage, Historic Environment Scotland and CADW). Unlike most of his drawings for the *ILN*, which were made in the heat and dust of new discoveries, these Ministry commissions were intended to encourage and inform increasing numbers of visitors who needed immediate help on which they could rely to understand what mazes of ruins, low walls and steps and bits of paving among manicured lawns, signified. Early on Robert Howarth, Chief Information Officer, indicated the end the Ministry had in view:

> "... I would stress that the success of this scheme depends entirely upon the artistic quality of the drawings produced and that drawings which are archaeologically correct but artistically poor would not serve the purpose at all. As Mr [Arnold] Taylor has pointed out we need an artist's impression and not an architectural drawing."[3]

And A. J. Taylor himself, in his comments, reveals a familiar process:

> "It is not so much that I have checked the drawings for historical 'accuracy', but rather that I have collaborated with the artist at every stage, visiting the monuments with him, and supplying sketches, photographs and documentary material with a view to achieving historical 'probability'..."[4]

FIG 98.

Top: a. *Framlingham Castle, Suffolk, the courtyard in the 13th century* (1960). Pen & ink, watercolour, gouache & chalks, 39 × 55.5 cm
(© CROWN COPYRIGHT. HISTORIC ENGLAND ARCHIVE)

Middle: b. *Castle Acre Priory, Norfolk, from the north-east, shortly before its suppression in 1537* (1958). Pen & ink, watercolour, gouache & chalks, 48 × 63 cm
(© CROWN COPYRIGHT. HISTORIC ENGLAND ARCHIVE)

Bottom: c. *Lullingstone Roman Villa, Kent, as it might have appeared c. AD 360* (1961). Pen & ink, watercolour, gouache, chalks, 41.5 × 60 cm
(© CROWN COPYRIGHT. HISTORIC ENGLAND ARCHIVE)

YEARS OF ACHIEVEMENT 153

With the aid of the Ministry's experts and with scrupulous attention to detail, Alan roofed buildings over again on paper, setting them in their landscapes, and let the light play on them, and peopled them as once they would have been. At each site a full-scale reproduction of the drawing was displayed in a waterproof case, as nearly as possible from the artist's viewpoint; they were also included in guide books and thousands of postcards were sold. The scheme achieved its purpose: the drawings had attractive power, although with consequences which were not universally welcomed. My father told us how, at Stonehenge once, watching the crowds thronging the stones and clambering all over them, Taylor turned to him and said ruefully (words to the effect that) "We have you to thank for this!" The subjects – more than 60 in a decade and a half – included the splendid intimidating castles of the Edwardian conquest of Wales: Harlech and Criccieth, Rhuddlan, Conway, Beaumaris; inland fortresses grown expansive in years of peace: Framlingham, Kenilworth, Raglan, Helmsley; business-like coastal defences, geometric and severe, at Deal and Tilbury. The great medieval monasteries and abbeys too, designed to be set apart from the world's corrupting influence but which, paradoxically, before the Dissolution, became the hubs of huge and very worldly estates: Tintern and Fountains, Rievaulx and Castle Acre; and the wild beauty of the Border abbeys in disputed country: Jedburgh, Dryburgh, Melrose. Roman Britain was represented by the military works along Hadrian's Wall, by a street in Caerwent and by Lullingstone's comfortable villa; and prehistoric sites by Avebury, Stonehenge, Grime's Graves.

When the spate of these commissions began to dwindle, Alan busied himself, with no loss of pace, with drawings of Roman London and, for regional museums, of Roman Colchester, Silchester, Wroxeter, St Albans, Bath, The Lunt at Baginton, Caister on the Norfolk coast and Anglo-Saxon Thetford (the industrial area); as well as with numerous book illustrations and work for television. It was a sustained achievement and so dense with information that I have been content to pick out interesting details here and there to show his range and versatility; and then let the drawings speak for themselves.

* * *

Years before there was any thought of their collaborating on reconstructions, apparently before he was even interested in Roman history, my father met I. A. Richmond, like Aileen Fox, in Rome. The British School was a good place for such meetings since student painters, engravers, architects, sculptors, archaeologists and historians lived and worked together under one roof. Ronald Syme, the future historian of *The Roman Revolution*, was there at the same time, and he and Richmond were great friends; but, writes Alan: "so comically different in appearance that a rude stranger had murmured 'Weary Willy and Tired Tim' on seeing them together." (Sorrell *c.* 1938, 76) (The reference is to two cartoon characters, fat and thin, in the *Comic Cuts* of his youth.) The manuscript of my father's Rome memoir, written with publication in mind, is salted with sharp observations of this kind, which no doubt explains why everybody in it appears under an alias. For himself, the protagonist, he chose the quavery-sounding *Quentin Evenden*, a name which contains, I believe, an ironic allusion to Walter Scott's romantic hero Quentin Durward, for the young self Alan portrays is full of romantic impulses struggling to find expression within his timorous breast: "diffident yet determined" as Aileen Fox so aptly described him.

Richmond is *George Elphinstone Johnstone*:

> "Johnstone was blond, broad and stout and slow moving, with a spotty, round child's face. His tones were dulcet soft but the sentences came jerkily for a man of his build and temperament" (Sorrell *c.* 1938, 76–7).

Richmond, alone among the archaeologists, endeared himself to the artists at the School by being prepared to take them seriously, sitting among them and listening to their views. Alan, who would have loved to join in and even lead these interesting discussions, felt compelled by his stammer, that self-limiting interruption of his natural flow, to forego them. Instead, he tells us, he withdrew enviously to the common room, where he played the *Kreutzer Sonata* endlessly on the gramophone.[5] And I have vivid memories of growing up at home without radio or television to entertain us, so that the sturdy gramophone with exchangeable needles which stood in the studio became our plaything. We had a dozen or so records, but the one my father seemed to listen to more than any other while he was working was Beethoven's *Kreutzer*, the returning theme of which he would greet with an ecstatic crescendo of toneless clicks, hums and whistles; and when the record had finished, turn it over and start again.

The unhappy feeling of exclusion continued until:

> "one day Johnstone came in softly and slumped into a nearby easy chair, and assuming the conventional expression of extreme mental agony, listened intently whilst Evenden changed the records without a word. At the end Johnstone said in his clipped jerky fashion 'What is it? Good music – very – who is it by?' – 'It's B-B-Beethoven's K-K-Kreutzer S-S-Sonata.' They got to know each other very well after that, and with a sympathetic audience of one, Evenden's silence gave place to a halting garrulity that would have driven away anyone less kindly and phlegmatic than George Elphinstone Johnstone." (*ibid.*).

By then (1930) Richmond was already an eminent Roman scholar. A couple of years earlier, as an offshoot of his vigorous writing activity, he had provided the introduction to Forestier's little book *The Roman Soldier* (1928), to the illustrations of which Nash-Williams referred my father when they were working on reconstructions of the legionary fortress at Caerleon (1939).[6] Probably archaeologist and artist did not meet again until 1950 but Richmond and the Foxes were well acquainted and we find Aileen Fox turning to him for advice, especially concerning Hadrian's Wall, when she and Alan began work on the book *Roman Britain* just after the war.

It was at the beginning of May 1946, within days of obtaining his release forms from the RAF, that my father proposed such a book – which he should both write and illustrate in the established Puffin format – to Noel Carrington at Puffin Books.[7] At this difficult but burgeoning time for him he needed to make money and headway. In Essex he had just found the disused chapel which would become our family home. My mother and he had argued furiously – both were strong-willed – but had come through those storms and were looking to marry as soon as possible. The future which she envisaged for them involved a move away from London, the focus of his professional career to that point, and from teaching into substantial creative work; *Roman Britain* would be an enabling step on that road. Commercially it looked like a good opening, with a print run of 50,000 copies or maybe more confidently expected;[8] and into it he was prepared to pour his energy and his heart.

FIG. 99. *Hadrian's Wall: Harrow's Scar Milecastle and Willowford Bridge* (1956). Pen & ink, watercolour, gouache & chalks, 34.5 × 53 cm
(© CROWN COPYRIGHT. HISTORIC ENGLAND ARCHIVE)

Negotiations with Carrington advanced promisingly. In high spirits my father told my mother that if he got one Puffin to do, he would give up some additional teaching he had planned to take on; if he got two (at one point there was even talk of five), he would buy a house of ill fame in Shaftesbury Avenue and live off the income; in the next breath apologising for being crude and silly! (Sorrell & Tanner 1944–7, June 1946).

In July, he mentioned the new project (not including the house of ill fame) to Cyril Fox, while making arrangements to begin work on his *Conversation Piece* of the Fox family, set in the study of the home they were soon to leave. Fox replied cautiously:

> "The 32 pages of pictures of Roman Britain in the Puffin you will do superbly. But writing about Roman Britain unless you have grown up with the literature may prove a grave of reputation. The Puffin people should not expect the same person to be expert in both fields."[9]

There was, as it happened, a confluence of interests here. For some little time Aileen Fox had been campaigning to have archaeology, more specifically the archaeology of Roman Britain, taught in schools. In an article just published (Fox 1946), she had advocated linking it with that old warhorse of the curriculum, Latin, but also, more engagingly, with class site visits, the handling of finds and imaginative reconstructions. In that article she had reproduced one of Alan's pre-war reconstructions for the National Museum of Wales, describing it as an example of "a happy collaboration between the excavators, the museum officials, and the artist". (It is only right to mention here that Alan's attitude to book illustration was more conflicted. He deplored a modern tendency to associate drawings only with books for children, to have photographs inevitably supplanting them in books for adults. A camera's eye view is not more "truthful" than the artist's selective eye, he contended (and took delight in demonstrating); and the corollary by implication that children will accept a lower level of proof. Nothing he ever drew was consciously "child-centred".[10]) So, when he joined them in Cardiff, it is not surprising that she should have expressed keenness to contribute by writing the text. And he agreed, for as he told my mother, it was after all her subject, and it would save him a lot of work of a not particularly congenial kind. She in turn replied that she expected he must "feel very relieved" (Sorrell & Tanner 1944–7, *c.* 4 & 6 Aug. 1946).

Roman Britain was to occupy them over the next several years, in the intervals of many other projects, as a labour which they brought finally to proof stage. Years later, Aileen Fox would recall her experience of the Sorrell method:

> "Sorrell demanded precise answers to many questions of detail. I remember hunting out the figure of a blacksmith in his leather apron, and the use of flails and winnowing baskets from provincial sculpture in the Rhineland; I never wholly approved of his version of the excavation of a late Roman buried treasure,[11] but in most of his pictures accuracy of detail was successfully combined with imaginative scenes and with a wonderful feeling for landscape." (Fox 2000, 102)

Every illustration, including maps and finds, was to be a Sorrell drawing; an immersive experience therefore. In due course he began submitting to the printer experimental plates of alarming colour; only to learn, towards the end of 1949, that Allen Lane at Penguin, reacting to "changing conditions in the book world", had cooled.[12] I do not believe Lane ever saw their material; certainly the business decision which he took affected more projects than this one. The story as I heard it at home was that he decided, while on a liner in mid-Atlantic, and cabled the order ahead of him to London, to cut his losses by cancelling all forthcoming non-fiction titles in the Puffin list. In the case of *Roman Britain* this meant a broken contract and a financial settlement; but meanwhile the artist was encouraged to complete the plates in the hope that conditions would improve; only for the agreement to be formally terminated in bleak mid-1950. At that point Alan wrote to Lane in a tone of understandable bitterness and frustration:

> "R[oman] B[ritain] is sufficiently scholarly to be used as a school book & lively enough to be enjoyed by anyone with any kind of interest in the subject. I have been ridiculously unstinting in making the drawings full as well as exciting ... The work is all done now, & I shall return all the plates to Cowells next week. They represent, I believe, an asset of considerable potential value. They represent at least 5 months of my time."[13]

So he was left with a product which was unmarketable in that form. Ten years were to pass before it saw the light and found the success it deserved, with a different publisher and with all the images redrawn and in black and white.

But it was not all lost time with this project, for through it and around it Alan continued his artistic development. A good way of demonstrating this is by comparing one well-loved and widely reproduced drawing from the published book (1961) – that of legionaries making a Roman road–with its forerunner in page proof of *c.* 1948. In terms of technical information there is little to choose between them. Here as elsewhere, Aileen Fox had been thorough in looking out sources, referring Alan to a road-making scene on Trajan's Column and to various German authorities. She had stipulated, since manpower would have been plentiful, that instead of wagons (no evidence), men should be shown carrying metalling for the road in baskets of a specified type, and baulks of timber in slings. Due prominence was to be given to the Roman surveyor with his groma, and to his pole-propping assistants, along whose line he could sight to the marker of smoke rising in the distance. She also asked Alan to alter his design so that, instead of the road running blind into the wildwood as he originally conceived it, it should advance through an open, park-like landscape. Interestingly, no doubt instinctively, he returned at last, with its mysteries, to a more elemental scene.[14]

FIG 100.
Left: a. Roman road making, page proof (*c.* 1948–9)
(ASA)

Right: b. Roman road making (1961). Pen & ink, ink washes & gouache, 27 × 21.3 cm. Produced for the book *Roman Britain* by Aileen Fox and Alan Sorrell published by Lutterworth Press 1961
(ASA)

So the work of analysis was done at an early stage, and it would have been easy for him to copy the existing drawing when the new contract was signed. Instead, to satisfy himself artistically, he rethought it and in so doing transformed it. To convey a true sense of distance and narrative progression, he introduces a dip in the middle distance, dividing the drawing into two planes, with the foreground road nearing completion and the background road still emerging, in potential; and at exactly the point of the dip, as if to emphasise it, he puts a man crossing, leading packhorses, whose action mimics the cloaked Roman officer crossing nearer at hand. In a larger sense, we see how harmoniously he has arranged the human actors who, in this later drawing, have lost all trace of the exotic. They are not simply ancient Romans any more, but everyday people like those "alive and active round us now", involved in and contributing to the task in hand, not imposed on the scene but inhabiting it. A work of information has become a work of art.

I would argue that Alan reached maturity as an artist in this decade. No doubt several factors combined to achieve the happy result; but an important one was his demonstrating to himself, in murals for the Festival of Britain (1951; see Fig. 40) and, even more effectively, for the school in Warwick (1953; Fig. 44), that he could work rapidly and successfully on a large scale, thereby satisfying ambitions he had nurtured since his student days.

FIG. 101. *Mawgan Porth, Cornwall: interior of long house, Dark Age settlement* (1955). Pen & ink, watercolour, gouache & chalks, 41 × 44.5 cm
(© CROWN COPYRIGHT. HISTORIC ENGLAND ARCHIVE)

Reconstruction drawings, I believe, now began to fill their place. They too were public art. Their compass was much smaller but through reproduction they reached a much wider audience; and did he not often tell us that it is not the size of paintings which matters– in reproduction many powerful ones appear larger than in fact they are – but the intensity which they distil? Such warmth and focus is apparent in the Jarlshof drawing already discussed, in an interior view of a Dark Age courtyard house at Mawgan Porth (1955) and increasingly throughout his work.

It had been Alan and Aileen's plan in the projected book to remodel as illustrations some of his pre-war reconstructions of Roman Caerleon and Caerwent. This meant reassessing the evidence, a natural step for a scholar but, for an artist (who, having completed his or her work, likes to regard it as finished), an ordeal, although it was one to which Alan always patiently submitted. For example, concerning the legionary fortress at Caerleon, Nash-Williams had suggested that the mural turrets should be given pitched, tiled roofs (Fig. 1). Aileen Fox sought the opinion of Ian Richmond, the acknowledged authority on Roman military architecture. In 1948 or 1949 (her letters are all without date), she told Alan:

> "I saw Richmond yesterday, and he thinks he may be able to arrange for you to do a Wall picture for the Housesteads Museum; I will write and remind him shortly – you would be able to stay at Chesters with the Birleys very probably, and it would all be very satisfactory, I am sure –
>
> I went into the vexed question of turret tops with him; he thinks they should be flat & crenellated on the Wall for certain. For the Fortresses it would vary, but there must be a look-out in any case, even with a roof, as on Trajan's Column ..."[15]

Here we see doors opening, for Alan would go on to work with both Eric Birley and his son Anthony – he had just completed a drawing of Roman Newgate with W. F. Grimes (*ILN* 12 March 1949, 337) – and make masterly reconstructions of Hadrian's Wall, including Housesteads, with Richmond. But all of this came later.

A more immediate result was a commission for drawings of the Mithraic temple at Carrawburgh which Richmond had recently excavated (*ILN* 24 March 1951, 454, 456–7): sealed beneath a peat bog, ephemeral items of Roman date including wood revetting and fronds of heather cut as a floor covering were preserved among the finds. In this instance, the discussions of artist and archaeologist have left little in the way of documentary material beyond a preliminary drawing (a fine one) and a handful of brief notes in Richmond's miniscule script – testimony to his belief that talking the thing over together was "better than reams of letters" (worse for us);[16] but shortly before publication, he wrote expressing pleasure at the result:

> "The photoprints of your splendid drawings arrived this morning. You have worked wonders with them and I now observe that although you have left the clerestory open and without shutters or louvres, this does not spoil the effect and it is certainly easier for the reader to understand. You have managed the ordeal scene very cleverly and I am enchanted with the whole thing ... Ultimately, when we get our museum, I hope you will be able to do us some cartoons on similar lines, but do not undertake this, of course, until I make a firm proposition ..."[17]

Exciting though they were, the discoveries at Carrawburgh proved in terms of public awareness and participation to be but a forerunner when a larger more fragmentary Mithraeum was brought to light by Professor

Fig. 102.

Top: a. Hadrian's Wall: Carrawburgh Mithraeum, working drawing (1951). Pen & ink, gouache & conté
(TULLIE HOUSE MUSEUM, CARLISLE)

Bottom: b. *Hadrian's Wall: Carrawburgh Mithraeum Interior* (1951). Pen & ink, washes, gouache & chalk, 29.5 × 46.5 cm
(IMAGE COURTESY OF THE SOCIETY OF ANTIQUARIES OF NEWCASTLE)

Grimes at Walbrook in the heart of London (*ILN* 2 Oct 1954, 534–5; 9 Oct, 594–5). That event, in a city still visibly scarred by wartime bombing, generated such huge interest it was almost a return to Tutankhamun fever, with thousands of people queuing daily to file past the excavation, rather as if they were doing honour to a statesman or monarch laid on a catafalque. Alan, naturally, was present, for in a few years he had established an unchallenged position for himself as a reconstruction artist. Richard remembers being on site with him and, as my father made sketches, some

FIG. 103.
Left: a. Walbrook Mithraeum: study of apsidal end (1954). Pencil (SKETCHBOOK D, ASA)

Right: b. Walbrook Mithraeum: advertisement board (1954) (ASA)

sumptuous Roman sculptures were unearthed which Grimes spirited away to the museum wrapped in towelling. The advertising men had enough confidence in his name to capitalise on it on their billboards, which was unprecedented recognition for him! And he was so versatile and speedy that anyone turning the pages of the *Illustrated London News* might expect, in another month or two, to see a different aspect of the past revivified by him, something equally strange and haunting and new.

Of course this indicates a degree of journalistic pressure. Alan acknowledged the fact in earlier correspondence with the cautious Grimes when, attempting to persuade him to collaborate with him on another subject for the *ILN*, he described the proposed drawing disarmingly but hardly reassuringly as "a preliminary canter for the one I hope to do for you one day. As you know, I don't scamp these things, but at the same [time] this I.L.N. needn't be quite as studied as a permanent drawing in the Museum …"[18] (The project went no further.) Undue haste explains why a narthex or vestibule at the eastern end of the Walbrook Mithraeum, although surmised, was omitted in the *ILN* exterior view because it lay outside the excavated area; in a second drawing, almost a copy of the first, which Alan made three years later for the developer and described as "revised to Professor Grimes' instructions", it was included.[19] He also later made, for the Guildhall Museum (1971), a new drawing of the interior which has several modifications, including the introduction of a plank floor.[20]

When the *ILN* was involved there was always a sense of hustle, of headlines and by-lines, which sat oddly with a paper which otherwise seemed immovably set in its ways. (Of Bruce Ingram, with whom his relations were cordial but never warm, my father wrote that "one always seemed to

YEARS OF ACHIEVEMENT 163

FIG. 104.
Top: a. *Walbrook Mithraeum, London: Exterior* (1957)
(WHEREABOUTS OF ORIGINAL UNKNOWN, ASA COPY)

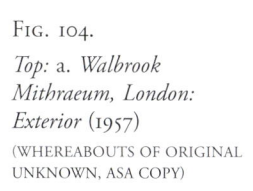

Middle: b. *Walbrook Mithraeum: Interior* (1954). *Illustrated London News*
(WHEREABOUTS OF ORIGINAL UNKNOWN, ASA COPY)

Bottom: c. *Walbrook Mithraeum: Interior* revised version (*c.* 1971). Pen & ink, watercolour, gouache & chalks, 32.38 × 45.72 cm
(© MUSEUM OF LONDON)

be conscious of the clop-clop-clop of a hansom cab when talking to him" (Sorrell *c.* 1974, 7). And it is understandable that an archaeologist who has devoted, maybe, several years of his or her life to the excavation and appraisal of a site, especially one where the buildings conform to no known type, should not take kindly to being bounced into making a firm statement about it before the time is right. Another season or two or several might alter one's whole conception of a thing so tentatively achieved that every new piece of evidence could reshape it.

I am thinking here in particular of a distinguished American archaeologist, Professor Carl Blegen, with whom Alan worked in Greece in the summer of 1954. Blegen was excavating an extraordinary structure at Pylos, by some called Nestor's palace – Nestor the wise old king and former companion of Odysseus at the siege of Troy. He had contributed a preliminary account to the *Illustrated London News* early that year, and Edward Bacon was keen to cap this by persuading him to collaborate with Alan, who would be visiting other sites in the country for a like purpose, in a reconstruction drawing. Blegen was politely disinclined for all the reasons previously mentioned, but Bacon was obstinate to push on with it – "the palace of a Homeric hero" had such tremendous romantic allure! – and Alan went anyway.

He and Blegen met (just the once) in Athens: in a letter home Alan mentioned having had "a very long discussion" with him.[21] What this actually amounted to becomes clear in a text which he wrote much later, in which he describes how, with Blegen beside him, he began to fashion and shape the reconstruction. It is a striking passage, both as a demonstration of his ability, honed by years of practice, to engage with material of baffling complexity and unlock it and give it imaginative coherence, and as a revelation of the archaeologist's fascinated response. Wittily (not without vanity), Alan compares Blegen's surprise at the sketch as it grew to that of a father presented soon after birth with his very own baby boy or girl: "He has no doubt about its paternity but is astonished to find it looks like *that*." It is my guess that, at the start, Blegen was girding himself to insist that the palace was in no fit state to be visualised, while my father was just as anxious that an opportunity should not be lost. But let him tell it in his own words. In August 1954 he visited Blegen's house in Plutarch Street:

> "It was a quiet street, and a great blind house, shuttered against the heat of the blistering sun. A manservant opened the door, and it was cool and empty and echoing inside. The Professor [was] very courteous as all Americans are, in the slightly old-world way which one always associates with the New World ... He took me into his study (I could not help noticing the indifferent paintings on the walls) and silently shewed me the plans of his excavations of the Palace of Nestor at Pylos. Then he became

even graver in manner, and said he thought there were very, very serious difficulties in the way of a reconstruction drawing of the site. Quite clearly it was necessary for me to demonstrate my competence in this matter and I proceeded to do so by developing, in my note-book, a three dimensional solid structure from the two dimensional plan that lay before us. It grew rapidly – it was just like building the palace – the ground floor first, then the first floor, after that the flat roof, and finally the crowning glory which was the extraordinary chimney to the great central hall. Professor Blegen had found its remains as it had fallen and shattered on the floor below when fire had destroyed the building about 1200 B.C.

All this time the Professor had been watching me intently and with growing interest; his reserve left him and he became voluble, enthusiastic and, more than anything else, surprised at what he saw. Yes, a reconstruction was indeed possible, and not only possible but desirable, a splendid idea. And now we must proceed to a discussion of how to get to Pylos, and we would join Mr Piet de Jong for tea downstairs ..." (Sorrell *c.* 1962, 52–3)[22]

Now, as it happens, I have found a drawing which appears to be this first sketch. It is a chance survival. For all that, late in life, Alan became the proud owner of a second-hand filing cabinet whose files he inscribed sedulously with letterbook As and Bs, he was not methodical with letters and preliminary drawings once a job was done. (With works in progress it was different: nothing on or around his apparently chaotic table was allowed to be touched.)[23] Rescued items, those kept back from his periodic hecatombs, the bodily carrying out of drawers of papers to bonfires in the lane, were likely to be found, as this was, buried in deep cupboards in portfolios under fallen clothes or flowed over into the carcase of a chest, making its drawers sit awkwardly with their fronts stepped out. And, as a matter of fact, it is not a notebook drawing. Most unusually for him, it is in blue biro and pencil on half a sheet of thin folded paper not of drawing quality – maybe from the Professor's study? – black-leaded on the reverse for transferral. The other half has details and times for the onward journey from Athens to Olympia (Professor Emil Kunze's excavations) and Pylos.

The sketch's viewpoint, giving prominence to the main building, became that of the final drawing. In Pylos, Blegen had assured him, he would find a landscape probably not much changed from Homeric times. Alan made a careful study of it, his usual practice; then, returning to Athens, he went to see Professor Homer Thompson, Director of the American Academy there, with whom he was working on another drawing. Thompson, to his pleasure, confirmed Blegen's excited response: "The Director said Professor Blegen ('who is rarely enthusiastic') *is* enthusiastic now about this reconstruction. Evidently my wonderful personality," he told Elizabeth.[24] Back home in England, he sent a tracing and letters were exchanged in which Blegen's

Fig. 105. Nestor's Palace, Pylos, working drawing (1954); see Fig. 17 for final version
(ASA)

natural caution returned, the words provisional, conjectural and interim featuring strongly; nevertheless he agreed that "It is certainly an impressive and well worked out reconstruction".[25] And so it was published (see Fig. 17), with a caption which falls neatly between two stools:

> "It is *not* claimed as a fully-authenticated reconstruction of a particular building; but it is intended rather as a most probable Homeric palace, set on a known site and to a ground plan, most of which has been established; and of a style and manner of building supported by the remains already discovered." (*ILN* 27 Aug 1955, 346–7)

With W. F. Grimes, in post-war London (remembering no doubt the abortive scheme of mural decoration for the archaeological gallery of the National Museum of Wales and attempting to realise something like it in a different place) Alan created a series of four panoramas for the London Museum (1956): they showed Roman London's haphazard development, its rather short life, from bridgehead settlement through to its apotheosis in a walled city. Here again the interval between excavation and reconstruction was short. Some distinctive structures in the drawings, including the fort in the north-western corner and the Walbrook Mithraeum, were discoveries Grimes himself had made. Since his appointment in 1946 as Director of the London Museum (in succession to Mortimer Wheeler), Grimes had supervised a deliberate search, the first ever undertaken, for the archaeology of the city's Roman and medieval past – a turning to positive account of the opportunity afforded by the large areas laid waste by bombing within the walls (Bruce-Mitford 1956, 111).

YEARS OF ACHIEVEMENT 167

In a letter, Alan described the set as "this important scheme of decoration (for such it is!)",[26] and I'm sure it pleased him to make this connection of different strands of his work, weaving together the warp and the weft of mural decoration and archaeological reconstruction. But the Renaissance muralists never faced the predicament implied in hovering imaginatively over a fitfully emerging lost city. It put Alan in the odd position, years later, of having to return to these drawings to insert new-old features subsequently revealed (although he did anticipate confirmation of the river wall).[27] No doubt, had he lived, he would have done the same for the large amphitheatre, visible on all but the cloudiest of days, which was found in 1988 in a place no one could have foreseen, outside the self-enclosed fort but within the city walls. Despite his strictures about the "colonial-type dullness" of Roman Britain (Mark Sorrell 1981, 25), the Romans continue to spring surprises.

With Grimes too he reconstructed an enigma, the "Heathrow temple", uncovered in 1944. Grimes had mentioned it as a possible subject for their collaboration as early as 1950[28] although, on the face of it, it seems a strange choice, given the uncertainties surrounding the rectangular building in the foreground, the "temple" itself. From its ground plan, which is that of a shrine surrounded by an ambulatory, it would appear to be an Iron Age precursor, built in wood, of Romano-Celtic temples like that at Caerwent.

FIG. 106. *Roman London, c. AD 400: the snowbound city, with houses burned by raiders beyond the walls* (1956). Gouache, ink & crayon, 70 × 130 cm
(© MUSEUM OF LONDON)

Grimes, however, preferred to see the influence of the classical Greek temple type, presumably impressed on the minds of Celtic traders and by them brought home to these remote shores (Grimes 1948, 77). Deciding on the type was crucial visually because it affected the form of the roof; but Heathrow has no clear provenance or parallels or votive finds or even an uncontested date. Grimes himself never wrote up a final report and that which was eventually published (Grimes *et al.* 1993), although it contains his findings, stands critically apart from them in this and other matters. The reconstruction, therefore, must be taken as an expression of Grimes's views at that time (1955), a lucid statement which, significantly, he wanted to see projected and distributed. That much is clear. What is more surprising, as the supporting correspondence shows, is the large input of Alan's prompts and suggestions as they worked towards realisation. As he wrote elsewhere:

> "Professor Grimes, who discovered the Walbrook Mithraeum, once spoke of 'the salutary experience of working with Mr Sorrell' but I believe the results have given some satisfaction to all concerned, though I have been conscious that, whilst I am not a fool, I have often trod where angels fear to tread."[29]

In July or August 1955, Alan sent off a tracing of the drawing thus far plotted (Fig. 107). On it he wrote such comments as (beside the temple): "would the trunks be without bark, coloured?"; on the swirl to the right, which is important artistically as a means of tying together the foreground and middle distance: "a chariot or two? men on ponies? flock of sheep? cattle?"; further back: "could you indicate hearths?"; beside the standing figures in the foreground: "costume? tunic? trousers?"; and in an accompanying letter, now lost, but to which Grimes's reply refers, he evidently questioned the spans of the roofs, both of the huts and the temple.

Grimes answered him point by point:

> "a) I don't think you need really worry about the span of the hut roofs: there may well have been additional internal supports but they need not necessarily have affected the external appearance ...
>
> b) I feel that the Romano-British type of construction for the Temple is unduly elaborate. On general grounds one would obviously expect the classical form to be followed and once again I don't think the span is unduly great, bearing in mind that the solid, central shrine would really be taking most of the weight. Taking up your question from the sketch, I think some, at any rate, of the timbers could be shown dressed roughly square, but some also were round in section so that the practice was not uniform. In general, I have a sort of feeling that your sketch shows the Temple rather more massive than in fact it was, and it may be this that is worrying you about the span of the roof.

c) I think we are almost forced to accept the view that the hut rings were indeed hut rings (rather than in some cases cattle shelters – at any rate until somebody provides really concrete evidence to the contrary) ...

As usual, the other questions are more difficult! You can certainly show some sheep and/or cattle and no harm could come from your group leading a bull towards the Temple for sacrifice. The odd horned skull attached to the facade would also not be out of place. Unfortunately, no hearths were actually found within the area covered by your drawing, but they must have existed and seem to have consisted on this site simply of burnt oval areas two or three feet across [0.6–0.9 m]. They do not appear to have had post holes or any other structures associated with them. I leave it to you to put in one or two somewhere near the hut entrances. Costumes should be quite simple and of the tunic and kilt order, with red and brown as probably the dominant colours ..."[30]

After the briefest of pauses, Alan replied:

"I don't want to start hares, but studying the Temple anew I am wondering whether there should be *four* posts in the porch? The post holes do rather suggest this. It would mean that the porch wd be much wider, of course. What do you think? The building wd become slightly more 'classical' in form [sketch]. You don't feel uneasy about the pitch of the temple as in the sketch? You don't mention carts or chariots? ..."[31]

[WFG, 6 Sept] "I'm a bit handicapped over the portico because you have the numbered plan & I don't know which p[ost] h[ole] is which! But I see no harm in 4 p[ost] h[oles]s if it seems to work to you, though in any case the portico must have been somewhat lopsided. But how does this affect the gullies? Could the roof then be [sketch of lean-to porch] rather than [sketch of 'classical' porch]? The roof pitch seemed alright to me. I left out carts and chariots for lack of evidence!"[32]

[AS, 7 Sept] "I much prefer form A for the porch [sketch of pitched roof] rather than B [sketch of lean-to]. It conforms quite well with the gulley. I didn't realise that I had the only plan! But I enclose a tracing of the relevant bit & a sketch for yr approval [Fig. 108]. If you sanction it I am putting in a little earth banked compound ... it's no good shewing sheep being driven if there's nowhere to drive them to! I suppose the fields (cultivated) outside wd be bordered with earth banks? I'm truly sorry to have to worry you (do you remember what a nuisance I made of myself with the Mithraeum) but it's all for the good of the cause ... I suppose you wd not mind some pack-horses [sketch]."[33]

[WFG, 9 Sept] "By all means go ahead with form A for the porch. I think this generally preferable, and if the gulleys are to be explained as drains they certainly suit the pitched roof rather than the lean-to variety ... I think I would be quite ready to have a compound of some kind

FIG. 107. Heathrow Temple, London, the Iron Age Settlement, preliminary tracing (1955). Pencil, watercolour washes on tracing paper (ASA)

for the sheep, but it ought to be a railed or wattled form rather than an earth bank which could only be made by digging some kind of trench or excavation, for which there is no evidence. With regard to the external fields, normally on the gravel terraces of the Thames, enclosures were of the bank-and-ditch variety: many such existed in the Oxford region, where the ditches now survive as crop marks in air photographs. Since no such traces have ever been observed in the Heath Row area, I think we had better assume a mainly pastoral economy, so that the fields should take the form of clearings with, once again, occasional wattle folds...The only weakness about the porch is of course the absence of the post-holes on the south side. On the other hand there is a hole in line with the oblique gully which could presumably have belonged to it: it more or less aligns with [post-holes] 131 and 132 but would have the effect of making the portico very nearly the same width as the main colonnade (see below) [sketch]. I don't know that that need worry us; nor need we concern ourselves particularly about the gully in the last resort: it is always possible that the gully did not relate to the Temple – and this applies also to the odd post-holes which are scattered about. No need to apologise for all the questions: I have always been delighted at the way in which you take trouble about these details! ..."[34]

With Roman and medieval architecture Alan was generally on much firmer ground. An opportunity to show what he was capable of soon arose. In 1956 the Ministry of Works was planning to mount a travelling exhibition at Newcastle to elucidate the Roman system of military defences along Hadrian's Wall. To this end they had photographs of the fragmentary

Right: Fig. 108. Heathrow Temple: sketch of portico with cows' skulls (1955). Pencil, gouache & ink washes
(ASA)

Below: Fig. 109 *Heathrow Temple*, the final drawing (1955). Pen & ink, watercolour, gouache & chalks, 47 × 62 cm
(© MUSEUM OF LONDON)

remains, captions, diagrams and models of milecastle, bridge, wall, ditch and vallum but the need was felt for something more vivid to connect the whole (Howarth 1959, 144, 146).

They also had, at Corbridge, but did not use for this purpose, some "dreadful coloured drawings" made by an unskilful artist previously employed who would not be guided.[35] I. A. Richmond, who acted as adviser for the project, seized the moment to suggest that Alan be brought in. Time was short. According to his diary, Alan first received news of the commission in mid-April for an exhibition to be held in late July. Four drawings were required: of the Roman fort at Housesteads; of the civil settlement of traders and camp followers which grew beyond its gate on the southern side; of the Roman supply station at Corbridge; and of the Willowford bridge flung over the river Irthing and carrying the wall on its spans (Fig. 99). In late May he travelled up to the Wall, met Richmond and spent two days with him at Corbridge, Housesteads and Birdoswald (for Willowford). Then, at his drawing table, he worked at tremendous speed – some years later he would tell the Ministry that he spent, on average, three weeks on each drawing made for them[36] – completing the Corbridge drawing in two days, the fort in three, the civil settlement and bridge in four each. By early June two of these were being passed around for comment at the Ministry. At the same time somebody asked that a file be started, mainly of internal memos, which allows us to see the impression they created:

> F.J. Root: "I think we might have more of these e.g. try one for Stonehenge instead of a model?"
>
> P.K. Baillie Reynolds (Chief Inspector): "These are very nice of their kind, that of Housesteads being more impressive. In a cursory glance I can detect no obvious flaws! They should have a good public appeal."[37]

Next the Minister saw and liked them, and suggested that consideration be given to having competent artists make similar reconstructions of other ancient monuments. Enquiries were made in the Ministry's drawing office but no suitable candidate was found to undertake such work, which meant it would have to be commissioned; and Alan, having demonstrated his extraordinary skill, became the obvious and only named choice. In September, therefore, he was asked to make six further drawings, including of Stonehenge and three Welsh castles, for £200. In the following year these were shown to the press at the Jewel Tower, Westminster; and a question put to the Minister, Hugh Molson, in the House of Commons (23 July 1957) enabled him to confirm the existence and intended expansion of the scheme. So began for my father a period of great productivity when reconstruction drawings, for the Ministry and the *ILN*, dominated his output.[38]

Richmond's feelings about the Roman Wall drawings were conveyed, as usual, in a brief telling private note:

> "... to say how very much I enjoyed your drawings in the Ministry of Works exhibition. I was particularly pleased with their verisimilitude and the very great care you had taken to stick to the evidence: and I marvelled how you had done so much so well in the time which you were given."[39]

All of this might suggest that Alan marched in unopposed with his drawings and found easy acceptance of them at the Ministry. True enough, they supplied a need keenly felt by some to connect with the public in insightful drawings of the highest quality; but to achieve this connection their supporters had to face down their own Chief Inspector. Baillie Reynolds opposed their use from the start. He wrote a four-page memo which survives in the official files, in which he becomes the conscious embodiment of a negative tradition:

> "It was an established principle in Sir Charles Peers's time that the Office of Works did not encourage or permit the exhibition of artist's reconstruction-drawings of monuments at the monuments in its care: it did not accept such drawings for display either as gifts, or on loan, or on sale-or-return terms or by any other means, and it did not include such drawings in any of its official publications.
>
> The reason for this principle is that in any reconstruction-drawing of a whole monument (as opposed to structural detail) there is so much that is missing for which there is no surviving evidence, and which has to be supplied by mere guesswork. Even well-informed guesswork is not certainty, and there is room for divergences of view, and artist A's reconstruction may very well differ in important respects from artist B's ... C.I.A.M. decided therefore...that the safe course for an official body was to eschew reconstruction-drawings altogether, and to be content with preserving the monument in the condition in which it was taken over.
>
> This decision was pretty consistently followed, and it applied *a fortiori* [even more so] to models, for which, since they are three-dimensional, even more accurate knowledge is necessary than for a drawing ..."[40]

Remarkably, reviewing more than 600 Ministry sites, he could call to mind only two present exceptions to this policy, each a special case: the aforementioned "dreadful coloured drawings" at Corbridge, and a scale-model made and presented by school children at Castle Acre, Norfolk (an object which was to be tolerated "rather as an example of the influence of A[ncient] M[onument]s on education than as a serious contribution to the study of the Priory"). Mistakenly it had been assumed that his tacit approval of the use of such drawings in a temporary exhibition (the Roman Wall) implied that he welcomed a wholesale departure from the position on which

Sir Charles had taken so resolute a stand. Decidedly this was not the case. He did not recall that he had been consulted. He would object most strongly to money being diverted for this purpose, or to the employment therein of any member of staff.

It took the genius of the Civil Service, since it was desirable to overrule him, to find a form of words to circumvent these difficulties. "Conjectural" and "probability", in all captions and relevant conversations, would cover the sin of representation and keep it decently clothed.[41]

These internal discussions soon left the question of accuracy (since to harp on it would have been to call in doubt the efficiency of the Ministry's own experts) and turned, in other hands, to criticism of Alan's style with its refusal to be insipid, his dark and stormy skies, in a carping note which gradually grew louder ("Like Mr Piper, Mr Sorrell seems to have had [no] luck with the weather!").[42] But my father found a defender at this stage in Baillie Reynolds's deputy, A.J. Taylor, who produced long lists of possible subjects with his own enthusiasms to the fore ("I should, personally, very much like to see in due course Sorrell drawings of *all* our North Wales Edwardian castles"[43]). These had to be whittled down to what the artist

FIG. 110. *Hadrian's Wall: Housesteads Roman Fort* (1956). Pen & ink, watercolour, gouache & chalks, 34.5 × 53 cm
(© CROWN COPYRIGHT, HISTORIC ENGLAND ARCHIVE)

FIG. 111.
Left: a. *Stonehenge, Wiltshire: the completed circle as it might have appeared c. 1400 BC* (1957). Pen & ink, watercolour, gouache & chalks, 41.5 × 60 cm
(© CROWN COPYRIGHT, HISTORIC ENGLAND ARCHIVE)

Right: b. Exhibition of Ministry drawings at the Jewel Tower, Westminster (1957). Alan Sorrell (right) and Hugh Molson
(ASA)

could cope with, 12 or eight or fewer a year (Alan, for his part, did his best: he was not one to turn down commissions[44]). Against the doubters, here was one whose word counted, who described the drawings to hand as "extremely fine pieces of work" and the artist as pre-eminently well qualified:

> "I do not think for a moment we could get better results from anyone else. Mr Sorrell has made himself the acknowledged leader in what is after all a highly specialised field, and he has gone to great pains to co-operate with us and to meet our suggestions as to how to treat the problems which are encountered with every one of the subjects selected."[45]

FIG. 112 *Tilbury Fort, Essex, from the south-west, as it might have appeared about 1725* (1958). Pen & ink, watercolour, gouache & chalks, 42.5 × 59 cm
(© CROWN COPYRIGHT, HISTORIC ENGLAND ARCHIVE)

At the Scottish Office, concerning a proposed reconstruction of St Andrews cathedral, Stewart Cruden put it more simply: "The [Scottish] Drawing Office started a drawing some years ago but it has made little progress. Since then Alan Sorrell has appeared upon the scene. He is the man for the job."[46] And Hugh Molson, standing a little apart as Minister, was instrumental in keeping up the momentum: his faith in my father's abilities is beyond praise. On one memo he scribbled: "I want to keep Mr. Sorrell steadily employed. What about Tilbury?",[47] referring to the fort on the Thames which the Ministry had just acquired and was preparing to open to the public. He took particular interest in the reconstructions of the three Border abbeys, which were near to his home, and wrote personally to my father about them. Alan replied:

> "Thank you very much for your letter. I am so glad you like the Scottish Abbey drawings, and it is extremely kind of you to tell me that you do. They were not easy subjects and I soon found that Scottish Gothic was not something I had experienced before! I very much appreciate your sympathetic and active interest in these reconstruction drawings ..."[48]

In a characteristic gesture, he visited Molson's country place, "Cherry Trees", to make a drawing of it, which he gave to him.

In the summer of 1958, a year after Alan and Professor Richard Atkinson had worked on an iconic reconstruction of Stonehenge, the Ministry performed some adjustments of its own at the site, controversially hoisting up from its recumbance a massive trilithon and some other stones which had fallen in historical times. The actual lifting and resetting involved much

FIG. 113.

Left: a. *Stonehenge: Lifting Gear in Position* (1958). Pen & ink, watercolour and chalks, 30.5 × 38 cm (ASA)

Right: b. Stonehenge: Alan Sorrell (left) and Professor Atkinson (1958) (© CROWN COPYRIGHT, HISTORIC ENGLAND ARCHIVE)

FIG. 114. *Buhen, Nubia: Reconstruction of the Middle Kingdom Fortress* (1959)
(WHEREABOUTS OF ORIGINAL UNKNOWN, ASA COPY)

preparation and weeks of delay, including that caused by bad weather, but Alan made a flying visit and produced drawings, not commissioned and never offered for sale, which showed stones of immemorial age trussed and caged in steel. All that summer crowds of people came and went to view the Ministry's undertaking, among them many photographers, and photographs survive in which he can be seen chatting and at work.

Meanwhile he was still making drawings for the *ILN*. One which had significance far beyond itself was a reconstruction of the mud brick Middle Kingdom fortress at Buhen in Sudanese Nubia, produced in collaboration with the archaeologist W. B. Emery (*ILN* 12 Sept 1959, 232–3). After the débâcle of the British intervention at Suez (when even he had thought it prudent to retire for a while across the border into the Sudan), Emery had continued, almost uniquely, to command respect in the country because of his lifelong commitment to Egyptology. It was a life of extraordinary endeavour, much of it bound up with terrain which lay within the water shadow of the first Aswan dam and its subsequent heightenings, and of the new monster dam which Nasser proposed to raise. Alan described Emery as an archaeologist of genius. He pictured his habit of traversing an apparently featureless site before, with pointed walking stick, commanding "Dig here!" with invariably rich results. (Sorrell *c*. 1974, 81). This was of course to underplay Emery's remarkable alertness to the subtleties of the Nubian landscape.

Working with him on Buhen in London, and reading the newspapers, Alan grew increasingly interested in Nubia, and wanted to go there and make a pictorial record of the temples, some of them already awash, and of the marvellous soon-to-be-drowned land. He wanted to go where, in the 19th century, Edward Lear and David Roberts had been before him and had left enticing descriptions and drawings, when Abu Simbel had still been buried to the neck in sand; but where no 20th-century artist of distinction had ventured.[49] (And I feel certain that the dire forebodings for Nubia chimed in his psyche with the earthquakes of cultural destruction which had long animated his imagination, although I do not know how far he was aware of this.)

With no funds of his own, he turned to the *ILN* to be his patron, but Bruce Ingram had already given extensive photographic coverage to the crisis and was not inclined to be generous in spite of their long association. He appealed to his Member of Parliament, only to learn of the coldness of the British government which had only just resumed diplomatic relations and still nursed hurt feelings after its failed adventure. He wrote to Mortimer Wheeler who was active in the International Committee – he and Wheeler had not worked together since the Festival commisions in 1951, but were friends. Wheeler returned him to source:

> "The ideal scheme would be for you to get yourself flown out to Wadi Halfa (opposite where Professor Emery is hard at work) and to begin there, working down the river subsequently to Abu Simbel ... 'The Illustrated London News' still seems to be the best bet; apart from the cost of transport to and from the Nile, the sums involved in the actual operation should not be large ..."[50]

Then the *ILN* commissioned him to make a cut-away drawing of Abu Simbel "in the prophetic vein" (*ILN* 10 June 1961, 980–1), illustrating an Italian plan to jack up the whole temple, all 300,000 tons of it, millimetre by millimetre to a height of 190 ft (*c.* 58 m). This would bring it above the new lake surface and it was the favoured proposal at the time – which explains why, in 1962, Swedish engineers were carrying out stress tests inside the hill (Fig. 68b). Its fantastic ingenuity, my father thought, would have delighted Leonardo – though it was hardly more fantastic than what was finally done to Abu Simbel by dissecting the whole thing with precise saw cuts and glueing it together again – leaving the reconstructed temples wrenched from context, sitting under the sky in the atmosphere of an outdoor museum.

FIG. 115.

Top: a. *Buhen, Nubia: the mud brick walls of the excavated fort* (1962). Pen & ink, watercolour & chalks, 34.9 × 51.43 cm

Bottom: b. *New Kalabsha, Nubia: blocks from the deconstructed late Ptolemaic–Roman temple stored ready for re-erection* (1962). Watercolour, chalks & pen & ink, 34.9 × 51.43 cm
(BOTH SOUTHEND MUSEUMS SERVICE)

But Ingram liked this drawing and met Emery, who urged him to expedite matters by writing to the Egyptian Minister of Culture, Dr Sarwat Okasha, to whom Emery had already recommended my father.[51] After a long pause Okasha, who was organising the international rescue operation, replied:

> "Mr. Sorrell's reputation is well known, and his drawings of Abu Simbel and Buhen have been much appreciated. I quite agree that for him to work on the Nubian sites could be both striking and valuable ... We should be pleased to supply Mr. Sorrell with air passage from Cairo to Aswan and back and to provide him with a boat and an assistant while he is in Nubia. I will do all I can to make his stay comfortable and to further his work."[52]

So the *ILN* became Alan's sponsor and gave him letters of introduction to 15 archaeological expeditions: Poles, Indians, Americans, Germans, Spanish, Italians, Russians and so on, amongst whom 200 miles (*c.* 320 km) of riverbank had been parcelled out for urgent exploration; and off he went and was away for months.

Nubia was a place of strange meetings at that time. In Aswan, Alan was run to earth by an Australian archaeologist, G. R. H. Wright, with whom he had worked on the ritual baths of Cyrene (*ILN* 16 July 1955, 113).[53] Wright was supervising the demolition and rebuilding on a higher site of the late Ptolemaic-Roman temple of Kalabsha for a German consortium. He drove Alan out one night to New Kalabsha to view the temple already felled and arranged in neat rows in the desert awaiting reconstruction. Alan recalled: "[W]e inspected long lines of moon-bleached temple stones laid starkly in ranks, like an unflinching old-time regiment struck down by the blast of war. I think we were awed ..." (Sorrell *c.* 1974, 20). Later, in daylight, he returned and made a drawing.

This was a foretaste of what was to come. At Abu Simbel he stayed for many days in front of the temples on a houseboat alongside the Documentation Centre; and, in the desert at Wadi Halfa, with the Emerys in the white-domed Expedition House which Sir Leonard Woolley had had built long years before. (It too, with the excavated fortress, has long since been drowned.) Then, on a government launch, the *Sheikh el-Beled*, he returned slowly northwards to Aswan making one or two complete watercolours every day. And he felt increasing anger, not at the huge and entirely laudable efforts to save the temples, but at the fate of the Nubians whom no one seemed to care much about, who would soon be resettled – the Egyptians in rows of concrete boxes at Kom Ombo and the Sudanese in an alien climate far to the south where many succumbed to disease.

When we saw him again, a gaunt dark exhilarated man, we hardly knew him. And inevitably, for him, what followed was something of an anti-climax. He compared his reception in an outer office at the *ILN*, where his precious drawings were hastily leafed through, to Apsley Cherry-Garrard's experience, returned from the howling wastes of the Antarctic, of being turned away from the Natural History Museum with a docket. It was painful, and painful years would pass as he tried to find a permanent home for the Nubian drawings, but in retrospect it hardly mattered.

Several times I heard him make the rather extraordinary statement that in Nubia he learned for the first time that he could draw. His sense of the journey as an accomplishment transformed him. It emboldened him to demand slightly better terms from the Ministry of Works.[54] It prepared him, when Sir Bruce Ingram died in the next year and the whole edifice of *The Illustrated London News* spectacularly collapsed, to find other patrons.

At the Ministry too, there had been for some time signs of an ending. The two tests which A. J. Taylor applied in each case before recommending the commissioning of a Sorrell drawing – the relative popularity of a monument and the possession of sufficient evidence to give its reconstruction a firm basis – had convinced him, as early as 1960, that nearly enough had been done. ("Nor would I care myself to provide the information that would be needed for a worthwhile reconstruction of Flint [Castle], where the things we most want to know about are those for which there is least evidence. Castell-y-Bere offers the opportunity for a wonderful fantasy, which I personally would like to see done: but it must be understood that this is what it will be …"[55])

These things were part of the problem. But part too, paradoxically, came from Alan's almost unchallenged dominance of the field, which led to charges of the imposition of a style on the past. This was the theme of Reyner Banham's cheeky article already referred to, although Banham I am sure

FIG. 116.
Left: a. *Anglo-Saxon Cheddar, Period I, pre-c. AD 930* (1966). Pen & ink & washes

Right: b. *Anglo-Saxon Cheddar, Period III, Late 10th to 11th Century* (1966). Pen & ink & washes
(BOTH © CROWN COPYRIGHT, HISTORIC ENGLAND ARCHIVE)

YEARS OF ACHIEVEMENT 181

would have been amazed had he seen the flutterings which his light words caused in the Ministry dovecotes, leading, in Taylor's case, as the files reveal, to a complete failure of nerve. So the years which followed saw a falling off in commissions from this source, but not in any way of the standards which my father required and imposed on himself – as can be seen, for example, in a late Ministry commission (1966) of a series of drawings asked for by Philip Rahtz, to give imaginative shape to the Anglo-Saxon and medieval timber palaces he had excavated at Cheddar.[56]

Fortunately Alan had the advantage of a hard-won reputation to balance the loss of these two important patrons. The success of the book *Roman Britain*, when it finally appeared, made it the model for others which were soon asked for, written by Henry Loyn, John Hamilton and Barbara Green, with drawings amply supported by scholarly evidence. Then he collected his Ministry reconstructions together and wove texts around them and, finding gaps in the pictorial record, sought out experts to guide him in the making of new works. Thus, for *British Castles*, he reconstructed Pevensey Castle (1970), a drawing which, later, the Ministry bought from him.[57] Similarly, a commission from the museum at St Albans for drawings of the Roman city (*Verulamium*), gave him the idea for a book on Roman towns in Britain. He soon discovered that many of the reconstructions he had long ago made of these subjects, mainly for the *ILN*, were speculative to the point of thinness and could not be used.[58] So he approached a younger generation of archaeologists to help him. They, having grown up with his work and been inspired by it, were pleased to find themselves collaborating with him and sharing the fruits of their excavations and research: Graham Webster at Wroxeter, Barry Cunliffe at Bath and Brian Hobley at The Lunt among

FIG. 117.
Left: a. *Medieval Cheddar, Period IV, Later 11th Century to 12th Century* (1966). Pen & ink & washes

Right: b. *Period V, Early 13th century* (1966). Pen & ink & washes
(BOTH © CROWN COPYRIGHT. HISTORIC ENGLAND ARCHIVE)

FIG. 118. *Roman Wroxeter, the bath complex* (1972). Pen & ink, watercolour, gouache & chalks, size 31.5 × 51.5 cm

(© SHREWSBURY MUSEUM & ART GALLERY)

others. Many of these drawings went to regional museums. And other individual commissions, such as a reconstruction of Bramber Castle (1972) for Worthing Museum, with the narrative suggestion of the former motte within its walls and the river estuary broadening magnificently beyond, produced intensely realised works. Another drawing of this subject, from a different viewpoint, was made for the National Trust.

He also busied himself with drawings for television. Among these, my favourites use a contemporary account as a voice-over to the events depicted. So we have a drawing of a disastrous clash between Vikings and Anglo-Saxons in a battle at Maldon (1967; the battle was fought in AD 991). The maker of the Anglo-Saxon poem on which the drawing is based, was close enough to the doomed fighters to call out many by name. The panning television camera, moving left to right, allowed my father to create a composite scene. Thus we see on the extreme left the first incursion and inpouring of the Vikings which began the battle:

> "They came with a rush, the wolves of war,
> Viking warriors; west over Pante,
> careless of water, carrying their shields high ..."
>
> (Mark Sorrell 2013, 48)

YEARS OF ACHIEVEMENT 183

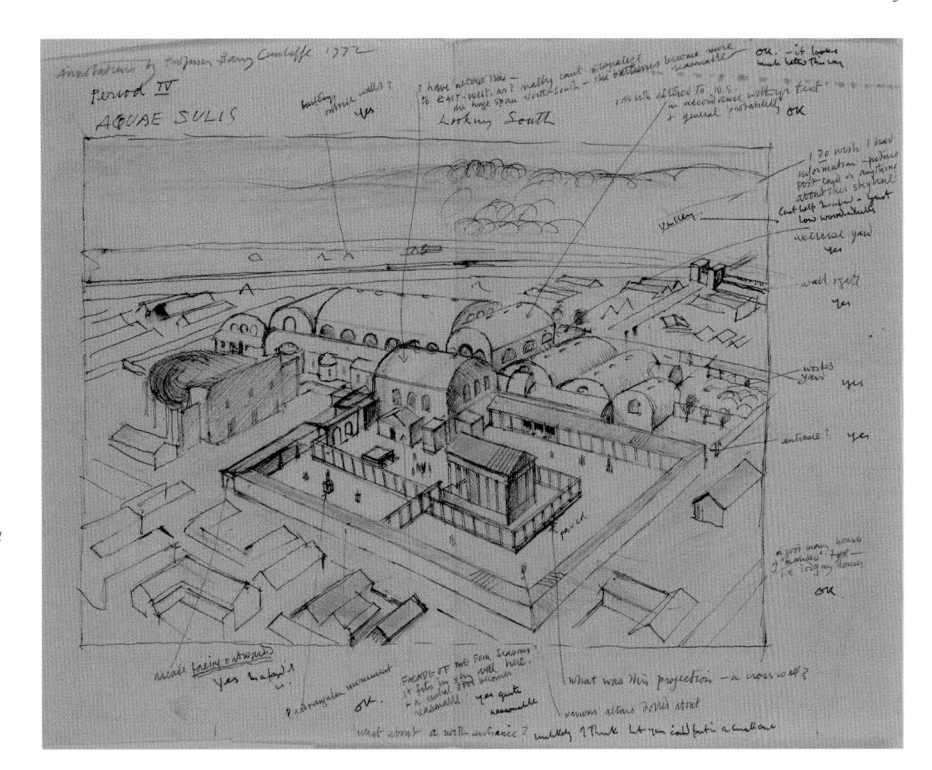

FIG. 119.

Right: a. Bath: Panorama of the Roman City, working drawing (1972). Pen work on paper

Below: b. *Bath: Panorama of the Roman City,* the final drawing (1972). Pen & ink, watercolour, gouache & chalks, 22.5 × 31.5 cm
(IMAGES ASA)

FIG. 120. *Bramber Castle, Sussex, as it might have appeared in the early 12th century* (1973). Pen & ink, watercolour, gouache & chalks, 40 × 58.42 cm (WORTHING MUSEUM AND ART GALLERY)

while the disintegration of the unsteady elements of the Anglo-Saxon army, which decided it, are shown on the right. The jigging camera moving backwards and forwards conveyed the sickening rhythms of battle in close combat with stab and counterthrust and falling bodies, bringing the whole action into one scene. Then it lingered, right of centre, on the Anglo-Saxon leader, Byrhtnoth as, dying, his head on his shield, he speaks his last prayer:

> "[M]y dear Master, great is my need
> of your mercy to receive my spirit.
> May my soul be allowed to come to you,
> Lord of Angels, passing in safety
> into your kingdom …"

The ethos of Anglo-Saxon society was of loyalty in war to a leader. Appalled by Byrhtnoth's death, and the scattering of his army, the courageous ones among them drew together to guard his body and refused to give ground, dying one by one – like Aescferth the Northumbrian bowman, to the right, committing himself although all hope is lost:

> "No weakness here in the play of battle.
> The frequent arrow sung in his bow,
> striking here in a shield, there in a man…"

Here too is Byrhtwold the old retainer, raising heroic spear and shield, who famously shouts defiance in this first elegy of an English last stand:

> "Now our spirits climb the higher, our hearts be the keener,
> our courage still increasing as our strength fails! …"

Rather different in tone but equally effective, was a drawing made with Barry Cunliffe for the BBC (1972).[59] This shows an exercise room in the Stabian Baths at Pompeii. The room has a substantial barrel vault and the walls, still surviving, have niches for storing clothes; but Alan's figures are conjured up in this case from Seneca, Letter LVI (Campbell 1969, 109: the translation they used) describing the privations suffered by a man unfortunate enough to live in too close proximity to a public bath-house. The air rings with thunderous noise, Seneca tells us, and so did the soundtrack. Here, close at hand, are the grunts of the naked gentleman swinging weights, the smack of the masseur pummelling the flesh of someone laid on a bench, the protests of the victim of the armpit hair-plucker. A hoarse-voiced dwarf hawks confections; the ball player runs in shouting the score, and the voices and splashes of bathers off-scene echo as they plunge into the pool.

In the year before his death, Alan received a large commission for sizeable drawings which were intended to be integrated into the design of the new Museum of London. They were many and varied, beginning with London as a *tabula rasa* – an ice-sheeted pre-human wilderness – and extending to Roman times. Now at last, he told us, it seemed as if he could be put in the way of making a lot of money; but he died before he was halfway through and Richard carried the project to completion.

But what he did manage to complete shows his style broadening. Some of these drawings, the pre-Roman ones, are built around no structures of any kind but only an isolated recovered object, a piece of treasure finely wrought – a gleaming ceremonial Bronze Age sword or ornamented shield not designed for use, fished out of the Thames in perfect condition – and are attempts to account for how they came to be there, what scene of sacrifice or burial or propitiation of a river god might have accompanied their deposition. Here groups of figures appear, larger than before in his reconstructions, and firelight and moonlight and a romantic atmosphere in tune with the old theme of mural decoration.

Towards the end of his life, writing about drawing, especially English drawing including his own contribution, Alan concluded with words which look beyond himself. With them we too may end this survey: "There is much to be done".[60]

> "We shall not cease from exploration
> And the end of all our exploring
> Will be to arrive where we started
> And know the place for the first time."
>
> (Eliot, *Little Gidding*, 239–42)

Anticlockwise from top left:

Fig. 121. *The Battle of Maldon* (1967). Pen & ink, watercolour, chalk & gouache, 25.5 × 72.5 cm
(ASA)

Fig. 122. Pompeii, Changing Room in the Public Baths, working drawing (1973)
(ASA)

Fig. 123. *Bronze Age funerary rites on the banks of the Thames* (1974). Pen & ink, watercolour, chalks & gouache, 37 × 62 cm
(© MUSEUM OF LONDON)

Fig. 124. *The Death of Hannibal* (1969). Pen & ink, ink washes & gouache 9.2 × 8.8 cm. The final image in *Stories from Livy* by R. M. Ogilvie, Oxford University Press (1970)
(ASA)

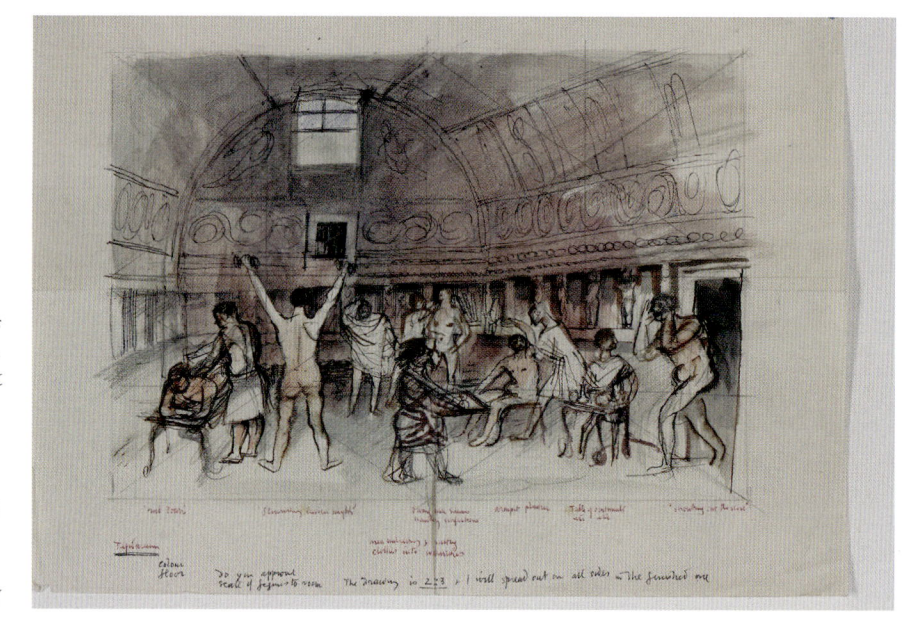

YEARS OF ACHIEVEMENT 187

Notes

1. Interview in *The Times Educational Supplement* 21 June 1968, 2079.
2. For dates see Appendix. The *ILN* drawings are now dispersed. The authors would be very pleased to hear from anyone who has bought, inherited or located an original drawing.
3. MoW (1956–74) WORK 14/2246, Memo 11 July 1956. Arnold Taylor was Assistant Chief Inspector, 1954–61; Chief Inspector, 1961–72.
4. MoW (1956–74) WORK 14/2246, Memo 26 April 1957. My father's diary (ASA) shows that, for example, in 1956 (7–9 Nov.), with Taylor driving, they toured north Wales, visiting Conway, Harlech and Beaumaris, a castle a day. In each place he made a watercolour drawing and took notes.
5. This and César Franck's *Symphony in D Minor* were the only records which the students at the School possessed (Lucas 2000, 40).
6. ASA, N-W to AS, 20 March 1939.
7. ASA, NC to AS, 24 May 1946. He was discharged from the RAF on 15 May and recommenced teaching at the College on 1 June.
8. ASA, H. Summers (for Penguin Books) to AS, 11 March 1947.
9. ASA, CF to AS, 1 July 1946.
10. Richard has suggested to me that, in making reconstruction drawings, one satisfaction for my father would have been to know that this was a field where the camera could not intrude or follow.
11. For a discussion of this, see Perry & Johnson (2014, 20–1).
12. ASA, AL to AS, 2, 8 Dec. 1949, *Roman Britain* file.
13. ASA, AS to AL (handwritten draft), 4 Aug. 1950, *Roman Britain* file. "Cowells" is the printing company W. S. Cowell.
14. ASA, various letters, all without date, *Roman Britain* file. I once asked him how the advance party, buried deep in woods, would have known where to build their fire.
15. ASA, *Roman Britain* file.
16. ASA, IAR to AS, 20 Jan. 1951.
17. ASA, IAR to AS, 21 Feb. 1951.
18. MoL 1950–78: 57.8. AS to WFG, 29 Jan. 1952.
19. ASA, Invoice book, 16 Dec. 1957. The changes are discussed in detail in ASA, correspondence, WFG to AS, 27 Nov. 1957.
20. MoL 1950–78: 76.16, Ralph Merrifield to AS, 5 Nov. 1971, and other letters.
21. ASA, AS to ES, Athens, 9–15 Aug. 1954.
22. Piet de Jong collaborated with Sir Arthur Evans in robust reconstructions of the Minoan palace at Knossos; and with Blegen.
23. In spite of these clearances, the Alan Sorrell Archive is substantial – a rich resource of sketches, working drawings and correspondence. By contrast, Forestier's working papers seem not to have survived (Smiles & Moser 2005, 78).
24. ASA, AS to ES, Athens, 15–19 Aug. 1954.
25. ASA, CB to AS, Cincinnati, 2 March 1955.
26. MoL 1950–78: 57.8, AS to WFG, 24 Aug. 1956.
27. "Alterations to drawings 2–4 were made by Alan Sorrell (10/5/67), revising the appearance of the basilica and inserting the so-called "'governor's palace' near the riverfront and a bath-building in Cheapside" (MoL 1950–78: 57.8).
28. MoL 1950–78: 50.70, AS to WFG, 10 July 1950: "At the same time I should like to learn something about the second subject you mentioned – an Iron Age drawing I think you said."
29. Sorrell *c.* 1962, 54, cancelled passage in one MS.
30. ASA, WFG to AS, 3 Sept. 1955.
31. MoL 1950–78: 55.89: AS to WFG undated (*c.* 5 Sept. 1955).

32   ASA, Postcard, 6 Sept. 1955.
33   MoL 1950–78: 55.89.
34   ASA. This is the top copy of a typed letter with Grimes's handwritten corrections and a diagrammatic sketch, neither of which are present in the carbon (MoL 1950–78: 55.89).
35   ASA, IAR to AS, 18 Dec. 1956.
36   MoW 1956–74: WORK 14/2934, Memo, R.W.B. Howarth, 21 May 1962. Most of his MoW drawings were made on standard imperial paper, about 22 × 28 in (*c.* 56 × 71 cm).
37   MoW 1956–74: WORK 14/2246, Memos, 11 June 1956. Baillie Reynolds was Chief Inspector, 1954–61, when A. J. Taylor succeeded him.
38   He also made a curious hieratic *Siege of Lachish* (1957) for the British Museum; and several batches of pleasing small historical drawings (1956, 1957, 1958, 1959, 1960, etc) for pamphlets to accompany BBC Schools programmes (ASA, Invoice book carbons).
39   ASA, IAR to AS, 29 July 1956.
40   MoW 1956–74: WORK 14/2246, Memo, P.K. Baillie Reynolds, 9 Oct. 1956.
41   Memo, F.J. Root, 19 Oct. 1956 MoW 1956–74: WORK 14/2246
42   MoW 1956–74: WORK 14/2247, Memo, N. Digney, 30 June 1959.
43   MoW 1956–74: WORK 14/2246, Memo. 25 April 1958.
44   "Mr Sorrell will be working at Tilbury on Jan. 7, Caerwent on Feb. 4, St Davids on Feb. 5 or 6, and Castle Acre during the week beginning Feb. 10 [1958]" (MoW 1956–74: WORK 14/2246, memo, A.J. Taylor, 3 Jan 1958).
45   MoW 1956–74: WORK 14/2246 and WORK 14/2247, Memos, 28 May 1957, 10 July 1959.
46   MoW 1956–74: WORK 14/2247, Memo, 10 Nov. 1958.
47   MoW 1956–74: WORK/2246, Memo, K. Nevis, 19 Sept. 1957.
48   MoW 1956–74: WORK 14/2246, AS to HM, 22 Dec. 1957
49   Emery did warn him that he had been forestalled by a Polish artist whom UNESCO had employed to travel throughout the affected areas of Nubia. The news was dashing; but when Alan learned that the artist had produced a series of abstracts "of such an advanced and incomprehensible nature that nobody could possibly describe them as recording anything at all", with vertical bars of pink to symbolise heat, and horizontal bars to symbolise the Nile, he was reassured (ASA, Notes, Sketchbook J, 54; Sorrell *c.* 1974, 84).
50   ASA, MW to AS, 27 Feb. 1961, Nubia file.
51   WBE to AS, at [Kasr] Ibrim, 2 Nov. 1961: "I am so glad all goes well with regard to your trip to Egypt. I saw Dr. Okasha in Cairo about it and, as you know he has arranged for you to receive all possible help. I would suggest the second half of January as the best time for your trip and don't fail to bring warm clothing with you, for it can be quite cold on the river in the Winter. Here at Kasr Ibrim we are making some very interesting discoveries and we are finding many very fine bronze objects, as well as glass and carved ivory and wood. All very encouraging …" (ASA Nubia file).
52   SO to Bruce Ingram, Cairo, 4 Oct.. 1961. AS to ES, Cataract Hotel, Aswan, 14 Feb. 1962: "I also was received [in Cairo] by the Minister. He could not have been nicer, he used phases like 'world wide fame' (me), 'honoured by my coming to do this work' & I was to let him know if I needed anything". (ASA Nubia file). See Okasha 2010 for his account of the whole Nubia rescue operation.
53   Wright, who had visited us, was remembered by my mother (who posed as one of the bathers) as enthusiastic and a little eccentric: "Yes, I remember the man Wright … You did a reconstruction of a women's ritual bathing place. He wanted you to go across Arabia or somewhere on a camel to do something or other …" (ES to AS, 21 Feb 1962, ASA Nubia file).

54 "Sorrell came to see me the other day on his return from Egypt and he tells me that he does not think he can continue to make these drawings for us at the present fee, which is 40 guineas, in addition to subsistence and travel allowances..." He had asked for 60 guineas, or, as a Ministry official calculated, "rather less than a Basic Grade Illustrator on maximum, allowing for holidays". However, the Treasury insisted that the increase be limited to 50 guineas per drawing, with copyright taken as usual. (MoW 1956–74: WORK 14/2934: Memo, R. W. B. Howarth, 21 May 1962; J. W. T. Pritchard to Mrs M. B. Sloman (Treasury), 18 July 1962; AS to R. W. B. Howarth, 12 Sept. 1962).

55 MoW 1956–74: WORK 14/2247, Memo, A. J. Taylor, 25 Feb. 1960. Nevertheless, in the case of Castell-y-Bere, where, in the opinion of the Inspector for Wales, O. E. Craster, a drawing "would be an enormous aid to comprehension" (19 Feb. 1960) a splendid one was made (1961). On holiday in Wales, we picnicked at the castle while my father sketched and took measurements.

56 Of periods I, III, IV and V. They had already worked together on a reconstruction of period II (*ILN* 30 March 1963, 464–5) which Rahtz saw no reason to alter (ASA, PR to AS, 28 April 1965). These drawings were not published until they appeared in the excavation report many years later (Rahtz 1979).

57 MoW 1956–74: WORK 14/2934, Memo, Ken Osborne, 14 June 1974.

58 Sheppard Frere, with whom he worked on reconstructions of Roman Canterbury (*ILN* 27 Dec. 1952, 1074–5), on the Bignor villa (*ILN* 29 Dec. 1956, 1114–5) and the Chesters section of Hadrian's Wall (*ILN* 31 Oct. 1959, 548–9), made exactly this point when the Canterbury drawing was in prospect: "I do hope they don't propose to do to Canterbury what they have just done to Bath (*ILN* 17 May 1952, 842–3). A purely hypothetical reconstruction (as that of Canterbury is bound to be), looking exactly like any other Roman town, without publishing any of the evidence or photographs of the excavations I am afraid leaves me quite cold." (ASA, SF to AS, 19 May 1952). Nearly 20 years later he returned to the theme: "It seems to me that it is not much use reconstructing buildings whose plan is incompletely known. Thus at Canterbury really the *only* thing worth reconstructing is the Theatre. For shops, town houses, temples, fora, baths etc one has to go to the towns which have them – i.e. really only Verulam, Silchester & Wroxeter ..." (ASA, SF to AS, 12 April 1971).

59 The image reproduced is the working drawing, with notes. The final drawing will, I hope, one day come to light.

60 Sorrell 1972c, 47.

Appendix: finding list of reconstruction drawings by Alan Sorrell

1. Reconstruction drawings (and other drawings) reproduced in the *Illustrated London News* (ILN)

Those reconstruction drawings marked* were commissioned by the Illustrated London News. *The pre-war commissioned drawings are presumed lost; the post-war ones were dispersed at the sale of the ILN archive. The names of the archaeologists with whom Sorrell collaborated in these projects are given in brackets.*

*13 Feb 1937, 254	Excavation of Roman remains at the Jewry Wall, Leicester
1936, *255	Reconstruction of Roman "basilica and forum" on same site in Leicester [Kathleen Kenyon]
*4 Dec 1937, 1013	Roman assault on eastern entrance of Maiden Castle, AD 43 [Mortimer Wheeler]
15 Oct 1938, 685	Post-Roman 5th century church [now believed to be post-medieval cottage] in Caerwent [V. E. Nash-Williams – see *National Museum of Wales* in this list]
686	Late Roman town houses in Caerwent under attack [V. E. Nash-Williams – see *National Museum of Wales*]
18 March 1939, 430–1	Roman Caerwent, 3rd century AD [V. E. Nash-Williams – see *National Museum of Wales*]
21 Aug 1943, 220	Reproduces "*8am parade, RAF*" exhibited with other War Artists' work at the National Gallery, London
8 April 1944, 415	Western corner of the Roman legionary fortress at Caerleon, *c.* AD 100 [V. E. Nash-Williams – see *National Museum of Wales*]
415	The amphitheatre, Caerleon, mid-2nd century AD [V. E. Nash-Williams – see *National Museum of Wales*]
416	The Roman legionary fortress and civil settlement at Caerleon [V. E. Nash-Williams – see *National Museum of Wales*]
12 March 1949, 337	Roman Newgate, London
*3 Dec 1949, 859	Interior of Viking longhouse, Jarlshof, Shetland [J. R. C. Hamilton]
*862–3	The Viking settlement, Jarlshof, Shetland, 11th century AD [J. R. C. Hamilton]
*15 July 1950, 102–3	Roman Colchester, *c.* AD 110 [M. R. Hull]
*3 Feb 1951, 172–3	Middle Stone Age hunting camp at Star Carr, near Scarborough, Yorkshire [Grahame Clark]
*24 March 1951, 454	Carrawburgh Roman Mithraeum, Hadrian's Wall, 3rd century AD: sealing an initiate into a living tomb [Ian Richmond]
*456	Mithraic ceremony in the Carrawburgh temple [Ian Richmond]

APPENDIX

*19 May 1951, 808–9	Viking coastal settlement with fishing boats drawn up, Jarlshof, Shetland, 11th century AD [J. R. C. Hamilton]
*29 March 1952, 539	The Roman city of Sabratha, Libya c. AD 200 with temple of Liber Pater in the forum [Kathleen Kenyon]
*17 May 1952, 842–3	Roman Bath [I. E. Anthony]
*27 Dec 1952, 1074–5	Roman Canterbury, 2nd century AD [Sheppard Frere]
*18 April 1953, 613	The siege of Paphos, Cyprus 498 BC: firing a cauldron in a counter-mine [J. H. Iliffe & T. B. Mitford]
*614–5	The siege of Paphos: the Persians' attack mound and the city wall [J. H. Iliffe & T. B. Mitford]
18 July 1953, 86–7	Reconstructions of the life of Cecil Rhodes at Oxford, 6 drawings for the memorial museum at Bishop's Stortford [with Geoffrey Jellicoe]
*17 April 1954, 614–5	Roman London, early 2nd century AD
*5 June 1954, 956–7	Funerary boats of Cheops at the Great Pyramid, Giza [Alan Rowe]
*2 Oct 1954, 534–5	Exterior of the Walbrook Mithraeum, London c. AD 150 [W. F. Grimes]
*9 Oct 1954, 594–5	A ceremony in the Walbrook Mithraeum, London 2nd century AD [W. F. Grimes]
*22 Jan 1955, 138–9	Roman Ghirza, Libya, 3rd century AD [Olwen Brogan]
*23 April 1955, 740–1	The Greek citadel and city at Emporio, Chios, 5th century BC [Sinclair Hood]
*16 July 1955, 113	Female celebrants at the Roman ritual baths at Cyrene, Libya [G. R. H. Wright]
30 July 1955 supplement	Three present-day drawings of Palladio's restored Teatro Olimpico at Vicenza
*27 Aug 1955, 346–7	Nestor's palace at Pylos before its destruction by fire, 2000 BC [Carl Blegen]
*1 Oct 1955, 566–7	Map view of Byzantine Constantinople [D. Talbot Rice]
*568	Constantinople: the Golden Gate c. AD 413 [D. Talbot Rice]
*19 May 1956, 554–5	Jericho: the walled Middle Bronze Age city 1800 BC [Kathleen Kenyon]
*7 July 1956, 22–3	The Agora of Athens c. AD 200 [Homer Thompson]
*29 Dec 1956, 1194–5	Bignor Roman Villa, Sussex, 4th century AD [Sheppard Frere]
9 Feb 1957, 220–1	Istanbul: four drawings of the present condition of the walls
*18 May 1957, 812–3	Clickhimin Broch, Shetland, end of 1st century AD [J. R. C. Hamilton]
3 Aug 1957, 191	Harlech, Beaumaris and Conway Castles; Roman Corbridge; the Jewel Tower, Westminster; Minster Lovell Hall [six Ministry of Works reconstructions reproduced]
2 March 1958 supplement	Three drawings of modern Athens
8 March 1958	Stonehenge [Ministry of Works reconstruction drawing reproduced]
28 March 1959, 524–5	*Londinium Romanum*, a mural painting for Roman House, Cripplegate Buildings, London reproduced
*12 Sept 1959, 232–3	The mud brick fortress of Buhen near Wadi Halfa, Nubia c. 2000 BC [W. B. Emery]
*249	The storming of the west gate of Buhen, c. 1675 BC [W. B. Emery]
*250	The fortress of Buhen in its New Kingdom phase 1570–1085 BC [W. B. Emery]
*31 Oct 1959, 548–9	Hadrian's Wall near Chester, in the first phase of its development [Sheppard Frere]
26 March 1960 supplement	Two drawings of the church of St Saviour, Chora, Istanbul in its present state
*8 Oct 1960, 608–9	Caister-on-Sea: the walled Roman town and port [Charles Green]

*10 June 1961, 980–1	The proposed (Italian) method of raising the Great Temple at Abu Simbel
*22 July 1961, 132–3	Peasant life in Xunantunich, British Honduras, a Mayan city abandoned after a natural disaster, *c.* AD 800 [E. W. Mackie]
30 June 1962 supplement	Five drawings of temples and sites in modern Nubia, threatened by the building of the Aswan Dam
7 July 1962, 31–3	Three further drawings of threatened temples and sites in modern Nubia
14 July 1962, 59–61	Two further drawings of threatened temples and sites in modern Nubia
21 July 1962, 105–7	Three further drawings of threatened temples and sites in modern Nubia
28 July 1962, 141–3	Three further drawings of threatened temples and sites in modern Nubia
4 Aug 1962, 180–1	Three further drawings of threatened temples and sites in modern Nubia
11 Aug 1962, 219–21	Three further drawings of threatened temples and sites in modern Nubia
18 August 1962 supplement	Two further drawings of threatened temples and sites in modern Nubia
*24 Nov 1962, 836–7	The Assyrian Fort Shalmaneser in Iraq, *c.* 600 BC [David Oates]
*30 March 1963, 464–5	The Anglo-Saxon palace of Cheddar, 10th century AD [Philip Rahtz]
13 April 1963, 554–5	Four further drawings of threatened sites and villages in modern Nubia
*31 Aug 1963, 310–1	The Roman cargo ship found at Blackfriars, London reconstructed [Norman Cook]
*16 Nov 1963, 816–7	Wharram Percy, Yorkshire, the early 15th century village reconstructed [J. G. Hurst]
*9 May 1964, 728–9	A funerary rite at Chatal Huyuk, Anatolia, 7th century BC [James Mellaart]
*11 Sept 1965, 34	The blockhouse at Clickhimin, Shetland in early Celtic times, 3rd–1st century BC [J. R. C. Hamilton]
7 May 1966, 25	*The Archaeologist [in Nubia]*, a drawing in the Royal Academy Summer Exhibition reproduced
2 July 1966, 14–15	Roman London; and the interior of the Roman fort at Cripplegate: two drawings for the new City of London police headquarters in Wood Street reproduced
29 April 1967, 33	*The Fallen Emperors*, an imaginative painting exhibited in R. A. Summer Exhibition reproduced
22 March 1969, 28	The Governor's palace, Roman London reproduced (accompanying a book review)
3 May 1969, 42	*An Ancient Place*, an imaginative drawing exhibited in R. A. Summer Exhibition reproduced
*31 May 1969, 26–7	The Megalithic mound at Knowth near Newgrange, Ireland [George Eogan]
*7 June 1969, 25	A priest depositing a chieftain's cremated remains within the Knowth mound [George Eogan]
*28 Aug 1971	Southend Pier
26 April 1980, 63	Roman London looking west, 2nd century AD, a Museum of London reconstruction reproduced
26 July 1980, 29	Harlech Castle, a Ministry of Works drawing reproduced
14 May 1992, 190	The Iron Age settlement at Jarlshof, Shetland, a Ministry of Works (Scotland) drawing reproduced

2. Reconstruction drawings commissioned by the National Museum of Wales, Cardiff

1938   Caerwent, Gwent: post-Roman 5th century church (now believed to be post-medieval cottage) [V. E. Nash-Williams]

1938   Late Roman town houses in Caerwent under attack [V. E. Nash-Williams]

1938   Roman Caerwent, 3rd cent AD [V. E. Nash-Williams]

1939   Western corner of the Roman legionary fortress at Caerleon, *c.* AD 100 [V. E. Nash-Williams]

1939   The amphitheatre, Caerleon, mid-2nd century AD [V. E. Nash-Williams]

1939   The Roman legionary fortress and civil settlement at Caerleon [V.E. Nash-Williams]

1940   Tinkinswood, South Glamorgan: burial ceremony at the Neolithic chambered tomb [Cyril Fox]

1940   Pond Cairn, Mid Glamorgan: the final stages of a Bronze Age burial [Cyril Fox]

1940   Llanmelin Iron Age hillfort, Gwent, the main entrance [Cyril Fox]

1940   [Maen Madoc, Ystradfellte, Powys: the son of Dervacus inspects his father's monument. Drawing made for Cyril Fox; now in the collection of the National Museum of Wales]

1949   Llantwit Major Roman villa, South Glamorgan as it might have appeared in the 4th cent AD [V. E. Nash-Williams]

1955   Caerwent, Gwent: the Roman forum and basilica [V.E. Nash-Williams]

1955   Caerwent, Gwent: the Roman town with Romano-Celtic temple [V.E. Nash-Williams]

3a. Reconstruction drawings commissioned by the Ministry of Works (now English Heritage/Historic England and Cadw: Welsh Historic Monuments) and Ministry of Works Scotland (now Historic Environment Scotland)

1951   Jarlshof Iron Age settlement, Shetland, as it might have appeared *c.* AD 450

1955   Exterior of courtyard house, Mawgan Porth, Cornwall looking north-west 10th century AD

         Interior of courtyard house, Mawgan Porth, 10th century AD

1956   Hadrian's Wall: Housesteads Roman fort 2nd century AD

         Hadrian's Wall: Housesteads civil settlement, 4th century AD

         Corbridge Roman station, Northumberland, 3rd century AD

         Hadrian's Wall: Harrow's Scar Mile-castle and Willowford Bridge

1957   Beaumaris Castle, Anglesey, late 13th century AD as it might have appeared had it been completed

         Conway Castle, Gwynedd about the year 1290

         Harlech Castle, Gwynedd about the year 1290

         The Jewel Tower, Westminster with Westminster Abbey, as they might have appeared in the early 16th century

         Stonehenge from the east as it might have appeared *c.* 1400 BC

         Minster Lovell Hall, Oxfordshire before it was dismantled in the 18th century

         Jedburgh Abbey, Roxburghshire, late 14th century

         Melrose Abbey, Roxburghshire, as it might have appeared in the 15th century

         Dryburgh Abbey, Berwickshire, 15th century

1958   Tilbury Fort, Essex, from the south-west, as it might appeared about 1725

         Castle Acre Priory, Norfolk from the north-east, shortly before its suppression in 1537

APPENDIX

Roman shops and houses, Pound Lane site, Caerwent 2nd century AD

The bishop's palace, St David's, Dyfed from the towers of the cathedral as it might have appeared *c.* 1530

1959 Goodrich Castle, Herefordshire at the end of the 13th century

Deal Castle, Kent, when newly completed in 1540

Hadrian's Wall: Walltown Crags looking east 2nd century AD

Rievaulx Abbey, Yorkshire (interior): the Frater as it might have appeared about 1320

Dundrennan Abbey, Kirkcudbrightshire, 13th century

Tintern Abbey, Gwent, the Cisterican monastery at it might have appeared before its dissolution

Raglan Castle, Gwent as it might have appeared at the time of Charles I's visit, 1645

Portchester Castle, Hampshire as it may have appeared in 1415 when it was the headquarters for Henry V's French campaign

Kenilworth Castle, Warwickshire, at the time of Queen Elizabeth I's visit in 1575

Bothwell Castle, Lanarkshire, in the 13th century, conjecturally completed

Caerlaverock Castle, Dumfriesshire, its likely appearance in the 15th century

Dirleton Castle, Lothian, early 14th century

1960 Carreg Cennen Castle, Dyfed, as it might have appeared before its dismantling in 1462

Framlingham Castle, Suffolk: the courtyard in the 13th century with chapel and domestic buildings

Conisbrough Castle, Yorskhire, early 13th century

1961 Lullingstone Roman villa, Kent about AD 360

Castell-y-Bere, Gwynedd before the end of the 13th century

Criccieth Castle, Gwynedd, late 13th century

Denbigh Castle, Clwyd, the gatehouse, late 13th century

Byland Abbey, Yorkshire

1962 Segontium Roman Fort, Gwynedd, 3rd century AD

Conway Castle, Gwynedd (interior): the Great Hall as it might have appeared when first built *c.* 1285

1963 Mount Grace Priory, Yorks, from the west, early 16th century

Valle Crucis Abbey, Clwyd, interior of the abbey church: Cistercian monks entering at dawn

Kidwelly town and castle, Dyfed, mid-15th century

Rhuddlan Castle, Clwyd, late 13th century

Helmsley Castle, Yorkshire, about 1500

1964 Pendennis Castle, Cornwall, as it might have appeared at the time of the Civil War siege, 1646

St Mawes, Cornwall, its probable appearance during the Civil War

1965 Totnes Castle, Devon, from the north-east, in the 14th century

St Andrews Cathedral Priory: bird's eye view to show the extent of the precincts

1966 Bolsover Castle, Derbyshire: the Earl of Newcastle's state rooms as they were about 1640

1967 Fountains Abbey, Yorkshire

1970 Rochester Castle, Kent, as it might have appeared in the later Middle Ages

Orford Castle, Suffolk: the Upper Hall as it might have appeared in the 14th century

1971 Restormel Castle, Devon: the gatehouse and adjacent buildings, as they might have appeared in the 14th century

Castle Rising, Norfolk: the forebuilding of the keep, as it might have appeared about 1200

3b. Reconstruction drawings commissioned for inclusion as illustrations in Ministry of Works official guides; and an excavation report

Atkinson, R. J. C. 1959. *Stonehenge and Avebury and Neighbouring Monuments: An Illustrated Guide*. London H.M.S.O.

Cover	Coloured drawing of part of Stonehenge in its present state (1958)
16–17	Two drawings and three vignettes showing five stages in the development of Stonehenge
32	Woodhenge
38	Avebury as it was in prehistoric times
49	West Kennet Long Barrow: offerings being made to the dead in front of the tomb
53	The building of Silbury Hill
57	A raft carrying a bluestone from Wales
58	Hauling a sarsen stone up to Stonehenge

Clarke, R. 1963. *Grime's Graves, Norfolk*: London: H.M.S.O. Official Guide

2	Section drawing showing how a flint-mine was probably worked
16–17	How the miners extracted flint
20	Ritual ceremony among prehistoric flint-miners
25	a stages in making a flint axehead b. felling a tree with a flint c. harvesting a corn crop

Birley, A. R. 1963. *Hadrian's Wall: An Illustrated Guide* London: H.M.S.O.

37	Activity in the principia, or headquarters building, at Chesters
39	The bath-house at Chesters in detail: diagrammatic, with tracing overlay
46–7	The fort at Birdoswald

Shortt, H. de S. 1965. *Old Sarum Illustrated Guide*. London: H.M.S.O.

17	What the earliest cathedral may have looked like in 1092
20–1	The cathedral as rebuilt by Bishop Roger probably appeared like this about 1130
24	What the Bishop's palace may have looked like about 1135

Hamilton, J. 1970. *The Brochs of Mousa & Clickhimin*. Edinburgh: H.M.S.O. Official Guide

17	[Clickhimin] Late Bronze Age farmstead and outhouse with enclosure wall
20	[Clickhimin] The Early Iron Age farmstead
22–3	[Clickhimin] Interior of Iron Age fort with blockhouse and wall ranges
28	[Clickhimin] The fort after flooding, showing landing stage, breakwater, inner ringwork under construction and temporary hut
30	[Clickhimin] View of broch showing temporary construction shelter, rebuilt blockhouse and builders' doorway in tower
35	[Clickhimin] Wheelhouse inside broch tower
37	[Clickhimin] Late wheelhouse settlement

Rahtz, P. 1979, *The Saxon and Medieval Palaces at Cheddar: Excavations 1960–62*. Oxford: British Archaeological Report 65

51	Reconstruction of period 1 complex
59	Reconstruction of period 3 complex
62	Reconstruction of period 4 complex
64	Reconstruction of period 5 complex
Plate III	Reconstruction of period 2 complex [*ILN* 30 March 1963]
Plate IV	Reconstruction of period 2 complex in winter [*Age by Age* (1967) 55]

4. Reconstruction drawings commissioned by the Museum of London (1974) and its predecessors: the London Museum and the Guildhall Museum

1955	Iron Age settlement at Heathrow
1955	Roman London: a street looking west towards Newgate [adapted in *Roman Britain* p. 27]
1956	Roman London: panorama *c.* 50 AD
1956	Roman London: panorama *c.* AD 100
1956	Roman London: panorama *c.* 200 AD
1956	Roman London: panorama of the snow-bound city *c.* AD 400
1967	Roman London: a typical street scene 1967 Roman London: interior of the basilica
1967	Roman London: wells west of Walbrook
1967	Roman London: the Cheapside bath building
1967	Roman London: the Blackfriars barge
1967	Roman London: the governor's palace
1967?	Roman London: Newgate
1971	Roman London: interior of the Walbrook Mithraeum [revised version of *ILN* 9 Oct 1954]
1974	Roman London: panorama of the city in the reign of Hadrian
1974	Roman London: a bastion
1974	London: the Thames valley in Mesolithic times
1974	Staines: a Neolithic causewayed camp
1974	London: a Neolithic encampment
1974	London: a Bronze Age farming settlement
1974	London: funerary rites on the banks of the Thames
1974	London: an accident at a ford
1974	London: a votive offering to the Thames

5. Some reconstruction drawings in other museums and art galleries

Maiden Castle from the west, at its fullest development [Dorset County Museum]
Caister-on-Sea: a panoramic view of *Venta Icenorum* [Castle Museum, Norwich]
Thetford: part of the industrial quarter of late Saxon Thetford, as it might have appeared in the 10th century AD [Castle Museum, Norwich]
Roman Colchester from the south [Colchester and Essex Museum]
Roman Colchester: the Balkerne Gate [Colchester and Essex Museum]
Verulamium, a panoramic view [Verulamium Museum, St Albans]
Verulamium: the forum and market scene [Verulamium Museum, St Albans]
Verulamium: the theatre [Verulamium Museum, St Albans]
Verulamium: the Triangular Temple [Verulamium Museum, St Albans]
Wroxeter: temple and houses in the Roman town [Shrewsbury Museum]
Wroxeter: the Roman baths [Shrewsbury Museum]
Silchester: panorama of the Roman town [Reading Museum]
Silchester: the Christian church in the Roman town [Reading Museum]
The Lunt, Baginton: the Roman fort from the north-east [Coventry Museum]
The Lunt Roman fort: the gyrus from the north, with the eastern gateway behind [Coventry Museum]
The Lunt Roman fort: the granary beside the principia [Coventry Museum]
Bramber Castle, as it might have appeared in the early 12th century [The Museum and Art Gallery, Worthing]
Southsea Castle, as it might have appeared in 1545 [Portsmouth City Museums]

References

Unpublished sources

Alan Sorrell Archive (ASA) General
Sketchbooks, all subjects, part indexed
Numerous loose sheets of working drawings, tracings, sketches, etc, for reconstruction drawings as well as some completed reconstruction drawings
Family and business correspondence files, all subjects, including much correspondence with archaeologists, historians, publishers, etc, concerning reconstruction drawings projected and in progress, indexed
Business diaries (1955–74)
Invoice book (100 carbons), kept fairly consecutively 1956–61
Seven sets of original book illustrations for *Roman Britain* (1961), *Saxon England* (1964), *Norman Britain* (1966), *Prehistoric Britain* (1968), *Stories from Livy* (1970), *Imperial Rome* (1970), *The Bible* (1970)

Alan Sorrell Archive (ASA) Short stories and book-length autobiographical typescripts & MSS
Sorrell, A. *c.* 1938. *Barbarians in Rome*.
Sorrell, A. *c.* 1940a. *The Shadow* also known as *The Gun*.
Sorrell, A. *c.* 1940b. *The Retired Life Of Henry Myers*.
Sorrell, A. *c.* 1940c. *Nothing Changes Except The Name*.
Sorrell, A. *c.* 1940d. *A Simple Story*.
Sorrell, A. *c.* 1962. *Walls Without Wages*
Sorrell, A. *c.* 1974. *Last Boat To Nubia*

Sorrell Family Collection Letters
Sorrell & Tanner 1944–7. Letters between Alan Sorrell and Elizabeth Tanner. These letters, his especially, were often undated, but the postmarks of the envelopes in which they were kept give a close date.

Unpublished archive materials in other collections
MoW 1956–74. Three Ministry of Works correspondence and internal memo files at the National Archives, Kew, concerned with the state's commissioning of reconstruction drawings by Alan Sorrell: WORK 14/2246, WORK 14/2247, WORK 14/2934.
NMW 1937–60. Letters in several departments at the National Museum of Wales, Cardiff, including correspondence with Sir Cyril Fox (1937–41) to and from Alan Sorrell concerning reconstruction drawings. Photocopies of many of these are in ASA.
MoL 1950–78. Five correspondence files concerning Alan (and Richard) Sorrell's reconstruction drawings for the Museum of London and its predecessors, the Guildhall and London Museums: 50.77; 55.89; 57.8/1-4; 57.26 (one letter); 76.16.
IWM 1940–6. Letters to and from Alan Sorrell at the Imperial War Museum concerning his work as a war artist: ART/WA2/03/193.

Theses
Cunliffe-Charlesworth, H. 1991. *The Royal College of Art, its Influence on Education, Art & Design 1900–1950*. PhD Thesis, Sheffield City Polytechnic.

Online resources
Illustrated London News Historical Archive 1842–2003. http://www.gale.com/c/illustrated-london-news-historical-archive

Published sources

Air Ministry. 1956. *The Royal Air Force Builds for War – A History of Design and Construction in the R.A.F. 1935–45*. London: H.M.S.O.
Atkinson, R. J. C. 1959. *Stonehenge and Avebury and Neighbouring Monuments: An Illustrated Guide*. London: H.M.S.O.
Bacon, E. (ed.) 1976. *The Great Archaeologists and their Discoveries as Originally Reported in the pages of The Illustrated London News*. London: Martin Secker & Warburg. [Reproduces three AS ILN drawings: Walbrook Mithraeum, interior; the fortress at Buhen, Nubia; ritual ceremony at Knowth, Ireland]

Banham, R. 1966. Wuthering Archaeology. *New Society* (3rd Nov.), 689.

Bell, C. 1914. *Art*. London: Chatto & Windus.

Birley, A. R. 1963. *Hadrian's Wall: An Illustrated Guide* London: H.M.S.O.

Blunt, A. & Fry, R. 1965. *Seurat*, London; Phaidon

Brewer, R. J. 1993. *Caerwent Roman Town*. Cardiff: CADW.

Brittain, V. 1944. *Seeds of Chaos: What Mass Bombing Really Means*. New Vision Publishing Company, London.

Bruce-Mitford, R. L. S. (ed.) 1956. *Recent Archaeological Excavations in Britain: Selected Excavations 1939–55 with a Chapter on air-reconnaissance*. London: Routledge & Kegan Paul. [Reproduces eight AS reconstruction drawings: Star Carr; Carrawburgh Mithraeum; Roman London panorama A.D. 100; interior and exterior of the Walbrook Mithraeum; Mawgan Porth, interior view of courtyard house; Jarlshof broch and wheelhouse settlement; Jarlshof Viking settlement]

Campbell, R. (trans.) 1969. *Seneca – Letters from a Stoic*. London: Penguin Books.

Clarke, R. 1963. *Grime's Graves, Norfolk*: London: H.M.S.O.

Collingwood, R. G. 1932. *Roman Britain*. Oxford: Oxford University Press.

Dykes, D. W. (ed.) 1980. *Alan Sorrell: Early Wales Re-created*. Cardiff: National Museum of Wales exhibition catalogue.

Foss, B. 2007. *War Paint – Art, War, State and Identity in Britain 1939–1945*. New Haven & London: Yale University Press.

Fox, A. 1946. The school teaching of Roman Britain. *Greece and Rome* 15 (71) 42–8.

Fox, A. 2000. *Aileen – A Pioneering Archaeologist*. Leominster: Gracewing.

Fox, C. 1940. The re-erection of Maen Madoc, Ystradfellte, Breconshire. *Archaeologia Cambrensis* 95, 210–16.

Frayling, C. 1987. *The Royal College of Art – One Hundred and Fifty Years of Art & Design*. London: Barrie Jenkins.

Gombrich, E. 1972. *The Story of Art* (12th edn). London: Phaidon.

Goodden, H. 2007. *Camouflage and Art – Design for Deception in World War 2*. London: Unicorn.

Grimes, W. F. 1948. A Prehistoric Temple at London Airport. *Archaeology* 1, 74–8.

Grimes, W. F., Clutton-Brock, J., Cotton, J., May, J. & Williams, D. F. 1993. The Excavation of Caesar's Camp, Heathrow, Harmondsworth, Middlesex, 1944. *Proceedings of the Prehistoric Society* 59, 303–60.

Hamilton, J. 1970. *The Brochs of Mousa & Clickhimin*. Edinburgh: H.M.S.O.

Hastings, M. 1979. *Bomber Command*. London: Michael Joseph.

Hauser, K. 2007. *Shadow Sites: Photography, Archaeology and the British Landscape*. Oxford: Oxford University Press.

H.M. Stationery Office. 1945. *Losses and Survivals in the War. Part I – South of Bologna*. London: H.M.S.O.

H.M. Stationery Office. 1946a. *Losses and Survivals in the War. Part II – North of Bologna*. London; H.M.S.O.

H.M. Stationery Office. 1946b. *Works of Art in Germany (British Zone of Occupation) – Losses and Survivals in the War*. London: H.M.S.O.

Horton, P. 1955. Alan Sorrell R.W.S. *The Studio* 150 (748) 18–21.

Howarth, R. W. B. 1959. Ancient monuments reconstructed: Alan Sorrell's drawings. *The Studio* 158 (800), 144–7.

Lambourne, N. 2001. *War Damage in Western Europe: The Destruction of Historic Monuments During the Second World War*. Edinburgh: Edinburgh University Press.

Llewellyn, S. & Sorrell, R. (eds). 2013 *Alan Sorrell: The Life and Works of an English Neo-Romantic Artist*. Bristol: Sansom & Co.

Lowther, A. W. G. 1976. Romano-British chimney-pots and finials. *Antiquaries Journal* 56 (1), 35–48.

Lucas, P. 2001. *Evelyn Gibbs Artist and Traveller*. Nottingham: Five Leaves Publications.

Maley A. E. B. 1937. *The Ancient Parish of Thundersley*. Southend, Washburn.

Merrifield, R. 1983. *London City of the Romans*. London, Batsford.

Miller, P. & Richards, J. 1995. The good, the bad, and the downright misleading: archaeological adoption of computer visualisation. In Huggett, J. & Ryan, N. (eds), *CAA94: Computer Applications and Quantitative Methods in Archaeology*, 19–22. Oxford: British Archaeological Report S600

(http://proceedings.caaconference.org/paper/03_miller_richards_caa_1994/)

Mories, F. G. 1939. Alan Sorrell, A.R.W.S. *The Artist* 17 (May), 84–6

Okasha, S. 2010. Rameses recrowned: the international campaign to preserve the monuments of Nubia, 1959–68. In D'Auria, S. H. (ed.), *Offerings to the Discerning Eye: An Egyptological Medley in Honor of Jack A Josephson*, 223–43. Leiden & Boston: Brill

O'Neil, B. H. St J. 1948. War and archaeology in Britain. *Antiquaries Journal* 28, 20–44.

Pearson, A. W. 2002. Allied model making during World War II. *Cartography and Geographic Information Science* 29 (3), 227–41. https://geography.wisc.edu/hoc/wpcontent/uploads/sites/3/2017/04/09pearson.pdf

Perry, S. & Johnson, M. 2014. Reconstruction art and disciplinary practice: Alan Sorrell and the negotiation of the archaeological record. *Antiquaries Journal* 94, 1–30.

Picture Post. 1939. Camouflage, *Picture Post* 15 April 1939, 28–9.

Piggott, S. 1978 *Antiquity Depicted: Aspects of Archaeological Illustration*. London: Thames & Hudson.

Quennell, M. & Quennell, C. H. B. 1924. *Everyday Life in Roman Britain*. London, Batsford.

Rahtz, P. 1979. *The Saxon and Medieval Palaces at Cheddar: Excavations 1960–62*. Oxford: British Archaeological Report 65.

Scott-Fox, C. 2002. *Cyril Fox Archaeologist Extraordinary*. Oxford: Oxbow Books.

Shortt, H. de S. 1965. *Old Sarum Illustrated Guide*. London: H.M.S.O.

Smiles, S. 2005. *Thomas Guest and Paul Nash in Wiltshire: Two Episodes in the Artistic Approach to British Antiquity*. Tate Papers 3 (Spring). http://www.tate.org.uk/research/publications/tate-papers/03/thomas-guest-and-paul-nash-in-wiltshire-two-episodes-in-the-artistic-approach-to-british-antiquity

Smiles, S. & Moser, S. (eds) 2005. *Envisioning the Past: Archaeology and the Image*. Oxford: Blackwell.

Smith, C. B. 1961. *Evidence in Camera: The Story of Photographic Intelligence in the Second World War*. London: Penguin Books.

Sorrell, A. 1934. The Mural paintings of historic Southend-on-Sea. *Transactions of the Southend-on-Sea Antiquarian & Historical Society* 2 (4), 1–6.

Sorrell, A. 1939a. Saying something with water-colour, part I. *The Artist* 18 (Sept.), 3–4.

Sorrell, A. 1939b. Saying Something with water-colour, part II *The Artist* 18 (Oct.), 35–6.

Sorrell, A. 1939c. Saying something with water-colour, part III. *The Artist* 18 (Nov.), 67–68.

Sorrell, A. 1939d. Saying something with water-colour, part IV. *The Artist* 18 (Dec.). 101–2.

Sorrell, A. 1940e. Saying something with water-colour, part V. *The Artist* 18 (January), 131–2.

Sorrell, A. 1940f. Saying something with water-colour, part VI. *The Artist* 18 (Feb.) 159–60.

Sorrell, A. 1942. The A–Z of mural painting, part I. *The Artist* 24 (Dec.), 86–8.

Sorrell, A. 1943a. The A–Z of mural painting, part II. *The Artist* 24 (Jan.), 104–5.

Sorrell, A. 1943b. The A–Z of mural painting, part III *The Artist* 24 (Feb.), 136–7.

Sorrell, A. 1943c. The A–Z of mural painting, part IV. *The Artist* 25 (Mar.), 8–9.

Sorrell, A. 1943d. The A–Z of mural painting, part V. *The Artist* 25 (Apr.), 46–7.

Sorrell, A. 1943e. The A–Z of Mural Painting, part VI. 25 *The Artist* (May), 64–5.

Sorrell, A. 1952a. Mural Painting, part I, *The Artist* 44 (Sept.), page nos unknown.

Sorrell, A. 1952b. Mural Painting, part II, *The Artist* 44 (Oct.), 34–5.

Sorrell, A. 1952c. Mural Painting, part III, *The Artist* 44 (Nov.), 68–9.

Sorrell, A. 1965. *Living History*. London: Batsford.

Sorrell, A. 1969. *Roman London*. London: Batsford

Sorrell, A. 1970. *The Bible*. London: Lutterworth Press.

Sorrell, A. 1972a. Some kinds of drawing, part 1 *The Artist* 83 (Aug.), 168–70.

Sorrell, A. 1972b. Some kinds of drawing, part 2 *The Artist* 84 (Sept), 24–7.

Sorrell, A. 1972c. Some kinds of drawing, part 3 *The Artist* 84 (Oct.), 44–7.

Sorrell, A. 1973a. *British Castles*. London: Batsford.

Sorrell, A. 1973b. The artist and reconstruction. *Current Archaeology* 4 (6), 177–81. [Quoted in full in Mark Sorrell (1981)]

Sorrell, A. 1976. *Roman Towns in Britain* (ed. G. Webster). London: Batsford.

Sorrell, A. with Fox, A. 1961 *Roman Britain.* London: Lutterworth.
Sorrell, A. with Green, B. 1968. *Prehistoric Britain.* London: Lutterworth Press.
Sorrell, A. with Ogilvie, R. M. 1970. *Stories from Livy.* Oxford: Oxford University Press.
Sorrell, Mark (ed.) 1981. *Alan Sorrell: Reconstructing the Past.* London: Batsford.
Sorrell, Mark. 2013. Sorrell on Sorrell: memories of the art and life of Alan Sorrell (1904–74). *British Art Journal* 14 (2), 81–5.
Sorrell, Mark. 2014. The Battle of Maldon, an Anglo-Saxon poem translated. *Long Poem Magazine* 11, 47–50.
Sorrell, Mary. 1969. *Out of Silence.* London: Hodder & Stoughton.
Spencer, G. 1974. *Memoirs of a Painter.* London: Chatto & Windus.
Sphere, The. 1964. Art in Industry – A series of watercolours by Alan Sorrell of the construction of Hinkley Point, The SPHERE (6 May), 208–9, 228–9.
Thurley, S. 2013. *Men from the Ministry: How Britain Saved its Heritage.* New Haven & London: Yale University Press.
Ward, J. 2006. *The Paintings of John Ward.* Newton Abbot: David & Charles.
Wheeler, R. E. M. 1928. A 'Romano-Celtic' temple near Harlow, Essex; and a note on the type. *Antiquaries Journal* 8, 300–26.
Wheeler, R. E. M. 1956. *Archaeology from the Earth.* London: Penguin Books.
Willsdon, C. A. P. 2000. *Mural Painting in Britain 1840–1940: Image and Meaning.* Oxford: Oxford University Press.

Further reading

Bacon, E. 1960. *Digging for History: A Survey of Recent World Archaeological Discoveries 1945–1959.* London: Adam & Charles Black. [Reproduces three AS *ILN* drawings: Walbrook Mithraeum, exterior; Clickhimin broch; the Agora of Athens]
Davies, D. G. & Saunders, C. 1986. *Verulamium.* St Albans Heritage, Tourism and Publicity.
Davison, B. 1997. *Picturing the Past Through the Eyes of Reconstruction Artists.* London: English Heritage.
Dobie, J. and Evans, C. 2010. *Archaeology and Illustrators: A History of the Ancient Monuments Drawing Office.* London, English Heritage Http://webcache.googleusercontent.com/search?q=cache:jOE2MQuGxLAJ:research.historicengland.org.uk/redirect.
Johnson, M. 2010. *Archaeological Theory: An Introduction* (2nd edn). Oxford: Wiley-Blackwell.
Mellor, D. (ed.) 1987. *A Paradise Lost: the Neo-Romantic Imagination in Britain 1935–55.* London: Lund Humphries.
Piggott, S. 1959. *Approach to Archaeology.* London: Adam & Charles Black.
Pitts, Mike. 2005. Hysteria gloom and foreboding. *British Archaeology* 83, 16–19. [on Alan Sorrell and Stonehenge]
Rahtz, P. 2013. *Invitation to Archaeology.* Oxford: Basil Blackwell. (reprint of 1991 edition).
Redknap, M. 2002. *Re-Creations: Visualizing our Past.* Cardiff: National Museum of Wales & CADW.
Sorrell, A. with Birley, A. 1970. *Imperial Rome.* London: Lutterworth.
Sorrell, A. with Drower, M. 1970. *Nubia: A Drowning Land.* London; Longmans Young Books.
Sorrell, A. with Hamilton, J. 1964. *Saxon England.* London: Lutterworth.
Sorrell, A. with Jessup, R. 1967. *Age by Age: Landmarks of British Archaeology.* London: Michael Joseph.
Sorrell, A. with Loyn, H. 1966. *Norman Britain.* London: Lutterworth.
Sorrell, A. with Loyn, H, 1977. *Medieval Britain* (additional illustrations by R. Sorrell). London: Lutterworth.
Stamp, G. 2014. Architecture. *Apollo* 616 (January), 70–1. [Reviewing AS exhibition at Sir John Soane's Museum, London]